KU-570-528

Principles of Geographical Offender Profiling

Edited by

DAVID CANTER
and
DONNA YOUNGS
Centre for Investigative Psychology, University of Liverpool, UK

ASHGATE

© David Canter and Donna Youngs 2008

All rights reserved. No part of this publication may be reproduced, stored in a retrieval system or transmitted in any form or by any means, electronic, mechanical, photocopying, recording or otherwise without the prior permission of the publisher.

David Canter and Donna Youngs have asserted their moral right under the Copyright, Designs and Patents Act, 1988, to be identified as the editors of this work.

Published by
Ashgate Publishing Limited
Gower House
Croft Road
Aldershot
Hampshire GU11 3HR
England

Ashgate Publishing Company
Suite 420
101 Cherry Street
Burlington, VT 05401-4405
USA

Ashgate website: http://www.ashgate.com

British Library Cataloguing in Publication Data
Principles of geographical offender profiling
  1. Criminal behavior, Prediction of 2. Crime – Regional
  disparities
  I. Canter, David II. Youngs, Donna
  364.3

Library of Congress Cataloging-in-Publication Data
Principles of geographical offender profiling / edited by David Canter and Donna Youngs.
    p. cm. -- (Psychology, crime, and law)
  Includes bibliographical references and index.
  ISBN 978-0-7546-2547-6 -- ISBN 978-0-7546-2549-0 (pbk)
  1. Geographical offender profiling. 2. Criminal investigation--Psychological aspects. I. Canter, David V. II. Youngs, Donna.

  HV8073.5.P75 2007
  363.25--dc22

ISBN: 978-0-7546-2547-6 (hardback)
ISBN: 978-0-7546-2549-0 (paperback)

Printed and bound in Great Britain by MPG Books Ltd, Bodmin, Cornwall.

Contents

List of Figures

Acknowledgements

The editors and the Publisher wish to thank the following for permission to use copyrighted material.

American Society of Criminology for George F. Rengert, Alex R. Piquero and Peter R. Jones, 'Distance Decay Reexamined', *Criminology*, 1999, 37 (2), 427–45.

Blackwell Publishing for F. Mizutani and P. A. Jewell, 'Home-range and movements of leopards (*Panthera pardus*) on a livestock range in Kenya', *J. Zool.,Lond.*, 1998, 244, 269–86.

Criminal Justice Press. for D. Kim Rossmo, 'Place, Space, and Police Investigations: Hunting Serial Violent Criminals' in *Crime and Place*, J.E. Eck and D. Weisburd (eds), 217–35.

David Canter and Karen Shalev for 'Putting Crime in its Place: Psychological Process in Crime Site Selection' paper for *Wheredunit? Investigating the Role of Place in Crime and Criminality*. Crime Mapping Research Center of the NIJ, San Diego.

The Forensic Science Society for David Canter and A. Gregory, 'Identifying the residential location of rapists', *Journal of the Forensic Science Society*, 1994, 34 (3), pp. 169–75.

Greenwood Publishing Group for David Canter and Samantha Hodge, 'Criminals' Mental Maps' in *Atlas of Crime: Mapping the Criminal Landscape*, E.H. Hendrix and B.D. Dent (eds), Oryx Press, 2000, pp. 186–91.

Home Office for Paul Wiles and Andrew Costello, 'The 'road to nowhere': the evidence for travelling criminals' section 5, *Home Office Research Study* 207, pp. 29–40.

John Wiley & Sons for Samantha Lundrigan and David Canter, 'Spatial Patterns of Serial Murder: An Analysis of Disposal Site Location Choice', *Behavioral Sciences and the Law*, 2001, 19, pp. 595–610.

Krieger Publishing Co. for Stanley Turner, 'Delinquency and Distance' in *Delinquency: Selected Studies*, T. Sellin and M. E. Wolfgang (eds), 1969, pp. 11–26.

Medico-Legal Society for David Canter, 'Geographical Profiling of Criminals', *Medico-Legal Journal*, 2004, 72 (2), pp. 53–66.

The Royal Institute of Navigation for Stuart S. Kind, 'Navigational Ideas and the Yorkshire Ripper Investigation', *Journal of Navigation*, 1987, 40 (3), pp. 385–93.

Sage Publications for Patrica L. Brantingham and Paul J. Brantingham, 'Notes on the Geometry of Crime' and William M. Rhodes and Catherine Conly 'Crime and Mobility: An Empirical Study', in *Environmental Criminology*, Brantingham and Brantingham (eds), 1981, pp. 27–54 and 167–243.

The Zoological Society of London for F. Mizutani and P. A. Jewell, 'Home-range and Movements of Leopards (*Panthera pardus*) on a Livestock Ranch in Kenya', *J. Zool., Lond.*, 1998, 244, pp. 269–86.

Series Preface

Over recent years many aspects of law enforcement and related legal and judicial processes have been influenced by psychological theories and research. In turn concerns that derive from investigation, prosecution and defence of criminals are influencing the topics and methodologies of psychology and neighbouring social sciences. Everything, for example, from the detection of deception to the treatment of sex offenders, by way of offender profiling and prison management, has become part of the domain of a growing army of academic and other professional psychologists.

This is generating a growing discipline that crosses many boundaries and international frontiers. What was once the poor relation of applied psychology, populated by people whose pursuits were regarded as weak and arcane, is now becoming a major area of interest for many students and practitioners from high school through to postgraduate study and beyond.

The interest spreads far beyond the limits of conventional psychology to disciplines such as Criminology, Socio-Legal Studies and the Sociology of Crime as well as many aspects of the law itself including a growing number of courses for police officers, and those associated with the police such as crime analysts or forensic scientists.

There is therefore a need for wide-ranging publications that deal with all aspects of these interdisciplinary pursuits. Such publications must be cross-national and interdisciplinary if they are to reflect the many strands of this burgeoning field of teaching, research and professional practice. The *Psychology, Crime and Law* series has been established to meet this need for up to date accounts of the work within this area, presented in a way that will be accessible to the many different disciplines involved.

In editing this series I am alert to the fact that this is a lively new domain in which very little has been determined with any certainty. The books therefore capture the debates inherent in any intellectually animated pursuit. They reveal areas of agreement as well as approaches and topics on which experts currently differ. Throughout the series the many gaps in our knowledge and present-day understanding are revealed.

The series is thus of interest to anyone who wishes to gain an up-to-date understanding of the interplays between psychology, crime and the law.

Professor David Canter,
Series Editor

Preface

There have been a growing number of studies, building up from the 1970s onwards relating to where offenders live and carry out their crimes. Some of these studies have helped in the identification of principles that are being drawn on for more and more police investigations worldwide. The studies and their applications have found a place under the common umbrella heading of *Geographical Profiling*.

This work has origins in disciplines as varied as zoology, epidemiology, psychology, criminology and, of course, geography, leading to important publications appearing in many and diverse journals that are not always readily available to academics and practitioners across the different disciplines. Some of the seminal papers are also now quite old and difficult to come by. It is therefore appropriate to bring together a collection of the key papers dealing with the origins and principles on which Geographical Offender Profiling is based so that researchers and investigators can consult the original source material in an easily available form.

The papers collected for the present volume are only a sample from the couple of hundred that could have been usefully drawn upon. Indeed, the number of important papers is now so great that a second volume is being published in tandem dealing with applications and opportunities for this area of study.

The papers have been selected to give a flavour of the range of studies that have been conducted in different times and different places as well as papers that provide an indication of the cumulative development of the methodologies and theories that people this area of research. This has meant that there is a conscious emphasis on papers that have emerged from the Centre for Investigative Psychology in the UK and those who have been associated with that Centre. This gives more coherence to the topics studied than might otherwise be the case, as well as showing how the collaboration between a variety of researchers over 15 years has produced the basis for a set of theories and methods that now are at the core of *Geographical Offender Profiling*.

The present volume focuses on the conceptual and theoretical developments. To facilitate teaching and professional training, this work is considered under 3 headings of i) Spatial Patterns in Behaviour ii) Offenders' Geography and iii) Key Concepts in Geographical Offender Profiling. The field now covers such a range of issues and results that it was also deemed appropriate to produce an extensive introduction to the present volume that will help the reader to understand the context of the various papers included and the different ways in which they contribute to our growing appreciation of the complex issues incorporated in what started as a simple, some would say naïve, belief in the possibility of locating an offender's base from a study of where s/he offends.

The introduction ranges beyond the papers in the present volume to provide an overview of value to students and practitioners who wish to gain a full understanding of this rapidly developing area of study and application. A full bibliography of the many relevant publications is also given at the end of this volume to further support research and development.

This is an exciting area of research that frequently attracts media attention even to the extent that fictional crime drama series on television such as *Numb3rs* and *The Bill* have constructed entire stories around the application of geographical profiling principles. This excitement, though, should not mask the very serious research that is at the heart of these dramas and the implications this research has, not just for criminal investigations but for the broader understanding of all human activity.

We are grateful to Michael Fusco for his assistance in preparing this volume.

David Canter and Donna Youngs

Chapter 1

Geographical Offender Profiling: Origins and Principles

David Canter and Donna Youngs

The Emergence of Geographical Offender Profiling

In the mid-1980s scientists assisting police investigations [Kind 1999, Canter 1994, Canter 2004, Rossmo 1995][1] realised that they could estimate where an offender was likely to be based from an analysis of the geographical locations of that offender's crimes. This process of indicating the possible area in which police should search for an offender eventually became known as 'geographical profiling' [Canter 2004], or in North America – where they worry less about syntactical niceties – 'geographic profiling' [Rossmo 1995].

The procedures for making such inferences grow out of studies of criminal spatial behaviour that can be traced back over a century and a half. It owes most, however, to the discovery first reported by Canter and Gregory [1994] for serial rapists, that an offender's home or base was more often than not likely to be within an area circumscribed by his crimes. This discovery was first put to practical use in the case of the Railway Rapist in London [Canter 2004]. In that case the location of the offender's residence was inferred from the geographical distribution of his offences. At that time a great deal of publicity was being given to the contributions which some FBI agents were claiming for how they solved crimes by drawing on a process that they called 'offender profiling'. It was therefore a small step to see the analogy to FBI 'profiling', which made inferences about the characteristics of the offender from crime scene behaviours. When deductions about where an offender may be found were derived from the distribution of offences on a map it seemed appropriate to call this process 'geographical profiling'.

There is now a recognisable field of geographical offender profiling that sits within the general discipline of Investigative Psychology and goes far beyond the 'wheredunit' search for an unknown offender's likely residential location. This field has, from its inception, and even before it was labelled, consisted of a number of different aspects:

---

1   Citations in [ ] are those included in these readings.

a) Studies of criminal spatial behaviour – basic research
b) Development of decision support tools that incorporate research findings
c) Explorations of how such tools may help police investigations and the effectiveness of these applications.

It thus straddles the divide that so often exists between, on the one hand, those purely academic studies that attempt to contribute to our knowledge about crime and criminals (as well as human behaviour more generally), and on the other, directly operational contributions to criminal investigations. An involvement at the borders between these academic and operational domains is also emerging out of the work on geographical profiling. Nowadays this is often characterised as 'strategic', policy development, in which a better understanding of criminals' activities informs how law enforcement agencies approach their overall tasks.

Although the direct study of the spatial distribution of individual offender's crimes only became a focus for research in the mid-1980s, some of the principles on which geographical profiling were based had been established over a century earlier. This had grown out of early criminological studies of the aggregate geographical distribution of crimes and criminals, most notably in the work of Guerry (1833). These studies revealed that offenders tended to live in distinct areas of a city and did not travel very far to commit their crimes.

The most graphic early description of this process was in the writings of Mayhew (1861) in which he described the areas in which there was a high concentration of criminals as 'Rookeries'. These criminal areas were located close to places that offered attractive opportunities for crime. For example, the St Giles rookery was situated between the City of London boundary and Oxford Street that was then, as now, one of the major shopping streets in the capital. From the Rookery, less than half a mile away, thieves could commit crimes in Oxford Street and never be too far from the sanctuary of their home.

Such findings were rediscovered over and over again in the following 150 years, being given considerable impetus by US sociologists (e.g. White 1932), and were reflected in the day-to-day experience of local police officers who knew the villains who lived and committed crimes on their beat. So, although the emergence of geographical profiling started with very serious crime series, notably serial rapists and serial murderers [Canter and Larkin 1993], its origins are in studies of general, volume crime. There therefore is no *a priori* need to assume that the findings and approach will only be of relevance to serious crimes or series of offences. The great majority of criminal investigations can be enhanced by considering the geographical aspects of criminality.

Indeed much general, non-criminal human activity is open to and informed by a spatial analysis. If routine activity holds sway then it can be assumed that criminal journeys will not be that different from other forms of legal journey. Certainly some of the patterns such as decay functions, are similar between legal and illegal activity. There is therefore a great deal to be learnt from studies of the spatial patterns of legal activities. This will enrich our models and theories of criminal behaviours in many ways.

One particularly powerful illustration of how studies of legal human spatial activities can enrich our conceptualisations of criminal geography are the very detailed studies of street traders reviewed by Bromley (1980). He explores the distinction between mobile and fixed traders and shows that quite different logical cycles can be modelled on the basis of different assumptions. One of the trader cycles he illustrates is remarkably similar to the 'marauding' pattern found for serial killers by Lundrigan and Canter [2001] and other types of criminals. So, the existence of other market cycles raises the possibility that we should be looking for them within criminal geographies. Many other issues raised by Bromley open up possible parallels with criminal activities. To take just one example, he draws attention to differences in part-time traders and those for whom it is a full time job. There are clear analogies here with casual offenders, who are often younger, and 'career' criminals whose life is devoted to crime. Are there similar important differences in how these different types of offender make use of their surroundings?

Some of the patterns of traders' spatial mobility can be seen as a natural result of the economy of opportunities. Traders wish to maximise their access to markets whilst minimising the effort involved. When the process has such a strong relationship between effort expenditure and benefits it is to be expected that there will be parallels in the animal kingdom. Mitzutani and Jewell [1998] show such parallels in the movement of leopards and their ranges of activities, as well as the location of their kills (Mitzutani 1993). These studies are conducted by monitoring electronic tags on the animals. Developments in criminal justice may make closely similar studies possible with criminals in the future.

These animal studies do show that some, at least, of the processes we have been summarising have a fundamental logic to them and are thus a consequence of natural activities. We should therefore not be surprised that more than a century and a half ago models of human spatial activity were proposed to help explain non-criminal phenomena. In particular the cause of an outbreak of cholera in London was explained by locating the patients on a map and relating that to the available water sources on well pumps [Snow 1855]. The clear correlation between the density of cholera cases and the location of particular wells was used to support the view that cholera was water borne. The assumption here was that people would use their nearest well, just as we assume offenders will not travel far to commit their crimes. The well plays a role analogous to the criminal's base and the cholera cases are distributed like crimes around that location. Snow's study is often heralded as the origin of modern epidemiology. It serves to show us that the patterns of criminal behaviour we are finding are not unique to criminals and, equally, that there is much that can be learnt about criminals' spatial activity from considering similarities in other domains of activity. These illustrations of approaches to spatial thinking drawn from other contexts then are important introductions to criminal geography.

Inferring a Criminal's Characteristics from Crime Scene Information

There are two distinct qualities of criminal spatial behaviour that make the inference of an offender's home location possible from examination of where the crimes are committed. One, already mentioned, is the common finding that the assumed journey from a base to a crime location, rather than being a lengthy one to an alternative city or locality, is often very short. This was well illustrated in a detailed study of young criminals in Philadelphia, drawn from a 10% sample of police records for 1960 by Turner [1969]. He reports that three quarters of offences took place within one mile of the juvenile's place of residence. Although Turner does not seem to be aware of the practical implications of his results, his study is the starting point for a more systematic and scientific contribution to criminal investigations. Such findings are the first step towards combining informal experience and academic scholarship into investigative support tools.

Using Turner's results to aid investigations is an example of a general process that can be summarised as using criminal psychology and criminology in the 'reverse' direction from that in which they are usually considered. Typically social scientists have information about people and are trying to relate that to their actions. The detective has the opposite task. He has information about the actions of an offender and he wants to infer from that crucial facts about the offender and his location. This is the process that Canter and Youngs (2003) describe as the $A \rightarrow C$ equation. A represents the Actions in a crime, more generally what is known to detectives when the crime is being investigated and before an offender is apprehended, which includes where and when the crime happened and to what or whom. The C describes the characteristics of the offender that the police can use to find him/her; most crucially, of course, where to look for the offender. The $\rightarrow$ is the science of investigative psychology. This arrow is a shorthand for the processes of inference that allow investigators to draw conclusions about offenders from information about the crime. In other words, from studies of criminals that are set up with the specific objective of finding patterns that could be applied to later investigations through the inference processes that are developed. The specificity of the information on the location of crimes and the residence of criminals make the study of criminals' geographical patterns especially feasible and instructive.

As Canter and Youngs (2007) note, Geographical Profiling is thus a special and very important example of how the $A \rightarrow C$ equation can be solved for the crucial context in which the A components are essentially where crimes occur and the C component is the location of the base of the offender. Of course, matters such as the nature of the location or locations of crimes and related issues such as the behaviour of the offender and the time and target of the offences need to be considered. Geographical profiling is not simply the consideration of the meaning of a dot on a map. The locations have to be understood in the context of as many other aspects of the crimes as can be harnessed to the inference process.

The discovery and rediscovery over the years, that many offenders often do not travel far to commit their crimes could not form the basis of a decision support tool for investigators until it was realised that this general trend could be applied to individual offenders. This is a small and logical step, but had not been immediately obvious to detectives. So, for example, if 75% of offenders are found to travel less than 2 kilometres to commit their crimes, then it must be the case that 3 out of 4 actual offenders will travel less than 2 kilometres. This is not a perfect prediction but it gives an investigator some framework within which to evaluate possible suspects. For instance, all else being equal, the suspects who live less than 2 kilometres from the crime scene should be given higher priority in the follow up investigation. Geographical profiling, then, generally moves the broad criminological consideration of aggregate crime processes on to the application to individual offenders. This has interesting, and important parallels to other questions in human spatial activity, as discussed by Bromley [1980] when attempting to model the mobility of street traders.

Kind [1987] was probably the first person to recognise the investigative potential of geographical analysis of crime locations. In 1980 he produced a report on the locations of the crimes attributed to 'The Yorkshire Ripper' who, over a five year period starting in July 1975, in the North of England, had murdered 13 women. As an ex-RAF navigator (Kind 1999) saw the task of locating the offender as a navigational task, likening the offence locations to fuel depots, with the challenge of discovering the optimal location of an aircraft's base by calculating the 'centre of gravity' of the crime locations. This proved reasonably accurate in determining where the convicted offender, Sutcliffe, was eventually found to live. Sutcliffe was arrested before the report could be acted upon, so Kind's discovery lay dormant until Canter rediscovered it independently five years later (see Canter 2005).

Kind showed that the short average distance travelled by many offenders is only one aspect of criminal spatial behaviour that makes geographical profiling possible. He introduced the second important aspect of criminal spatial behaviour, i.e. the possibility that many offenders have a base within the area circumscribed by their crimes. This has been shown to be a quite distinct finding from the shortness of the distance between home and crime [Canter et al. 2000]. Indeed, the finding that criminals tend to operate over a particular size of area, having a particular 'criminal range' [Canter and Gregory 1994] helped to broaden the whole perspective beyond just those offenders who travel small distances. It opened the way to considering the patterns of offending in relation to the home rather than simply focusing on offenders whose base is close to the crime. These spatial patterns of offending, notably the significance of the home, drawing attention to the environmental psychological and perceptual processes that had to be involved in criminal spatial behaviour, and the characteristic range of offending, led to the recognition that under some circumstances the criminal's base could be inferred with a useful degree of accuracy from relatively simple geometrical calculations. This encouraged the development of software systems that allowed precise predictions to be made, and tested, applying various geometrical models to the distributions of crimes [Rossmo 1995].

These early studies also demonstrated that there was enough replicable structure in criminal spatial behaviour to make this a fruitful area of research (see Canter and Youngs 2007e for a review). Furthermore, they showed that offence location patterns were relative, and needed to be adjusted, to the scale over which the offender operated. Very similar patterns were found for offenders who travelled large distances to those that travelled small distances (Canter 2005). This meant that geographical profiling could be much more than merely drawing attention to the many offenders having bases near their crimes. Rather broader models of offending could be derived that explored the geographical patterns independently of the range of any given offender.

The generality of these results suggested that they reflect general mental schemata (Bartlett 1930) of how offenders conceptualise their environment. These internal representations are often referred to as 'mental maps' (cf. Canter 1977). They have been explored by environmental psychologists such as Ladd (1970) using the device of getting people to draw a sketch map of an area. As Down and Stea (1977) and many others have shown, building on the seminal work by Lynch (1960), these mental representations do differ from person to person, relating closely to their actual experience of particular environments. The implication of this is that experience shapes understanding of places which in turn influences where a person does what. The findings open the way to exploring how the spatial distribution of offences may reveal fundamental cognitive processes that criminals share with law abiding citizens. The direct exploration of offenders' 'mental maps' [Canter and Hodge 2000] as a way of predicting and understanding the spatial distribution of their activities thus became a further area for research. By this route, then, from application to theory, rather than the other way round, an arena of psychological study emerged from attempts to solve practical investigative problems.

Assumptions Underlying Geographical Offender Profiling

In building on models of criminals' spatial behaviour and developing them as part of geographical profiling, a number of fundamental assumptions about criminal behaviour are made (Canter and Youngs 2007). These assumptions underlie any attempt to draw inferences about an offender's location from details of where crimes have been committed. If these assumptions are not valid then the inferences drawn will be unsafe. It is therefore of value to summarise what the major assumptions are.

Locatedness

The first assumption is that the crimes have a distinct location. This may seem an obvious assumption for a burglary or a robbery, but it becomes more open to question if, for example, the crimes consist of telephone calls or fraud carried out over the internet. However, there are examples of these crimes, which apparently lack a specific geographical location in physical terms but that, nonetheless, still reveal meaningful spatial patterns (Canter 2005). These crimes exist in a 'virtual', or cognitive, space that the offender makes use of. For instance he may only telephone local numbers, or even though the fraud is perpetrated over the internet the fraudster will still use local banks to establish fraudulent accounts.

The issue of locatedness also becomes more complicated when there are a number of different locations associated with any given crime. For instance in a murder case there may be a point of first contact with a victim; a location to which the victim was taken and assaulted; another location where the victim was murdered, and yet another location where the body was disposed of. All of these locations are of interest to investigators, as is the relationship between them. All of them may also have some systematic relationship to where the offender is based.

The locatedness of the offender's base is a further complication. Generally it is assumed that what we are trying to indicate with geographical profiling is where the offender lives, or at least typically sleeps at night. But the term 'base' or even 'anchor point' is often used because the focal point for his crimes may not be accommodation. The offender may be a vagrant with 'no fixed abode', or be venturing out from a friend or partner's house. Criminals may also use pubs or nightclubs as a base, or commit their crimes more directly in relation to where they can obtain a supply of illegal drugs than to where they are living. All of these possibilities, and many others, add challenges to the geographical profiler.

Systematic Crime Location Choice

A further fundamental assumption underlying geographical profiling is that the locations at which crimes occur are not random. Of course the whole of geography and psychology are based on the premise that human behaviour has some patterns and structure to it, but it is only in recent years that there has been a determined, systematic search for the geographical patterns within crime locations. Additionally, it has to be assumed that the patterns are not solely a function of the opportunities for crime or broad social processes. There has to be some aspect of any given individual offender's ways of dealing with any possibilities for crime that influences where his criminal acts take place.

Canter and Shalev [2000] and Canter and Hodge [2000] explored the mental representations people have of their surroundings, following up the studies of non-criminal populations mentioned above, (Canter 1977, Downs and Stea 1977). They studied the strategies offenders use for choosing crime locations by asking them to draw 'mental maps' of their offence areas. This did show the mixture of locational decision processes on which offenders draw, ranging from impulsive, opportunistic strategies to those that are carefully planned.

Brantingham and Brantingham [1981] had referenced the significance of criminals' mental maps, with direct citation of the original work of Lynch (1957), but did not give as much emphasis to the psychological implications of the process of cognitive representation of environments as was articulated by Canter (1977). They drew heavily on what has become known as 'routine activity' theory (Clarke and Felson 1993) which is based on the hypothesis that criminals learn of opportunities for crime, or seek them out, as part of their daily legitimate actions, visiting friends, going to work, shopping and the like. Recently Wiles and Costello [2000] have reported results from interviews with burglars and those stealing cars that lend support to the earlier speculations of the Brantinghams. The interviewees indicated that even when they travelled some distance from their place of residence to carry out a crime the places they went to were influenced by contacts they had in those areas.

Routine Activity Theory puts the offender in a rather passive role in relation to the environment, only becoming aware of opportunities for crime by what the environment reveals whilst the offender is going about non-criminal activities. According to Canter (1977) this is only one aspect of how people come to understand and make sense of places. He emphasised that there are two interacting psychological processes that contribute to a person's internal model of his/her surroundings. One is the process of encoding the information. This leads to various forms of distortion in the mental image. The second is how people make use of their surroundings.

The mental image or 'map' is derived from the interaction between the active storing of information and the passive availability of environmental cues. The mental image that is formed influences what a person thinks is possible and where that possibility lies. This is a developing, cyclical process. The direct interaction with the surroundings in turn shapes the person's conceptualisations. Where a person does various things is consequently partly a product of what that person knows to be possible and where. Their experience shapes what they know to be possible. This will be a dynamic process that takes the offender beyond their 'routine activities' as they get to explore the possibilities for crime. It is out of these dynamic processes that the offender selects opportunities for crime. Therefore the more we understand of these environmental psychological processes the more we will be able to model and predict criminal spatial behaviour (Canter and Youngs 2007).

Centrality (Commuters and Marauders)

One of the implications of the mental mapping approach to understanding how people act on their surroundings is that the places with which they are familiar exert a great deal of influence over where they are likely to go. As mentioned, Brantingham and Brantingham [1981] imply that this familiarity relates very strongly to the key locations in a person's routine activities; home, work, recreation and the routes between them. Rhodes and Conly [1981] had explored a similar parallel between the journeys criminals took to crimes and more conventional journeys, such as a commuter's travel to work, showing that even some of the mathematical modelling of commuter journeys could fit criminal journeys.

However Canter's (1977) model, with its greater emphasis on the person's internal representations, gives more weight to where the people live, as this is likely to be at the core of their cognitive representation of the places they know and are familiar with. Some support for this stress on what is sometimes called 'domocentricity' can be derived from the remarkable finding that in many cases the offender's home or base is within the geographical distribution of his offences. Canter and Gregory [1994] proposed that the simplest way to define the area circumscribed by the crimes was to identify the two crimes furthest from each other and use the line joining them as the diameter of a circle. They then hypothesised that the offender's home would be within the circle so defined. They labelled such offenders 'marauders'. This notion has been so widely adopted that it is important to note that the assertion was not that the circle was necessarily the most precise geometry for describing an offender's domain, just that it was the simplest and most direct way of indicating the area covering offenders' 'mental maps' of criminal opportunities.

Various studies have lent support to this 'circle' hypothesis. The proportion of offenders who are 'marauders' in this sense varies for different studies, as shown in Table 1.1. This can vary within one area of Australia from 35% for a sample of burglars to 93% for a sample of sex offenders (Meaney 2004). The reasons for such variations have not been explored, but as more studies emerge a clearer picture will become possible.

But even at lower proportions there are still enough offenders with bases within the areas of their crimes for this finding to provide a systematic basis for prioritising offenders, or the places to look for them. This assumption of 'domocentricity' helps to demarcate the area to be searched in order to find an offender. As a consequence, the general principle of crimes being centred on the home of the offender has been at the heart of geographical profiling systems. Thus most of geographical decision support systems work on the assumption that the offender is operating within the area of his/her crimes.

There are ways of modelling offenders' actions that do not rely on the assumption of 'domocentricity' (as discussed in Canter 2005). However at present these are more speculative, have been less studied and have not been applied in any direct way to actual investigations, other than the loose suggestion that offences carried over considerable distances along transport routes may well have been committed by someone whose job takes them along such routes, for example as a delivery van driver.

One challenge to research, therefore, is to determine whether offenders are commuters or marauders from aspects of their criminal activity. There has been little success in doing this, although the study by Warren et al. [1998] gives an interesting pointer by showing that serial rapists who are 'commuters' tend to travel further from home (a mean of 4.03 miles) than those who are 'marauders' (a mean of 2.36 miles). This accords with the findings reported by Lundrigan and Canter [2001] that

Table 1.1 Summary of proportions of Marauders and Commuters found in various studies

	Location of Offence	When Offence Occurred	Type of Offence	Percentage in Each Group	
				Marauder	Commuter
Meaney, R. (2004)	NSW, Australia	2000–2003	Burglary (N=83)	35	65
			Arson (N=21)	90	10
			Sexual Offences (N=32)	93	7
Canter and Larkin (1993)	Greater London and SE England	1980s	Serial Rape (N=45)	87	13
Canter and Gregory (1994)	Greater London and SE England	1980s	Serial Rape (N=45)	87	13
Tamura and Suzuki (2000)	Tokyo and its surrounding suburban area and Osaka (urban arsonists)	1989–1995	Arson (N=107)	70	30
Warren et al. (1998)	U.S.A.	Not stated	Serial Rape (N= 64)	57	43

serial killers who travel long distances tend to carry out consecutive crimes closer together than alternate crimes, but for those who travel shorter distances, it is the alternate crimes that tend to be closer than the consecutive crimes. This implies that when travelling larger distances there is more of a tendency to focus intensely on a given area, as a commuter does, rather than spread out over a particular area, as appears to be more typical of marauders.

Comparative Case Analysis (Linking Crimes)

Some principles of geographical profiling can be applied to one, single crime. However, the more crimes that can be linked to a common offender, the more information there is to work with and so the more powerful can be the application of this approach. This requires that crimes can be effectively linked, which is not always feasible, especially in the absence of forensic evidence.

The process of linking crimes to a common offender is thus an important, sometimes crucial, basis for developing an offender's geographical profile. It is not necessary to have details of all the crimes an offender has committed to be able to analyse their geography, but any spatial bias in the sampling of offences that are considered will of course distort any conclusions drawn from the analysis. So if, for example, crimes are only drawn from one police jurisdiction, but the offender has also committed crimes in another jurisdiction in, say, an adjacent area, then any geographical conclusions drawn will be misleading. Also crimes wrongly attributed to a person can distort the spatial interpretation. That is why some software systems, such as Dragnet [Canter 2004] allow exploration of subsets of offences, deleting those that may have been inappropriately linked, to determine the relative impact of any particular crimes on the geographical conclusions reached.

However, one intriguing possibility has been overlooked by researchers in this area. If offenders commit crimes close to home then they must be committing crimes close to each other. This has the significant implication that crimes committed near to each other may well have been committed by the same person. With the appropriate analyses it should therefore be possible to demonstrate that crimes close to each other are actually linked to a common offender. Support for this use of spatial distribution of crimes comes from Grubin et al's (2001) study of serial stranger rapists. They found that by far the most fruitful way of linking crimes to a common offender was by looking at crimes close to each other. They were working with a national sample for a rare crime so localisation might be expected. But in a much more focused test of the effectiveness of linking with different distance criteria, Bennell and Canter [2002] showed that commercial burglaries in the UK could be effectively linked by the distance between crimes. Bennell and Jones (2005) showed that other forms of burglary could be linked in the same way and these findings have been repeated in other regions also for burglary (Ewart et al. 2005). There is thus growing evidence that rather than rely on linking crimes before carrying out geographical profiling, the actual geographical analysis itself could help to link the crimes.

Challenges of Data Sources

Before we get too carried away with the exciting prospects that geographical profiling offers crime analysis and detection, a number of important cautions need to be emphasised. Many of these cautions derive from the fact that the whole domain of geographical profiling is based on the development of empirically tested principles. This means that it draws from information about crime and criminals. But the challenge is that illegal activities, of course, are not normally in open public view. They can thus usually only be turned into data once the crime has been identified. Also, much information – notably where the offender lives – only becomes available once the offender is apprehended. This means that many of the studies may be biased because they must ignore those crimes that are not reported to the police or solved.

Broadly the crime and criminal can give rise to data for research in one of two general forms. The most common is when the details become part of official records, held by the police, various legal agencies or government departments. Although, as Canter and Alison (2003) have argued, these records have a great deal of value for research and subsequent operational use, they are not normally produced with the idea of detailed analysis in mind. They are typically incomplete and often unreliably recorded. Their greatest weakness is that they only record information about crimes that have been drawn to official attention and the full details are only present for crimes for which an offender is known. It is certainly possible that the offenders who are not caught have different patterns of behaviour to those who are. This possibility however, assumes that offenders are caught through very focused and systematic police processes, rather than the random trawls that will catch offenders if they commit enough crimes.

A second source of information is the offenders themselves. This relies on the vagaries of offenders' memories as well any particular distortions they may introduce by way of justification or caution, or even to make themselves appear to be more significant criminals than they actually are. This source of information therefore probably has different biases from the official sources. Fortunately the few studies that compare these two sources of information indicate that they do not contradict each other, but rather the self-reported activities tend to be a clarification and elaboration of the much sparser official records (Farrington 1989, Youngs et al. 2004).

Weaknesses in Study Methodologies

One further assumption that it would be disingenuous to ignore is that the researchers in this area are all working at the highest standards. As the discerning reader will quickly become aware the various papers cited have a mixture of strengths and weaknesses. For example, often information that we now know to be of great interest is just not reported. Sometimes basic facts like the exact nature of the crime or the average distances travelled will not be reported in studies that otherwise have very useful ideas and findings. In some cases overly complex statistics are presented that hide more basic results which are theoretically of considerable significance. No study or the report of it is perfect. However, it is by drawing on the strengths of very different published reports that consistent and enlightening theories and findings are emerging.

There are many reasons why research in this area and accounts of it will be weak. Often studies are funded for direct practical reasons so the researcher has to balance an exploration of some relatively straightforward set of facts with the development of a richer understanding of what is giving rise to those facts. Another complication is that the data are never collected under the purified and controlled conditions of laboratory research. This can give rise to curious anomalies. For instance police records may only allow the ages of offenders to be extracted in sub-groups rather than the actual ages, so the researcher is doomed to work with these sub-groups that may not allow some important differences in behaviour to be revealed. Or the police recording of addresses may be so vague that only general areas can be indicated rather than precise points.

Such problems and difficulties are ever present, so it is noteworthy that so many consistent and clear findings have been produced. It is also the case that as law enforcement agencies around the world become aware of the potential practical values of studies of criminal geography, and researchers become more aware of the contributions to our understanding of human behaviour that can be made from studying criminals' geography, that an ever more productive interaction between researchers and the police is developing. Out of these interactions much more reliable, precise and detailed information is emerging so that the quality of research is constantly improving.

Mental Maps and Environmental Decision Making

The theoretical basis for geographical profiling has been much less fully explored than its possible practical applications. This has meant that a number of core, implicit assumptions that may complement or contradict each other have not been clearly stated or their implications fully explored. These assumptions can be traced back to two rather different fundamental models of how people build up mental representations of their surroundings and thus the processes that will give rise to how criminals will chose crime locations (Canter and Youngs 2007).

These two different ways of conceptualising people's transactions with their surroundings reflect earlier debates in psychology from the middle of the twentieth century. This debate was often characterised as between Hull (1943) and Tolman (1948), although these two psychologists were actually articulating two different traditions in psychology. In essence, Hull (1943) proposed that learning was based on the build up of a series of habits derived directly from experience. In contrast, Tolman (1948) argued for the development of internal representations ('mental maps') that allowed the individual to make choices that go beyond his/her immediate experience.

Detailed consideration of their arguments reveals that Tolman and Hull had much more subtle ways of considering human learning, than this over-simplification of 'habit' learning versus 'map' learning, but the broad differences between them offers a way of thinking about distinctions between models of criminals' spatial activity. Both approaches draw on the assumption that, rather than being entirely opportunistic, offenders do make some sort of choice as to where to commit a crime, even if below their level of awareness. The processes that are assumed to give rise to these choices are rather different, however.

The model favoured, at least implicitly, in North America, notably by Brantingham and Brantingham (1982) is more Hullian, in that the assumption is made that the offender moves along well-known paths and learns of criminal activities along these paths. It is out of this perspective that the popular but possibly psychologically misleading notion of a 'Journey to Crime' emerges. Offenders' spatial decision making is assumed to relate very strongly to established routes and actual journeys. Within this framework researchers will tend to put greater emphasis on the actual streets and pathways that offenders may follow. In contrast, the European perspective, most readily described by Canter (2005), explicitly takes the Tolmanian viewpoint that the offender makes choices on the basis of his/her mental map of the opportunities for crime. The exact journey will, from this perspective, be less significant than the overall knowledge of the offence area. The straight line distance here is regarded as reflecting this overall conceptualisation of what is where rather very specific routes between places.

The idea that an offender builds up knowledge of an area by moving through it and carrying out crimes can be taken a step further if it is assumed that what the offender is doing is not just learning a route with opportunities along it, but, in line with the Tolmanian perspective, is also building up a mental picture of the area that will fill in gaps between locations that s/he has visited. In other words, rather than just knowing a linked set of routes, the assumption is that the offender has some notion of a domain, or region, of activity. These domains are clearly illustrated in D's map and P's map in Canter and Hodge [2000a] and in the drug supplier's map in Canter and Shalev [2000]. The offenders may not even have a clear notion of a specific route of relevance to their crimes, but they do have an idea of general locations and the broad directions in which they need to travel to get to them. Furthermore, because they are part of a general cognitive representation the offender has they are open to influence from many different sources, including comments and suggestions from other offenders.

Running through all these considerations is the idea that the offender has some influence over where he commits his crime. It also does assume that the crime location is not totally random. Even if it were a spur of the moment impulse, it would still have to be in a location where the offender was when that impulse is acted on. True randomness would only be possible if the offender was randomly in a variety of locations. However, the patterns themselves that emerge out of these implicit choices are not necessarily assumed to be under any conscious control of the offender. There may be conscious choices about avoiding an area where the criminal may be recognised, or seeking out an area where particular targets are possible, but how this shapes the spatial geometry of the crimes is not usually likely to be something the offender considers.

There has been hardly any research on how the distribution of possible opportunities for crime helps to shape the geographical distribution of a criminal's activity, although Bernasco and Luyxk (2003) have done some theoretical studies to show the potential power of such considerations. Clearly, the influence of opportunities will depend on how focused is the offender's targeting. If the criminal is seeking out rare or unevenly distributed targets, such as street level prostitutes, or antique clocks, then where they are located will produce distortions in the offence behaviour, provided the offender is aware of the geographical possibility of such targets.

One interesting and more elaborate pattern of the way opportunities may distort activities in relation to the objectives of the offender is emerging in relation to property crime. This is the finding that the greater the value of the property stolen the further the offender is likely to have travelled [van Koppen and Jansen 1998]. This fits with the idea that if offenders have specific targets then they will search further to find those targets, being likely to build up very rich mental maps of the areas in which such targets exist. So, the particular nature of the individual's transactions with his/ her surroundings will be reflected in the form that their mental representation will take. This differentiation between offenders in their mental maps of areas reflects findings central to the whole environmental image literature. Canter (1977) referred to 'environmental roles' as the particular reasons a person has for being in a place, arguing that each of these roles will harness different mental representations of an area. House burglars may be regarded as having different environmental roles from street robbers or car thieves so they would be expected to have distinguishable mental maps. Much research with actual offenders is necessary to understand these processes more fully.

From Principles to Applications

Work concerned with the specification and elaboration of the principles underlying geographical offender profiling was initially a response to the potential investigative applications that a number of high profile cases drew attention to (e.g. see Canter 1994). This movement from potential application to principle, although consistent with Canter's notion of investigatory rather than applied disciplines, runs contrary to the direction of influence associated with the traditional model of applied science. Yet, of course, now, as the principles are clarified and established empirically, the range and power of potential applications to investigations is increasing. However, in evaluating the science of Geographical Offender Profiling, the distinction between the robustness of the principles of criminal spatial behaviour and the effective harnessing of these in police investigations sometimes gets confused. In an attempt to clarify this distinction, research exploring the potential investigative uses is considered in a separate, companion volume to the current book, *Applications of Geographical Offender Profiling*. The recommendation is that any program of study or professional training course based on these volumes retain this distinction explicitly.

References

Bartlett, F. (1932, Reprinted 1964). *Remembering: A Study in Experimental and Social Psychology*. London: Cambridge University Press.

Bennell, C., and Jones, N. J. (2005). Between a ROC and hard place: A method of linking serial burglaries. *Journal of Investigative Psychology and Offender Profiling*, 2, 23–41.

Bennell, C., and Canter, D. V. (2002). Linking commercial burglaries by modus operandi: Tests using regression and ROC analysis. *Science and Justice*, 42 (3), 1–12.

Bernasco, W., and Luyxk, F. (2003). Effects of Attractiveness, Opportunity and Accessibility to Burglars on Residential Burglary Rates of Urban Neighborhoods. Criminology, 41, 981–1001.

Brantingham, P. J., and Brantingham, P. (1981). *Environmental Criminology.* Waveland Press Inc: Prospect Heights, Illinois.

Bromley, R. J. (1980). Trader mobility in systems of periodic and daily markets. In D. T. Herbert and R. J. Johnston (eds), *Geography and the Urban Environment* (pp. 133–174). New York: John Wiley & Sons Ltd.

Canter, D. (2005). Confusing operational predicaments and cognitive explorations: Comments on Rossmo and Snook et al. *Applied Cognitive Psychology*, 19(5), 663–668.

Canter, D. (2004). Geographic profiling of criminals. *Medico-legal Journal*, 72, 53–66.

Canter, D. (1977). *The Psychology of Place.* London: The Architectural Press.

Canter, D., and Alison, L. J. (2003). Converting evidence into data: The use of law enforcement archives as unobtrusive measurement. *The Qualitative Report*, June, 8, (2).

Canter, D. V., and Gregory, A. (1994). Identifying the residential location of rapists. *Journal of the Forensic Science Society*, 34, 169–175.

Canter, D., and Hodge, S. (2000). Criminals' mental maps. In L. S. Turnbull, E.H. Hendrix and B. D. Dent (eds), *Atlas of Crime, Mapping the Criminal Landscape* (pp 187–191). Phoenix, Arizona: Oryx Press.

Canter, D., and Larkin, P. (1993). The environmental range of serial rapists. *Journal of Environmental Psychology*, 13, 63–69.

Canter, D., and Youngs, D. (2008). Geographical offender profiling: Applications and opportunities. In D. Canter and D. Youngs: *Applications of Geographical Offender Profiling*. Aldershot, England: Ashgate.

Canter, D., and Youngs, D. (2007). Beyond geographical offender profiling: The investigative psychology of criminal spatial activity – an emerging research agenda *(Submitted)*.

Canter, D., and Youngs, D. (2003). Beyond offender profiling: The need for an investigative psychology. In R. Bull and D. Carson (eds), *Handbook of Psychology and Legal Contexts*, (pp. 171–205).

Canter, D., Coffey, T., Huntley, M., and Missen, C. (2000). Predicting serial killers' home base using a decision support system. *Journal of Quantitative Criminology*, 16, 457–478.

Canter, D., and Shalev, K. (2000). Putting Crime in its Place: Psychological Process in Crime Site Location. Paper for *Wheredunit?* Investigating the Role of Place in Crime and Criminality. Crime Mapping Research Center of the NIJ, San Diego.

Clarke, R., and Felson, M. (eds) (1993). *Routine Activity and Rational Choice*. New Brunswick: Transaction Publishers.

Downs, R. M., and Stea, D. (1977). *Maps in Minds*. London: Harper and Row.

Ewart, B. W., Oatley, G. C., and Burn, K. (2005). Matching crimes using burglars' *modus operandi*: A test of three models. *International Journal of Police Science and Management*, 7, 160–174.

Farrington, D. P. (1989). Self-reported and official offending in adolescence and adulthood. In M. W. Kelin (ed.), *Cross-National Research in Self-Reported Crime and Delinquency,* Dordrecht: Kuwer, 399–423.

Grubin, D., Kelly, P., and Brunsdon, C. (2001). *Linking Serious Sexual Assaults Through Behaviour*. Home Office Research Study 215.

Guerry, A. M. (1833). *Essai sur la Statistique Morale de la France*. Paris: Crochard.

Hull, C. L. (1943). *Principles of Behavior.* New York: Appleton Century Croft.

Kind, S. (1999). *The Sceptical Witness: Concerning the Scientific Investigation of Crime Against a Human Background*. Harrogate: The Forensic Science.

Kind, S. (1987). Navigational ideas and the Yorkshire Ripper investigation. *Journal of Navigation* 40, 3, 385–393.

Ladd, F. C. (1970). Black youths view their environment: Neighbourhood Maps, *Environment and Behaviour* 2, 1, 74–99.

Lundrigan, S., and Canter, D. (2001). A multivariate analysis of serial murderers' disposal site location choice. *Journal of Environmental Psychology*, 21, 423–432.

Lynch, K. (1960). *The Image of the City*, Cambridge, Mass: MIT Press.

Mayhew, H. (1861). *London Labour and the London Poor: A Cyclopaedia of the Condition and Earnings of Those That Will Work, Those That Cannot Work, and Those That Will Not Work*.

Meaney, R. (2004). Commuters and marauders: An examination of the spatial behaviour of serial criminals. *Journal of Investigative Psychology and Offender Profiling*, 1(2), 121–137.

Mizutani, F. (1993). Home range of leopards and their impact on livestock on Kenyan ranches. *Symposium Zoological Society London*, 65, 425–439.

Rhodes, W. M., and Conly, C. (1981). 'Crime and mobility: An empirical study'. In Brantingham, P. J. and Brantingham, P. (eds). *Environmental Criminology*. Waveland Press Inc: Prospect Heights, Illinois.

Rossmo, K. D. (1995). Place, space and police investigations: Hunting serial violent criminals. In J. E. Eck and D. Weisburd, (eds), *Crime and Place*, NY: Criminal Justice press, 217–35.

Snow, J. (1855). *On the Mode of Communication of Cholera*. Explanation of the map showing the situation of the deaths in and around Broad Street, Golden Square. Retrieved February 25th, 2006, from http://www.ph.ucla.edu/epi/snow/snowbook2.html.

Tamura, M., and Suzuki, M. (2000). Characteristics of serial arsonists and crime scene geography in Japan. In A. Czerederecka, T. Jaśkiewicz-Obydzińska and J. Wójcikiewicz (eds), *Forensic Psychology and Law: Traditional Questions and New Ideas*, (pp. 259–264). Kraków, Poland: Institute of Forensic Research in Cracow, Poland.

Tolman, E. C. (1948). Cognitive maps in rats and men, *Psychological Review*, 55, 189–208.

Turner, S. (1969). Delinquency and distance. In Sellin, T., and Wolfgang, M. E. (eds). *Delinquency: Selected Studies* (pp. 11–26). New York: John Wiley & Sons.

Van Koppen, P. J., and Jansen, R. W. (1998). The road to robbery: travel patterns in commercial robberies. *British Journal of Criminology*, 38(2), 230–246.

Warren, J., Reboussin, R., Hazelwood, R. R., Cummings, A., Gibbs, N., and Trumbetta, S. (1998). Crime scene and distance correlates of serial rape. *Journal of Quantitative Criminology*, 14(1), 35–59.

White, R. C. (1932). The relation of felonies to environmental factors in Indianapolis, *Social Forces*, 10, 498–509.

Wiles, P., and Costello, A. (2000). *The 'Road to Nowhere': The Evidence for Travelling Criminals*. Home Office research study 207. Section 5, pp. 29–42.

Youngs, D., Canter, D., and Cooper, J. (2004). The facets of criminality: A cross-modal and cross-gender validation. *Behaviormetrika* 31, 2, 1–13.

PART 1
Spatial Patterns in Behaviour

Chapter 2

Navigational Ideas and the Yorkshire Ripper Investigation

Stuart S. Kind

Introduction

Navigational ideas are useful in crime investigation. This is particularly so in those examples ('multiple' or 'series' crimes) where several offences are suspected as having been committed by the same criminal. Such a series is exemplified by the Yorkshire Ripper series of attacks.

The writer's involvement in the Yorkshire Ripper investigation falls into two parts. The first part was as a member of an advisory team, which included four senior police officers. In December 1980, before the arrest of the killer, for a period of seventeen days, this team examined the progress of the investigation.

The second part took place the following year after the arrest of the killer when, with the same four police officers, the writer spent several months reviewing the investigation under the chairmanship of Mr Lawrence Byford, HM Inspector of Constabulary (now Sir Lawrence Byford, HM Chief Inspector of Constabulary).

It would be tempting to illustrate part of this presentation by knowledge which came through membership of the Byford review team (post arrest); hindsight is a powerful ally in argument. However, this chapter will be restricted to some aspects of the first period which took place before the arrest of Peter William Sutcliffe.

On Friday, 22 March 1981, Sutcliffe was convicted of thirteen murders and seven attempted murders in the Yorkshire Ripper series. He was sentenced to 20 concurrent terms of life imprisonment with a recommendation that he should serve a minimum of 30 years.

The Investigative Process

A scientist produces hypotheses by inductive inference. That is to say he combines a number of individual findings into a general statement which, he believes, accounts for the individual facts. The mental procedure of producing hypotheses is extremely complex and does not concern us here. Our approach will be strictly pragmatical.

The scientist next deduces some logical consequences of his views. These he then subjects to experimental test. Likewise the police investigator may produce

LIVERPOOL JOHN MOORES UNIVERSITY
LEARNING SERVICES

a hypothesis (called in his case a 'hunch') which he subjects to test by adopting particular lines of enquiry. The logical pattern is the same in both examples.

If the hypothesis or hunch survives the test then one may consider it confirmed, or at least supported, keeping in mind that logically speaking one can never totally establish a hypothesis (the next experiment may prove you wrong). However, the essence of the matter is that one commits oneself to a particular view in advance of the facts being established.

Einstein predicted the gravitational bending of light rays as a deduced result of the Theory of Relativity. The predicted bending was observed experimentally and this was taken as support for the theory. An air navigator (of which the writer was a wartime example) may predict his track and estimated time of arrival. He may arrive where and when he predicts. Error in the first example may lead to a rethinking of scientific concepts. Error in the second, like errors by crime investigators, may lead to fatal consequences.

The Yorkshire Ripper Series

At the end of November 1980, except for a single meeting with some colleagues who were professionally involved in the investigation, the writer's entire knowledge of the Yorkshire Ripper investigation stemmed from newspaper reports since, although a professional forensic scientist, he had held a research job for the previous four years.

There was widespread public disquiet at the time. The female population of the North of England was terrorized to a degree which it is hard to conceive so long after the events. Personal disquiet at the situation was expressed by the Prime Minister and the Home Secretary, and it was as a result of this that a visit was made by Mr Lawrence Byford to the Chief Constable of the West Yorkshire Metropolitan Police (Mr Ronald Gregory) during November 1980.

The immediate consequence of this visit was that an advisory group was set up to review the Yorkshire Ripper investigation, as it had unfolded during the previous five and a half years, with a view to making recommendations for any change of direction which might be thought necessary in the pattern of enquiries.

The Advisory Group consisted of Mr Leslie Emment (Deputy Chief Constable, Thames Valley Police), Mr David Gerty, (Assistant Chief Constable, West Midlands Police), Mr Ronald Harvey, (Assistant to Her Majesty's Chief Inspector of Constabulary), Mr Andrew Sloan (Assistant Chief Constable, Lincolnshire Police) and the writer (Director, Home Office Central Research Establishment).

The work of the advisory group started on 1 December 1980 and continued until 17 December 1980 when, with the production of an interim advisory report for the Chief Constable of the West Yorkshire Metropolitan Police, the work temporarily ceased. An intention to return to the task the following month proved superfluous because Sutcliffe was arrested in Sheffield on 2 January 1981. It is necessary to point out here that the circumstances of Sutcliffe's arrest owed nothing to the work of the advisory group but were simply a consequence of good routine police work by South Yorkshire Police aided by efficient radio communications and by the excellent Home Office Police National Computer Unit.

The situation found by the five-member team as work began at the beginning of December 1980, was that there were seventeen established Ripper victims of which thirteen were murders and four were assaults (see Table 2.1). 'Established' simply means those cases which, at that time, for the purpose of the investigation, were accepted as belonging to the series. Of those seventeen cases, fifteen of them were accepted with some confidence as belonging to the series but two of them, No. 4 (Harrison, Preston, 20 November 1975) and No. 12 (Pearson, Bradford, 21 January 1978) were considered as doubtful members of the series.

Over the seventeen days of the exercise the group read many case files and reports, interviewed many police officers (singly and in groups), visited scenes of Ripper crimes and conferred together at length.

The Ripper offences, as far as then known, were restricted to the North of England and consideration was given to cases throughout West Yorkshire and in Greater Manchester and in Preston. At the time the group started work the Yorkshire Ripper investigation involved several hundreds of police officers and it had been under way in one form or another since 1975. Table 2.1 gives date, location and time of each of the seventeen attacks. Figure 2.1 gives the geographical location of the attacks.

At the end of 1980 the pattern of the investigation was substantially polarized by the view of the chief investigating officer that certain letters and a tape recording which he had received originated from the Yorkshire Ripper. From this view arose the idea that the Ripper had a Geordie (Sunderland) accent and much of the investigation was based upon this assumption. The argument for adopting this view was that certain information in the letters and the tape could only have been known to the Ripper himself.

After considering the content of the letters and the tape, together with various reports which had appeared in the media throughout the several years of the Yorkshire Ripper investigation, the group concluded that it was by no means established that the tape and letters came from the killer. All the information which was supposedly private to the Ripper had been available, somewhere or other in the press, although it is true to say that it would have taken a degree of dedication for a person unassociated with the investigation to search for and to assemble it. There was, furthermore, some evidence which positively indicated that the letters and the tape were a hoax. It is only fair to add that this was a view which was fairly widespread amongst many of the investigating police officers themselves.

Having disposed of the necessity to assume that the Ripper was a Geordie the view gradually developed amongst the members of the advisory group that the Ripper was a local man. 'Local' in this sense meant the Bradford and Leeds areas with preference for Bradford. The reasons this view was adopted were many and complex and no attempt will be made to analyse and present them here except to say that it developed gradually and as a consequence of a barrage of information imposed

Table 2.1   The 17 assumed Yorkshire Ripper attacks which were considered by the advisory team

Offence no.	Day	Date	Location	Time victim last seen/assaulted		Offence	Victim
				Clock	GMT		
1	Saturday	5 July 1975	Keighley	0110	0010	Assault	Anne Roglkyj
2	Friday	15 Aug. 1975	Halifax	2300	2200	Assault	Olive Smelt
3	Thursday	30 Oct. 1975	Leeds	0115	0115	Murder	Wilma McCann
4	Thursday	20 Nov. 1975	Preston	2220	2220	Murder	Joan Harrison
5	Tuesday	20 Jan. 1976	Leeds	1900	1900	Murder	Emily Jackson
6	Saturday	5 Feb. 1977	Leeds	2330	2330	Murder	Irene Richardson
7	Saturday	23 Apr. 1977	Bradford	2315	2215	Murder	Patricia Atkinson
8	Sunday	26 June 1977	Leeds	0145	0045	Murder	Jayne MacDonald
9	Sunday	10 July 1977	Bradford	0100	2400	Assault	Maureen Long
10	Saturday	10 Oct. 1977	Manchester	2130	2030	Murder	Jean Jordan
11	Wednesday	14 Dec. 1977	Leeds	2000	2000	Assault	Marilyn Moore
12	Saturday	21 Jan. 1978	Bradford	2130	2130	Murder	Yvonne Pearson
13	Tuesday	31 Jan. 1978	Huddersfield	2110	2110	Murder	Elena Rytka
14	Tuesday	16 May 1978	Manchester	2200	2100	Murder	Vera Millward
15	Wednesday	4 Apr. 1979	Halifax	2330	2230	Murder	Josephine Whitaker
16	Sunday	2 Sep. 1979	Bradford	0215	0115	Murder	Barbara Leach
17	Monday	17 Nov. 1980	Leeds	2120	2120	Murder	Jacqueline Hill

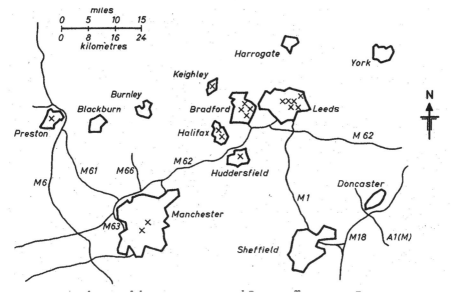

Figure 2.1   Distribution of the 17 assumed Ripper offences as at December 1980

upon fresh professional minds. But whatever the reasons for the hypothesis it was one which was intuitively held by the group. So, having formulated the hypothesis that the Ripper was a local man, was there any way it could be tested?

There were seventeen cases to work on where the locations of the attacks were known to a high degree of confidence. The times of the attacks were less precisely known since in some instances the body was not discovered until some time after the attack. However one factor was exactly known in each case where the time of attack was doubtful. This was the 'time-last-seen-alive'. There were good reasons in most cases for assuming this to be shortly before the attack.

The Two Navigational Tests

For the purposes of this chapter we must disregard the exact nature of the welter of information, much of it conflicting, which led the group to formulate the idea that the Ripper was a local man. It is, however, useful to note two pieces of valuable physical evidence which were available at the time.

The first of these was that in three of the cases, No. 6 (Richardson, Leeds, 5 February 1977), No. 11 (Moore, Leeds, 14 December 1977) and No. 14 (Millward, Manchester, 16 May 1978) motor-car tyre tracks had been left at the scenes of crime. The tyre tracks were sufficiently informative to suggest that the same vehicle had been used on each occasion.

The other piece of physical evidence was that a new five-pound note had been found in the handbag of victim No. 10 (Jordan, Manchester, 1 October 1977). This had been issued between Thursday 29 September and Saturday 1 October 1977 by one of two banks both of which were located in North Bradford (Manningham and Shipley). This was the only money in the deceased's handbag. It was assumed to be payment for prostitution since five pounds in advance was the going rate for that class of prostitute in that area at the time. The fact that the note had been issued in Yorkshire, where eight of the previous nine Ripper cases had occurred, was taken to be highly significant.

The First Navigational Test

The first test to be applied to the hypothesis that the Ripper was a local man was to compute the 'centre of gravity' of the offences without regard to when they occurred. 'Centre of gravity' in this context can best be visualized by the following example.

Take a map of the area in which the seventeen Yorkshire Ripper offences occurred and mark the location of each by a pin. Next take an eighteenth pin and join it to each of the seventeen locations by a piece of thread. That location of the eighteenth pin which minimizes the amount of thread required is the centre of gravity of the seventeen offences.

In fact the exercise was carried out on computer at the Home Office Central Research Establishment. The calculations were performed on the basis of the simplest possible pattern, that is distances as the crow flies. Six different exercises were carried out. These were based on six different sets of assumptions as to which of the seventeen cases were in fact Ripper cases. The centre of gravity proved to be in all cases near the City of Bradford (see Figure 2.2).

The justification for the test was simply that criminals, like non-criminals, are subject to the constraints of time and space in all their activities. The possibility that a criminal may act in such a way as deliberately to cover his tracks must be balanced against the natural human tendency to gain results with minimum effort. Neither should one forget the fourteenth-century dictum of William of Ockham (Occam's Razor), 'entities should not be multiplied without necessity' or, put another way, keep hypotheses as simple as the data permit.

The Second Navigational Test

The second test made on the seventeen sets of data points concerned the possible effect on the timing of the crimes if the Ripper operated from a single location. The reasoning behind this test went thus: If the killer seeks his victims wherever he can find them and then returns to his base as quickly as possible, he will have the tendency to attack later in the day the closer he is to base. The reason for this

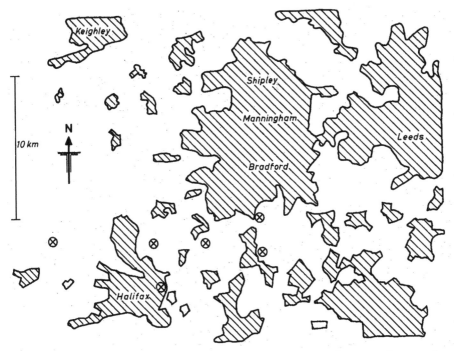

Figure 2.2 The centres of gravity for six different sets of assumptions made at the time as to which of the seventeen offences were, or were not, Ripper offences. This is an exact reproduction of the locations noted in December 1980

tendency is to minimize the risk of being held up on the way home should the crime be swiftly discovered.

In the seventeen established cases the Ripper had attacked exclusively after sunset. Because of this, in the summer-time the attacks tended to be later. The question to be asked was therefore 'if this trend were compensated for, would any correlation of time and location be discernible?'

The method adopted was simply to plot a graph with clock time on the ordinate and day length on the abscissa. This method was adopted because the assessment was carried out in haste, in the early hours of the morning, in an hotel bedroom. No diary with sunset times was available so day length was computed roughly by taking December as the month of the shortest days, June as the month of the longest days and the other ten months were paired in five groups of two. The intention was to refine the hastily performed calculation when sunset times became available but, in the event, this was not done before the arrest of the Ripper.

Certain questions will doubtless occur to the navigator on reading the above paragraph but they will not be dealt with here simply because they did not occur to the writer at the time. Those who have experienced the necessity to perform quick approximate calculations, when fatigued, will doubtless understand why.

The graph so produced (of which Figure 2.3 is a legible and quantitatively precise reproduction) showed a distinct seasonal trend in attack times. Allowing for this seasonal trend it appeared to the writer, at the time, that the later attacks were those located near Leeds and Bradford just as the hypothesis demanded.

The Broad Basis Document

Having absorbed a large amount of information, and having seen the hypothesis pass two metrical tests, the conviction grew upon the writer that the Ripper was indeed a local man. This view was transmitted to the Operational Services Division of the Home Office Central Research Establishment and was reproduced as a Broad Basis document which was circulated on 10 December 1980. Among a number of clauses, the relevant ones were:

(2)   The centre of gravity of the incidents, weighted and unweighted, tends to be near Bradford.
(3)   Time of offence correlates well with day length but the late 'fliers' tend to be in Leeds and Bradford.

The document also contained the suggestion that the Ripper lived in or near Bradford, possibly in the Manningham or Shipley area.

The human mind tends to rationalize conclusions arrived at on a purely intuitive basis and so the reader must decide for himself how convincing he finds the Broad Basis document clauses as a reflection of the reasoning processes involved. But whatever view is taken of the matter one must accept the fact that the document was drafted, filed and distributed before the matter was finally determined by the arrest of the Ripper.

Readers may find it instructive to work on the data in Table 2.1 in their own ways and to see what conclusions they arrive at. These may, of course be additional to (or even different from!) those of the writer.

Interim Report and the Arrest

On 17 December 1980 the group produced an interim report for the Chief Constable of the West Yorkshire Metropolitan Police. *Inter alia* the report recommended that a special team of high-grade detectives be dedicated to enquiries in the Bradford area. It was the intention of the group to return to its task early in the New Year and to monitor how effectively the recommendations had been put into effect. This return proved unnecessary.

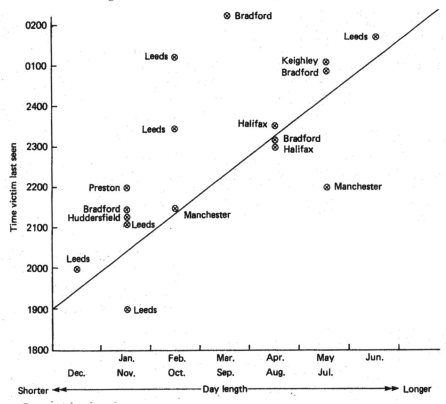

Figure 2.3   The data from Table 2.1 plotted as clock time (ordinates) and day length (abscissa). The data for attack No. 9 (see Table 2.1) was plotted too early in error. Correct plotting lends added strength to the hypothesis. It is instructive to rework the data in the form of a simple rank order after sunset, particularly in the light of the special status of attack No. 4. This was the only one of the 17 attacks to which Peter William Sutcliffe did not plead guilty

At 10.50 p.m. on Friday 2 January 1981, Sergeant Robert Ring and Constable Robert John Hydes of the South Yorkshire Police were on motor-patrol duty in the City of Sheffield. There they questioned, and later arrested, Peter William Sutcliffe. Sutcliffe was later charged with and convicted of, *inter alia*, all the crimes listed in Table 2.1 with the exception of No. 4. Sutcliffe was a native of Bradford who spoke with a Bradford accent. He lived in the district of Heaton in Bradford. Heaton is located midway between Manningham and Shipley.

Discussion

Such results as were obtained in the exercise described above were a consequence of the work of the group as a whole. The expertise of the forensic scientist cannot be applied in a vacuum. Experience clearly shows that the closer the cooperation between the investigator and his scientific advisers the more efficiently may specialist techniques be applied. Indeed it may even be said that given sufficient and sufficiently expert briefing, the way to proceed for the scientific adviser becomes so obvious as to be trite. Certainly one could hardly claim any measure of originality for the tests used here as scientific methods *per se*.

Yet the investigation had been under way in one form or another for five and a half years. As the investigation developed, more data points (if one is ever justified in describing human tragedy in such a way) became available. At what stage of the investigation might the same methods have been applied to demonstrate the same ideas discussed here? Perhaps some navigator with an interest in crime investigation might care to rework the data available after each crime! Certainly it appears no one applied the approach described here yet hundreds of competent police investigators, and dozens of expert forensic scientists had been involved in the investigation and millions of pounds of taxpayers' money had been spent.

Criticism is sometimes made that the applications of the lessons to be learned from the failures in the Yorkshire Ripper investigation have been placed entirely in the hands of those who failed in the first place. But it is difficult to see how things could, for the most part, be otherwise. Were every failure in human affairs to be the signal for a purge of those who failed then it is doubtful if lessons could ever be learned.

It is only fair to say 'that the agencies involved in the matter (for the most part the Home Office and the police service itself) have made great efforts to identify and teach the lessons to be learned to those involved in crime investigation. Much of this work has been attended by success. Few would dispute that the computer facilities now available are much superior to those which were available throughout the Yorkshire Ripper investigation. The HOLMES (Home Office Large Major Enquiry System) computer facility for the police is a case in point. Much of this success stems from the work of the Major Crime Working Group of the Association of Chief Police Officers, a group which was set up by ACPO as a consequence of the Byford Review.

Yet there currently seems to be an overwhelming view that the lessons to be learned can be distilled in their entirety in the form of 'procedures' and 'guidelines'. This attitude seems to be a consequence of it being produced by agencies whose main business it is to produce policy as distinct from operational solutions.

Doubtless policy is extremely useful but only if it does not automatically exclude the application of incisive and entreprenurial investigation techniques. The navigator who loses his aircraft despite having strictly followed the rules, but showed no imagination, is hardly free from blame. Habits of bureaucratic thought must not resist the free introduction of new ideas into crime investigation and it is here that the navigator (be he professionally a sailor, a flier, a scientist or a policeman) can help.

Was the application of navigational concepts into the Yorkshire Ripper Investigation a legitimate extension of their use? Might such ideas be applicable in other multiple-crime investigations either in the same or in a modified form? Are such concepts only of use where several crimes, suspected of being committed by the same person, are involved?

On the other hand are parameters such as locations and times relating to victims and suspects in the single crime, amenable to 'navigational' treatment? Take for example the following case which, although hypothetical, has sufficient similarity to real problems to render any solution practically useful.

A woman leaves her house by car at a known time and is not seen again. Her car is found in a lay-by in a sparsely populated moorland area of the country. The man with whom she is associating is seen at a certain location and time and subsequently at another location and time. If he is responsible for the disappearance of the woman in the intervening period then can navigational ideas be used to optimize the search for the body?

Such a problem as this, given to a scientist, may well lead to elegant solutions. For all the writer knows it may be a type of problem already worked on by scientists but, to be practically useful, not only must the solution be 'correct' but it must also be framed in a way useable by those whose job it is to solve practical problems. In the real situation it is better to be master of a little science rather than the slave of much. The approximate methods of the navigator are far more likely to be useful in crime investigation than the elegant solutions of the mathematician.

Acknowledgements

The credit for any potential usefulness, or for any apparent originality, of the views expressed here, is largely due to the professional competence, friendship and stimulating company of the police colleagues named earlier in this article. The inadequacies are entirely the writer's.

Chapter 3

Excerpt from *On the Mode of Communication of Cholera*

John Snow

Instances of the Communication of Cholera through the Medium of Polluted Water in the Neighbourhood of Broad Street, Golden Square

The most terrible outbreak of cholera which ever occurred in this kingdom, is probably that which took place in Broad Street, Golden Square, and the adjoining streets, a few weeks ago. Within two hundred and fifty yards of the spot where Cambridge Street joins Broad Street, there were upwards of five hundred fatal attacks of cholera in ten days. The mortality in this limited area probably equals any that was ever caused in this country, even by the plague; and it was much more sudden, as the greater number of cases terminated in a few hours. The mortality would undoubtedly have been much greater had it not been for the flight of the population. Persons in furnished lodgings left first, then other lodgers went away, leaving their furniture to be sent for when they could meet with a place to put it in. Many houses were closed altogether, owing to the death of the proprietors; and, in a great number of instances, the tradesmen who remained had sent away their families: so that in less than six days from the commencement of the outbreak, the most afflicted streets were deserted by more than three-quarters of their inhabitants.

There were a few cases of cholera in the neighborhood of Broad Street, Golden Square, in the latter part of August; and the so-called outbreak, which commenced in the night between the 31st August and the 1st September, was, as in all similar instances, only a violent increase of the malady. As soon as I became acquainted with the situation and extent of this irruption of cholera, I suspected some contamination of the water of the much-frequented street-pump in Broad Street, near the end of Cambridge Street; but on examining the water, on the evening of the 3rd September, I found so little impurity in it of an organic nature, that I hesitated to come to a conclusion. Further inquiry, however, showed me that there was no other circumstance or agent common to the circumscribed locality in which this sudden increase of cholera occurred, and not extending beyond it, except the water of the above mentioned pump. I found, moreover, that the water varied, during the next two days, in the amount of organic impurity, visible to the naked eye, on close inspection, in the form of small white, flocculent particles; and I concluded that, at the commencement of the outbreak, it might possibly have been still more impure. I requested permission, therefore, to take a list, at the General Register Office, of the deaths from cholera, registered during the week ending 2nd September, in the subdistricts of Golden Square, Berwick Street, and St. Ann's, Soho, which was kindly granted. Eighty-nine deaths from cholera were registered, during the week, in the three subdistricts. Of these, only six occurred in the four first days of the week; four occurred on Thursday, the 31st August; and the remaining seventy-nine on Friday and Saturday. I considered, therefore, that the outbreak commenced on the Thursday; and I made inquiry, in detail, respecting the eighty-three deaths registered as having taken place during the last three days of the week.

On proceeding to the spot, I found that nearly all the deaths had taken place within a short distance of the pump. There were only ten deaths in houses situated decidedly nearer to another street pump. In five of these cases the families of the deceased persons informed me that they always sent to the pump in Broad Street, as they preferred the water to that of the pump which was nearer. In three other cases, the deceased were children who went to school near the pump in Broad Street. Two of them were known to drink the water; and the parents of the third think it probable that it did so. The other two deaths, beyond the district which this pump supplies, represent only the amount of mortality from cholera that was occurring before the irruption took place.

With regard to the deaths occurring in the locality belonging to the pump, there were 61 instances in which I was informed that the deceased persons used to drink the pump-water from Broad Street, either constantly, or occasionally. In six instances I could get no information, owing to the death or departure of every one connected with the deceased individuals; and in six cases I was informed that the deceased persons did not drink the pump-water before their illness.

The result of the inquiry then was, that there had been no particular outbreak or increase of cholera, in this part of London, except among the persons who were in the habit of drinking the water of the above-mentioned pump-well.

I had an interview with the Board of Guardians of St. James's parish, on the evening of Thursday 7th September, and represented the above circumstances to them. In consequence of what I said, the handle of the pump was removed on the following day.

Besides the eighty-three deaths mentioned above as occurring on the three last days of the week ending September 2nd, and being registered during that week in the sub-districts in which the attacks occurred, a number of persons died in Middlesex and other hospitals, and a great number of deaths which took place in the locality during the last two days of the week, were not registered till the week following. The deaths altogether, on the 1st and 2nd of September, which have been ascertained to belong to this outbreak of cholera, were one hundred and ninety-seven; and many persons who were attacked about the same time as these, died afterwards. I should have been glad to inquire respecting the use of the water from Broad Street pump in all these instances, but was engaged at the time in an inquiry in the south districts of London, which will be alluded to afterwards; and when I began to make fresh inquiries in the neighborhood of Golden Square, after two or three weeks had elapsed, I found that there had been such a distribution of the remaining population that it would be impossible to arrive at a complete account of the circumstances. There is no reason to suppose, however, that a more extended inquiry would have yielded a different result from that which was obtained respecting the eighty-three deaths which happened to be registered within the district of the outbreak before the end of the week in which it occurred.

The additional facts that I have been able to ascertain are in accordance with those above related; and as regards the small number of those attacked, who were believed not to have drank the water from Broad Street pump, it must be obvious that there are various ways in which the deceased persons may have taken it without the knowledge of their friends. The water was used for mixing with spirits in all the public houses around. It was used likewise at dining-rooms and coffee-shops. The keeper of a coffee-shop in the neighbourhood, which was frequented by mechanics, and where the pump-water was supplied at dinner time, informed me (on 6th September) that she was already aware of nine of her customers who were dead. The pump-water was also sold in various little shops, with a teaspoonful of effervescing powder in it, under the name of sherbet; and it may have been distributed in various other ways with which I am unacquainted. The pump was frequented much more than is usual, even for a London pump in a populous neighbourhood.

There are certain circumstances bearing on the subject of this outbreak of cholera which require to be mentioned. The Workhouse in Poland Street is more than three-fourths surrounded by houses in which deaths from cholera occurred, yet out of five hundred and thirty-five inmates only five died of cholera, the other deaths which took place being those of persons admitted after they were attacked. The workhouse has a pump-well on the premises, in addition to the supply from the Grand Junction Water Works, and the inmates never sent to Broad Street for water. If the mortality in the workhouse had been equal to that in the streets immediately surrounding it on three sides, upwards of one hundred persons would have died.

There is a Brewery in Broad Street, near to the pump, and on perceiving that no brewer's men were registered as having died of cholera, I called on Mr. Huggins, the proprietor. He informed me that there were above seventy workmen employed in the brewery, and that none of them had suffered from cholera – at least in a severe form, – only two having been indisposed, and that not seriously, at the time the disease prevailed. The men are allowed a certain quantity of malt liquor, and Mr. Huggins believes they do not drink water at all; and he is quite certain that the workmen never obtained water from the pump in the street. There is a deep well in the brewery, in addition to the New River water.

At the percussion-cap manufactory, 37 Broad Street, where, I understand, about two hundred workpeople were employed, two tubs were kept on the premises always supplied with water from the pump in the street, for those to drink who wished; and eighteen of these workpeople died of cholera at their own homes, sixteen men and two women.

Mr. Marshall, surgeon, of Greek Street, was kind enough to inquire respecting seven workmen who had been employed in the manufactory of dentists' materials, at Nos. 8 and 9 Broad Street, and who died at their own homes. He learned that they were all in the habit of drinking water from the pump, generally drinking about half-a-pint once or twice a day; while two persons who reside constantly on the premises, but do not drink the pump-water, only had diarrhea. Mr. Marshall also informed me of the case of an officer in the army, who lived at St. John's Wood, but came to dine in Wardour Street, where he drank the water from Broad Street pump at his dinner. He was attacked with cholera, and died in a few hours.

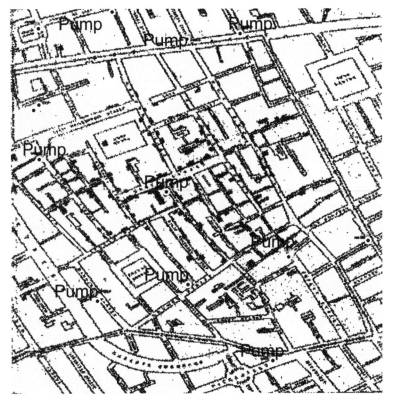

Map 3.1   **Showing the deaths from cholera in Broad Street, Golden Square, and the neighborhood, from 19th August to 30th September 1854. A black mark or bar for each death is placed in the situation of the house in which the fatal attack took place. The situation of the Broad Street Pump is also indicated, as well as that of all the surrounding pumps to which the public had access.**

Explanation of the Map Showing the Situation of the Deaths in and around Broad Street, Golden Square

The deaths which occurred during this fatal outbreak of cholera are indicated in the accompanying map, as far as I could ascertain them.

There are necessarily some deficiencies, for in a few of the instances of persons who died in the hospitals after their removal from the neighborhood of Broad Street, the number of the house from which they had been removed was not registered. The address of those who died after their removal to St. James's Workhouse was not registered; and I was only able to obtain it, in a part of the cases, on application at the Master's Office, for many of the persons were too ill, when admitted, to give any account of themselves. In the case also of some of the work people and others who contracted the cholera in this neighbourhood, and died in different parts of London, the precise house from which they had removed is not stated in the return of deaths. I have heard of some persons who died in the country shortly after removing from the neighbourhood of Broad Street; and there must, no doubt, be several cases of this kind, that I have not heard of. Indeed, the full extent of the calamity will probably never be known. The deficiencies I have mentioned, however, probably do not detract from the correctness of the map as a diagram of the topography of the outbreak; for, if the locality of the few additional cases could be ascertained, they would probably be distributed over the district of the outbreak in the same proportion as the large number which are known. The dotted line on the map surrounds the sub-districts of Golden Square, St. James's, and Berwick Street, St. James's, together with the adjoining portion of the sub-district of St. Anne, Soho, extending from Wardour Street to Dean Street, and a small part of the sub-district of St. James's Square enclosed by Marylebone Street, Titchfield Street, Great Windmill Street, and Brewer Street. All the deaths from cholera which were registered in the six weeks from 19th August to 30th September within this locality, as well as those of persons removed into Middlesex Hospital, are shown in the map 1[1] by a black line in the situation of the house in which it occurred, or in which the fatal attack was contracted. In addition to these the deaths of persons removed to University College Hospital, to Charing Cross Hospital, and to various parts of London, are indicated in the map, where the exact address was given in the "Weekly Return of Deaths," or, when I could learn it by private inquiry. The pump in Broad Street is indicated on the map, as well as all the surrounding pumps to which the public had access at the time.

It requires to be stated that the water of the pump in Marlborough Street, at the end of Carnaby Street, was so impure that many people avoided using it. And I found that the persons who died near this pump in the beginning of September, had water from the Broad Street pump. With regard to the pump in Rupert Street, it will be noticed that some streets which are near to it on the map, are in fact a good way removed, on account of the circuitous road to it. These circumstances being taken into account, it will be observed that the deaths either very much diminished, or ceased altogether, at every point where it becomes decidedly nearer to send to another pump than to the one in Broad Street. It may also be noticed that the deaths are most numerous near to the pump where the water could be more readily obtained. The wide open street in which the pump is situated suffered most, and next the streets branching from it, and especially those parts of them which are nearest to Broad Street. If there have been fewer deaths in the south half of Poland Street than in some other streets leading from Broad Street, it is no doubt because this street is less densely inhabited.

In some of the instances, where the deaths are scattered a little further from the rest on the map, the malady was probably contracted at a nearer point to the pump. A cabinet-maker, who was removed from Philip's Court, Noel Street, to Middlesex Hospital, worked in Broad Street. A boy also who died in Noel Street, went to the National school at the end of Broad Street, and having to pass the pump, probably drank of the water. A tailor, who died at 6, Heddon Court, Regent Street, spent most of his time in Broad Street. A woman, removed to the hospital from 10, Heddon Court, had been nursing a person who died of cholera in Marshall Street. A little girl, who died in Ham Yard, and another who died in Angel Court, Great Windmill Street, went to the school in Dufour's Place, Broad Street, and were in the habit of drinking the pump-water, as were also a child from Naylor's Yard, and several others, who went to this and other schools near the pump in Broad Street. A woman who died at 2, Great Chapel Street, Oxford Street, had been occupied for two days preceding her illness at the public washhouses near the pump, and used to drink a good deal of water whilst at her work; the water drank there being sometimes from the pump and sometimes from the cistern.

The limited district in which this outbreak of cholera occurred, contains a great variety in the quality of the streets and houses; Poland Street and Great Pulteney Street consisting in a great measure of private houses occupied by one family, whilst Husband Street and Peter Street are occupied chiefly by the poor Irish. The remaining streets are intermediate in point of respectability. The mortality appears to have fallen pretty equally amongst all classes, in proportion to their numbers. Masters are not distinguished from journeymen in the registration returns of this district, but, judging from my own observation, I consider that out of rather more than six hundred deaths, there were about one hundred in the families of tradesmen and other resident house-holders. One hundred and five persons who had been removed from this district died in Middlesex, University College, and other hospitals, and two hundred and six persons were buried at the expense of St. James's parish; the latter number includes many of those who died in the hospitals, and a great number who were far from being paupers, and would on any other occasion have been buried by their friends, who, at this time, were either not aware of the calamity or were themselves overwhelmed by it. The greatest portion of the persons who died were tailors and other operatives, who worked for the shops about Bond Street and Regent Street, and the wives and children of these operatives. They were living chiefly in rooms which they rented by the week.

Chapter 4

Home-range and Movements of Leopards (*Panthera pardus*) on a Livestock Ranch in Kenya

F. Mizutani and P. A. Jewell

Introduction

Territoriality is one of the most important behavioural traits affecting the spatial organization of animal populations. Kruuk (1972) showed that spotted hyena (*Crocuta crocuta*) were territorial in one population but not in another. This difference was determined by the nature of their food supplies. Davies (1978) recognized territoriality where animals were spaced further apart than would be expected from a random occupation of suitable habitats. Territories are often considered as spatially stable and this is made explicit, for example, in Brown and Orians' (1970) definition as 'a fixed, exclusive area with the presence of defence that keeps out rivals'. Home-range is defined as 'that area traversed by the individual in its normal activities of food gathering, mating and caring for young' (Burt 1943). The concept has been refined by several authors (Mohr 1947; Jewell 1966; Baker 1978): home-range is not the whole area that an animal traverses during its lifetime (Jewell 1966), but rather the area over which an animal normally travels in pursuit of its routine activities.

In most Felids, female home-ranges are usually smaller than those of males, and are used to provide sufficient prey and denning sites for rearing kittens every year, including years of low prey density. Male home-ranges overlap with two, three, or more female ranges, presumably to provide an area where they can mate with as many females as possible without interference from surrounding males (Kitchener 1991). The social system among tigers (*Panthera tigris*) is typical for a wild cat: two or more non-overlapping female resource territories of 16–20 km^2 being overlapped by a larger male home-range of 60–72 km^2, exclusive of other males (Sunquist 1981). In contrast, home-ranges of male jaguar (*Panthera onca*) overlap by up to 80% with those of neighbouring males in the Cockscomb Basin, Belize (Rabinowitz and Nottingham 1986), and individuals commonly occupy areas of as little as 2.5 km^2 for several weeks out of their annual home-range of 30 km^2. This unusual situation probably reflects abundant and atypical prey.

In this study, radio telemetry was used to investigate the size of the home-ranges and movement of leopards living on the ranch and the manner in which they used their ranges, to help identify individual leopards that were responsible for killing livestock, and to determine the density of the leopard population on the Lolldaiga Hills ranch. A preliminary analysis of the radio-telemetry (Mizutani 1993) has been presented, and now more data allow a full analysis of the home-range of the leopards.

Study Area

The Lolldaiga Hills ranch, 16 km north of the equator, is 200 km² (19,890 ha) in extent and lies between 0°07′N and 0°21′N, 37°04′E and 37′11'E. It is set amongst the Lolldaiga Mountains, north-west of Mount Kenya. North of the ranch is the Mukugodo Reserve, which is used by Samburu pastoralists, and to the south the land is intensively used for agriculture by new small-scale settlers. Along the eastern boundary of the ranch is a hilly ridge on which stands a telecommunications microwave station.

The Lolldaiga Mountains are part of the African Basement Complex (Ahn and Geiger 1987). Igneous rocks and overlying surface deposits have contributed to the present day soils (Hackman 1988; Hackman et al. 1989). The soils are mainly light, sandy and infertile, being derived from rocks high in quartz. The soils in the lowlands include reddish brown, sandy-clay loams that are moderately permeable and have medium to low natural fertility. The mean annual rainfall over the years between 1976 and 1992 was 690 mm. There are three rainy seasons (long, continental, short rains) and dry seasons between them. Continental rains in July and August are one of the most unpredictable but rather important rains for the growth of grasses. January, February and March are the driest months in the year.

Vegetation in the area was classified as scattered tree grassland (*Acacia–Themeda*) by Edwards and Bogdan (1951) and as *Themeda–Hyparrhenia* grassland by Heady (1960). Much of Laikipia district was classified in ecological Zone IV (the semi-arid eco-climatic zone with marginal agriculture) by Pratt and Gwynne (1977). In all these classifications, *Themeda* sp. has been indicated as a common important grass. The Lolldaiga Hills ranch covers a variety of natural and semi-natural habitats. The southern part of the ranch (the Hills and Valley, 104 km²) lies in Zone III (the agricultural eco-climatic zone) of Pratt and Gwynne (1977) and has a preponderance of evergreen shrubs and trees: common species include *Themeda triandra, Cynodon dactylon, Pennisetum straminium, Juniperus procera, Olea* sp., *Euclea divinorum*, and *Acokanthera* sp. The northern area of the ranch (the Low Country, 95 km²) is in ecological Zone IV and tends towards Zone V (arid with ranching and pastoralism) at the north-eastern part of the ranch, where it borders with Kamwaki ranch and Mukugodo Reserve: *Pennisetum straminium, Acacia drepanolobium, Acacia nilotica, Balannites* sp. and *Boscia* sp. are the common plants of this savannah area. Full details are presented by Mizutani (1995).

Some 60 species of large mammals live on the ranch, including 23 species of ungulates; Buchell's zebra, steenbok, Thomson's gazelle, Grant's gazelle, impala, fringe-eared oryx, Coke's hartebeest, eland, and giraffe are the commonest species. The total biomass density of the wild animals on the ranch was, at the time of the study, 1,543 kg km^{-2} and within this the natural prey for leopards, which includes smaller species and young of larger species, was 443 kg km^{-2}. Five species of large carnivores, namely lion, spotted hyena, striped hyena, leopard, and cheetah, also live on the ranch. The ranch carries over 4,500 head of cattle (0.23/ha), mainly a crossed breed of red poll and boran, and 4,000 head of merino and dorper sheep (0.20/ha). When the average body masses of each age, sex and type of livestock derived from the ranch records of body masses were used to calculate the *actual* biomass of livestock on the ranch *during the study*, then the figures were, on average, 257 kg per head of cattle and 40 kg per head of sheep. Using these figures, the biomass density of domestic stock was 6511 kg km^{-2} (65.11 kg ha^{-1}). Only calves and sheep are potential prey for leopards. These comprise a biomass of 545 kg km^{-2}.

Methods

Radio-tracking data

Methods of analysing radio-tracking data have been reviewed by Harris et al. (1990) and White and Garrott (1991), and Linn and Key (1996) have examined further the concept of home-range and considered the problems of 'autocorrelation', and of 'outliers', that arise in the collection of field data.

Because we were aware through the work of Pollock (1975) of the dangers of autocorrelation in serial fixes of an animal's movements (as discussed by Swihart and Slade 1985), we took the precaution at an early stage of the work of examining the daily behaviour of the leopards and allowing appropriate time intervals between fixes. Leopards usually lie-up resting for part of the daylight hours but move continuously at night. (Lair 1987, in analysing radio-tracking data, has emphasized that if an animal chooses not to move this is meaningful information for the biologist). We had only one vehicle and receiver and it took some time to drive to new positions suitable for triangulation. On a typical day tracking started at 05.00 h before first light, with 2 or 3 collared leopards perhaps being located by 11.00 h, and continued until after dark or through the night if a leopard was near a sheep boma. In this hilly terrain there were frequent times when a particular leopard could not be located at all. One fix a day became usual.

When measuring the extent of an animal's homerange, the calculation may be greatly exaggerated by what appear to be a few unusually wide movements or 'outliers' that Burt (1943) originally called 'occasional sallies'. Even when defined by statistical procedures (Samuel et al. 1985; Breitenmoser et al. 1993), these outliers cannot be removed without misgivings about their biological relevance (Linn and Key 1996). We have followed Kenward (1987) and Todd (1993) in retaining the

95% of plotted points that lies closest to the arithmetic mean centre of the range, and have 'peeled' the outlying 5%. However, all such peeled points were examined in the context of their actual position in the terrain, and the possible activity of a leopard there, before accepting their rejection as reasonable.

We chose robust non-parametric methods to calculate the home-range size and centre of activity of animals: the minimum convex polygon method (Mohr 1947) WILDTRAK (Todd 1993); the grid-cell method WILDTRAK (Todd 1993); and the harmonic mean method (Dixon and Chapman 1980; Spencer and Barrett 1984) RANGES IV (Kenward 1990). The results from all these methods are presented to facilitate comparison with published work. If only one method were to be used, we think the harmonic mean gives most useful information but the minimum convex polygon method is the one commonly encountered in the literature.

The grid-cell uses the counts of locations within gridcells on a map of an animal's home-range. Disjoint areas (areas that are not connected) may be added together (following the Queen's rule) to form the home-range estimate. Thus, the disjointedness is assumed to be due to reduced sampling intensity. The method is useful for a representation of habitat usage but not so useful for calculating home-range areas. Complete counts of gridcell areas do not allow for removal of the outliers and so a 95% confidence area is not defined. The greatest problem with the grid-cell approach is selecting the size of grid square to be used, which determines the number of grid squares on the map. In the present analysis, after examining the home-range estimates of different individuals by using different sizes of grid cells (e.g. of side length 250 m, 500 m, 750 m and 900 m) and comparing these to the results from the minimum convex polygon method, a grid cell of 500 m was chosen.

The harmonic mean method estimates the density distribution of fixes, which is equivalent to the probability of encountering the animal. Contours are developed that indicate the areas of greatest activity and so several 'centres of activity' may be revealed. This is important in comparing females' and males' ranges.

The manner in which 2 animals living as neighbours relate their activities to each other is an important aspect of territorial and social behaviour. An attempt has been made to unravel some of this behaviour. Estimations of range overlap were made by 3 methods. These were monocular polygon area (peeled polygon area) RANGES IV (Kenward 1990); harmonic mean method RANGES IV (Kenward 1990); and static interaction analysis WILDTRAK (Todd 1993). Kenward's method allows a range of percentages to be selected, depending on the particular data available. Two types of overlap matrix will be presented for the static interaction analysis; one represents the home-range used by animals irrespective of the time sequence; the other represents the range during the period that both animals were radio-tracked concurrently. In all the analyses of overlap, if less than 10% overlap was found it was treated as non-overlap.

The spatial overlap of two home-ranges and congruence in at least part of their utilization distributions is termed 'static interaction'. The manner in which overlap of ranges affects the individual animals concerned may be different according to circumstance. For example, 2 ranges might overlap by less than 50%, although the shared area contains the most utilized parts of both ranges. Alternatively, 2 individuals may concentrate their activities in different parts of a large shared range. These differences can be accounted for by testing for correlation in the utilization distributions of each range. Positive correlation indicates similar utilization (attraction) and negative correlation indicates different utilization patterns (repulsion). Spearman's coefficient of rank correlation (termed r_s) is used as an index of concordance in the utilization of home-ranges, because it takes into account both the overlap of two ranges and their utilization (Doncaster 1990).

For static interaction analysis, 3 kinds of analyses were carried out. First, using all the fixes; second using fixes from the period of time when both animals were being radio-tracked; and third using only the fixes from both animals that were obtained on the same day.

Analyses of movements were carried out by dynamic interaction analysis (Doncaster 1990) and drift movement analysis (Doncaster and Macdonald 1991). The drift analysis is one of the grid-cell methods used to estimate a range that has not reached an asymptote and where an animal is shifting continuously into new areas. Some animals have ranges that change slowly over the course of time whilst others have remarkably stable homeranges. Still others have home ranges which switch very suddenly from one area to another.

Age of Leopards

Adult leopards had bright coats, teeth that were white or slightly yellow with tips only slightly worn. Female nipples were darkly pigmented. *Old leopards* were large, scarred and with somewhat faded coats and worn teeth. *Subadult leopards* were lighter and smaller than adults of the same sex with white and sharp-pointed teeth and pink nipples. A subadult female F5 became adult during the study; she produced cubs. Similarly, a subadult male M9 matured on the ranch during the study, but a second animal, M2, moved away and disappeared (See Table 4.1).

Results

The total time spent radio-tracking was 942 hours over 30 months between 29 March 1990 and 20 September 1993. The accuracy of fixes was determined to be within a mean polygon area of 208.8 m^2 with standard error of 43.3 (n= 5). The period of radio-tracking and total number of fixes used for each leopard are given in Table 4.1. Since the seasons are not clear on the ranch, it was impossible to discern a seasonal effect on homerange size. Therefore, all fixes were combined to examine the overall home-range of each individual during the period that it was under study.

Comparison of Home Ranges by Different Methods

Data were obtained from 11 leopards but only nine of these gave adequate data to permit the set of analyses described above. These methods gave rather different results that require appropriate interpretation. It will therefore be helpful to explain the procedures adapted step-by-step before making a comparison between all leopards. To do this, the results obtained with just one leopard, female leopard F5, will be presented as an example.

Using the results from subadult female leopard F5 as an example
When F5 was caught, she had small pink nipples and her mammary glands were not enlarged. She was classified as a subadult. Two and a half years later, at the end of August 1993, she was seen fully pregnant and she visited a particular sheep boma everyday. She killed two sheep just before she gave birth. During the 9 months that she was followed, F5 occupied the range around the top of Microwave station ridge and sometimes went down to the Low Country.

By the minimum convex polygon method
Her maximum home-range, using 100% of fixes, was 24.69 km². Figure 4.1 shows the 95% minimum convex polygon area, and the clumping of fixes indicates her centre of activity. Table 4.2 gives range information for leopard F5. Figure 4.2

Table 4.1   Basic information on radio-tracking for estimating sizes of home-range of leopards

Leopard no.	Sex	Age	Date of capture	Total no. of fixes used	Date range start	end
F5	female	subadult	19/12/90	136	19/12/90	19/9/93
F6	female	adult	19/12/90	109	19/12/90	4/12/92
F7	female adult	24/12/90	96	23/12/90	23/1/92	
F8	female adult	5/1/91	62	4/1/92	6/5/92	
F10	female	old adult	21/7/91	3*		
F11	female	young	11/9/92	39	10/9/92	19/9/93
M1	male	adult	23/9/90	3	29/3/90	31/3/90
M2	male	subadult	7/4/90	47	7/4/90	20/8/90
M3	male	adult	2/5/90	92	2/5/90	14/5/90
M4	male	old adult	20/7/90	24	20/7/90	18/11/90
M9	male	subadult	24/1/91	52	24/1/91	12/1/92

*Shows fixes based on sightings

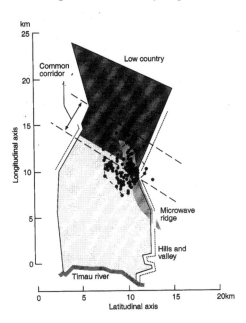

Figure 4.1 **Minimum convex polygon (95%) for subadult F5 and plot of all fixes (see Table 4.2). The orientation of the *x* and *y* axes is that of latitude and longitude which are taken from the grid lines on the Survey of Kenya map. The point of origin is arbitrary. The solid black line represents the boundary of the ranch. When a dotted line is shown, parallel to it a conventional fence (easily crossed by animals) is in place. Elsewhere (in the west and north) the fence is electric. The wavy line at the bottom in the south is the river along the boundary of the ranch. Two larger dotted lines are showing 'Common corridor' (see text).**

examines whether her home-range reached an asymptote. It appeared to have reached an asymptote around 70 fixes, by April 1991, but one year later, around 120 fixes, she was found in new locations, showing some change of her home-range, perhaps reflecting her being pregnant (see drift table: Table 4.10). After this, the size of her range again appeared to reach an asymptote at around 136 fixes (when field work stopped). Figure 4.3 and Table 4.3 reveal that there is a sharp change in the rate of increase in range size when about 90% of the fixes have been plotted. This, according to the WILDTRACK manual (Todd 1993), gives the best representation of the regularly used range of the animal.

By the grid-cell method
Figure 4.4 shows the home-range of F5 by the grid-cell method. Black cells contain 6–16 fixes in each cell and show her core area on the Microwave Station Ridge

Table 4.2   Basic information on the home-range estimated by the minimum convex polygon method for subadult leopard F5

Range (km²)	Fixes		Range centre*	Date range†	Distance (km)	
	Used	Total			Fixes	Polygon
24.69	136	136	x = 10.0	12/12/90	3[1]	5[3]
			y = 10.2	19/9/93	8[2]	6[4]

*Co-ordinates as seen in Figure 4.11
†Dates of start and end of radio-tracking
[1]Mean distance of all the fixes from the range centre
[2]Maximum distance of the furthest fix from the range centre
[3]Mean distance of polygon corners from the range centre
[4]Maximum distance of furthest polygon corner from the range centre

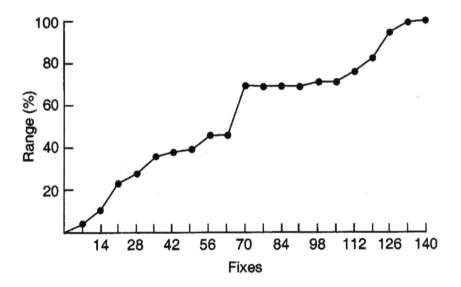

Figure 4.2   The relationship between the number of fixes and the percentage of total home-range estimated by the minimum convex polygon method of subadult leopard F5

Table 4.3 **Minimum convex polygon areas for subadult leopard F5**

% fixes	Area (km²)
100	24.694
95	16.115
90	12.270
85	11.646
80	9.469
75	8.221
70	7.332
65	6.282
60	5.255
55	5.052
50	4.405
45	3.341
40	2.709
35	2.146
30	1.790
25	1.480
20	1.050
15	0.887
10	0.408
5	0.125

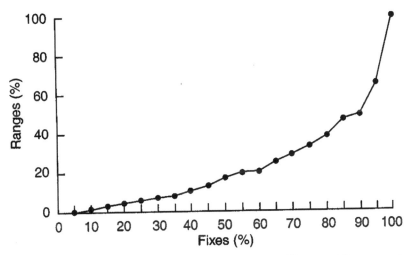

Figure 4.3   The relationship between the percentage of fixes and the percentage of total home-range estimated by the peeled minimum convex polygon method for subadult leopard F5

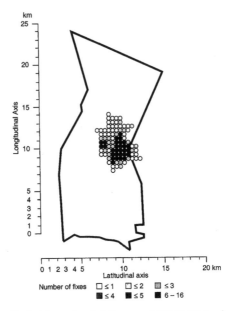

Figure 4.4   **Grid-cell plot for subadult leopard F5 (0.25 km² cells with influence cells trimmed). For further details see legend in Figure 4.1**

Table 4.4   **Basic information on estimating the size of the home-range of subadult leopard F5 by the grid-cell method**

Range (km²)	Fixes		Cells	Date range	Max. score
	Used	Total			
23.75	136	136	95	19/12/90 19/09/93	16

where the sheep boma was often located. Table 4.4 gives information on her range. The home-range included 95 grid cells and the maximum number of fixes in a grid cell was 16; the area, using all the fixes, was estimated to be 23.75 km². Figure 4.5 shows the relationship between the number of fixes and the percentage of her homerange area: two asymptotes are reached.

By the harmonic mean method
For the harmonic mean method, the areas of computed harmonic means are drawn in Figure 4.6 and the relationship between fixes and area is examined in Figure 4.7.

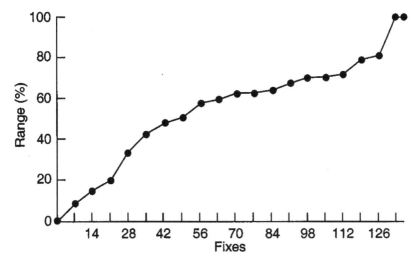

Figure 4.5 **The relationship between the number of fixes and the percentage of total home-range estimated by the grid-cell method for subadult leopard F5**

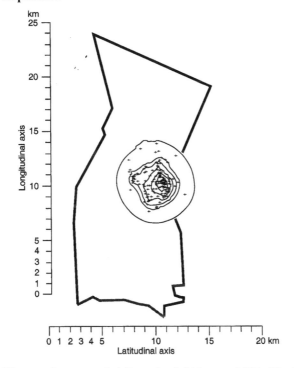

Figure 4.6 **Harmonic mean plot for subadult leopard F5: 20, 40, 60, 80, 95 and 100% isopleths. For further details see legend in Figure 4.1**

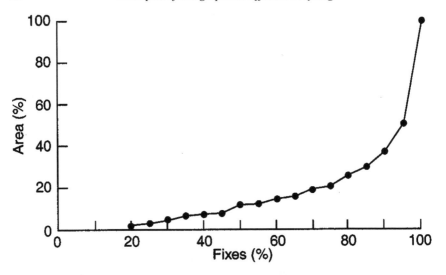

Figure 4.7   **The relationship between the percentage of fixes and the percentage of harmonic mean areas for subadult leopard F5**

Table 4.5   **Harmonic mean areas for subadult leopard F5**

% fixes	Area (km²)
100	43.868
95	22.090
90	16.199
85	12.882
80	11.106
75	9.085
70	8.256
65	6.824
60	6.330
55	5.442
50	5.171
45	3.579
40	3.328
35	2.874
30	1.892
25	1.441
20	1.262

Her total home-range was 43.87 km² and 22.09 km² using 95% of total fixes (Table 4.5). Examination of the areal parameters derived from this method show that the relative dispersion of the fixes around the activity centre was small; the skewness of the distribution was positive, meaning that more fixes were found on the right-hand end of the distribution; the value of kurtosis was more than 2, meaning that it was leptokurtic and the peak was 'dominant' (expression used by Spencer and Barrett 1984). This indicates that she used the places around the core area intensively.

Summary of comparison of home range by all methods

There are similarities between the three methods. In relating the revealed area of the home-range to number of fixes, both the minimum convex polygon method and the grid-cell method show two asymptotes. Using 100% of fixes these two methods also give similar areas: 24.69 km² and 23.75 km², respectively. The harmonic mean method yields a much bigger area at 43.87 km², but a small deletion of only 5% of the most distant fixes reduces this to 22.09 km². This concordance of areas at somewhat over 20 km² still begs many questions of its usage by leopard F5. However, most workers who use the minimum convex polygon method prefer to exclude an outermost zone and when this is done taking the convention of 90% of fixes (Figure 4.3 and Table 4.3), a homerange of 12.27 km² is determined.

The calculated centres of activities were similar by the minimum convex polygon and by the harmonic mean method (see Figure 4.11).

a. Amongst females

All radio-tracking results obtained for each leopard were treated in the several ways that have just been described for F5. The home-range sizes of leopards by different methods are summarized in Table 4.6.

In the minimum convex polygon method all females' ranges reached an asymptote (Table 4.6), indicating that their energy requirements were fulfilled within the ranges revealed. Even in the case of the young female leopard F11, whose home-range size was relatively small, an asymptote was reached, suggesting that at her age at that time her requirements were fulfilled. On the other hand, by the grid-cell method, although the calculated sizes of home-range were similar to those of the minimum convex polygon method, only two females reached an asymptote. When these two methods are compared with the third one, the harmonic mean method (Table 4.6), it is seen that maximum size by the harmonic mean method is larger, but when adjusted, by being peeled, the actual sizes of home-range are not dissimilar.

The grid-cell analysis revealed that female leopards did not use their home-ranges uniformly. Some of the grid cells were used intensively whilst other areas were avoided. This is seen in Figure 4.8 which shows the homerange for F6 and reveals that two sites within her homerange were used more frequently than others. This emphasis on particular sites developed after she had had cubs, and it was noted that the intensively used cells had conspicuous features such as rock outcrops and thick vegetation.

Table 4.6   Comparison of home-range size estimated by different methods

Leopard no.	Minimum convex polygon				Grid-cell				Harmonic mean	
	Reached asymptote	Maximum	Peeled	Chosen (%)	Reached asymptote	Maximum	Maximum	Chosen (%)	Peeled	Chosen (%)
F5	yes	24.69	12.27	90	yes	23.75	43.87	95	22.09	95
F6	yes	16.66	11.46	90	yes	16.75	25.22	95	17.05	95
F7	yes	24.66	12.62	95	no	17.25	76.53	95	17.89	95
F8	yes	31.20	26.56	95	no	20.75	46.06	90	27.22	90
F11	yes	9.66	7.00	85	no	9.50	10.73	85	5.50	85
M2	no	69.97	31.02	90	no	12.75	160.40	90	49.63	90
M3	yes	109.75	43.10	75	no	29.75	212.61	95	118.92	95
M4	no	46.18	31.16	75	no	7.75	35.23	95	27.42	95
M9	yes	63.88	25.71	80	no	16.25	102.03	75	16.82	75

Note: home-range size is shown in square kilometres
0.25 km² was used as the grid-cell size in the grid-cell method
40 × 40 grid cells were used in the harmonic mean method
Insufficient data were obtained from leopard F10 and M1

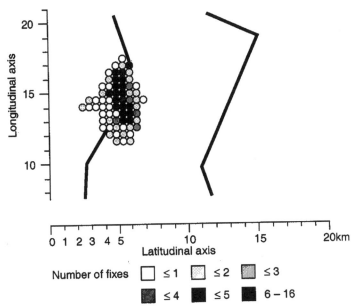

Figure 4.8   Grid-cell plot for adult leopard F6 (0.25 km² cells with influence cells trimmed). For further details see legend in Figure 4.1

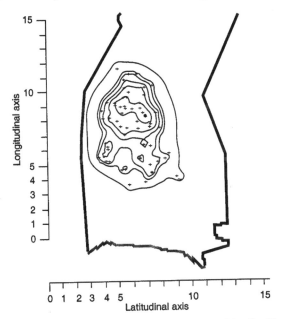

Figure 4.9   Harmonic mean plot for adult leopard F8: 20, 40, 60, 80, 90 and 100% isopleths. Heavy black lines show the ranch boundaries

The description of the ranges by the harmonic mean method revealed that female leopards were found less than 1000 m on average from the activity centre and hence the dispersion of the fixes was small, the skewness of the range was positive, and the peak in home-range use around the activity centre was 'dominant', indicating intensive use. Spread in the range was around 1250 m. An exception was adult leopard F8 (see Figure 4.9). The value of spread in the range was almost 2000 m and the value of dispersion was also greater than that of other females. This may be a reflection of the prey availability in her home-range. Her home-range occupied the south-west part of Lolldaiga mountains where the estimated biomass of natural prey was low (170 kg km^{-2}, Mizutani 1995) and she used a lower plain some way to the west. This leopard F8 used this lower plain, in the same way that other females (F5, F6 and F7) sometimes used the Low Country to the north.

b. Amongst males
Amongst males, the minimum convex polygon method indicated that two (M3 and M9) reached an asymptote, but it has to be recognized that, amongst males, the situation was highly dynamic. Prior to his death, M4, an established male, had moved widely and erratically. The movements of M3, another established male, were similar. The percentage of fixes chosen for the peeled polygon was as low as 75% for these individuals (Table 4.6).

Turning to results from the grid-cell method, no male leopards reached an asymptote (see Table 4.6). For male leopards, the number of 0.25 km^2 grid cells a leopard used gave a lower estimate of the size of the home-range than did the minimum convex polygon method. No intensively used cells were revealed in males' home-ranges, indicating that males were always on the move.

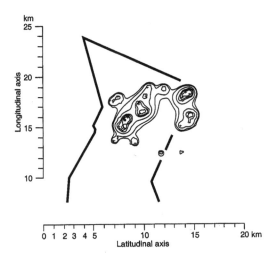

Figure 4.10   Harmonic mean plot for old adult leopard M4: 20, 40, 60, 80, 95 and 100% isopleths. Heavy black lines show the ranch boundaries.

The harmonic mean method using 100% of fixes gave rather different results from either the minimum convex polygon or the grid-cell methods, as was seen to a smaller extent amongst females (Table 4.6). Home ranges generated by the harmonic mean are larger than ones generated by the minimum convex polygon and by the grid cell. However, the size of home-range for an old male, M4, by the harmonic mean method (35.23 km^2) was smaller than the estimate by the minimum convex polygon method (46.18 km^2). This is partly because M4 was found dead after 5 months so that results by different methods are influenced directly by the small sample size (24 fixes, Figure 4.10). Males travelled from the activity centres less than 1000 m on average and hence the dispersion of the fixes was small, the skewness of the range was positive and the peak of fixes around the activity centre was very 'dominant'. These parameters appear similar to those of females but it must be noted that the males have more 'centres of activity' than females. Spread in the range was on average 2200 m. These results indicate that they used a wide range and the intensive use around the activity centre was prominent, which is emphasized by the great skewness of the range. A subadult male M2 had the greatest skewness which was due to his persistent movement from the study area.

c. Between sexes and age classes
The mean sizes of home-ranges between sexes by the peeled polygon, grid-cell, and peeled harmonic mean methods are summarized in Table 4.7. In the peeled polygon method, the mean home-range for female leopards was significantly smaller than that for males. By the grid-cell method the areas were similar, and although apparently markedly dissimilar by the harmonic mean method, this difference was not significant.

The description of home-ranges by the harmonic mean method revealed that females' home-ranges were less dispersed, less positively skewed, less in extent and had less leptokurtosis, than males' home-ranges. This indicates that the females use their home-ranges in a more concentrated way, using each part more intensively. The manner of use of home-ranges of males was more varied than that of females.

Figure 4.11 shows centres of activity calculated by the minimum convex polygon and by the harmonic mean methods. Most of the calculated range centres were concentrated in a small area for each individual, for all females and for three of the males. An exception was the old male M4. As mentioned above, he died 5 months after capture and the sample size of fixes for him (Table 4.1) may be insufficient for the calculation of his range centre.

Comparisons of home-range in different age classes in each sex are shown in Table 4.8. All methods suggest that younger leopards have smaller home-ranges than older leopards. According to the minimum convex polygon (MCP) and harmonic mean (HM) methods, the size of the home-range is positively correlated with body mass (MCP: *P*<0.05), total length (MCP: *P*<0.01, HM: *P*<0.05) chest girth (MCP: *P*<0.01, HM: *P*<0.05), and neck girth (MCP: *P*<0.05). When sex is controlled as a variable, only total length is positively correlated in the harmonic mean method. This suggests

Table 4.7   Comparison of the sizes of home-range (in km²) between female and male leopards

Sex	Sample size	Peeled minimum convex polygon		Grid-cell		Peeled harmonic mean	
		mean	S.D.	mean	S.D.	mean	S.D.
Both combined	9	11.32	12.06	17.17	6.91	33.62	34.17
Female	5	13.98	7.38	17.60	5.34	17.95	8.05
Male	4	32.75	7.35	16.25	9.42	53.20	45.90
Mann–Whitney U-Wilcoxon Rank Sum test		$P = 0.028$ ($Z = 2.205$)		NS	NS		

Table 4.8 Comparison of the sizes of home range (in km²) in different age classes of leopards

Sex	Age	Sample size	Peeled minimum convex polygon		Grid-cell		Peeled harmonic mean	
			mean	S.D.	mean	S.D.	mean	S.D.
Female	young	5	7.00		9.50		5.50	
	subadult	1	12.27		23.75		22.09	
	adult	3	16.88	8.40	18.25	2.18	20.72	5.64
Male	young	4						
	subadult	2	28.37	3.75	14.50	2.47	33.23	23.2
	adult	2	37.13	8.44	18.75	15.56	73.17	64.7

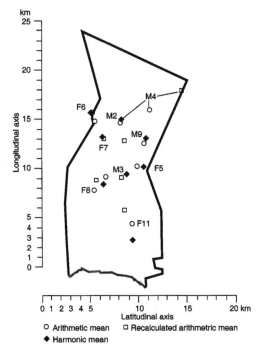

Figure 4.11   Centres of activities as calculated by three different methods: 1) The arithmetic mean of range centre determined by the minimum convex polygon method; 2) the recalculated arithmetic mean of range centre determined by the peeled minimum convex polygon; 3) the harmonic mean of range centre determined by the harmonic mean method. For further details see legend in Figure 4.1

that difference in the size of home-range between the sexes is generated by sex and it is partly due to the difference in body size, hence in the energy requirements.

Comparison of overlap of home-ranges by different methods

Measures of overlap can best be described by examining the percentages of home-range overlap estimated by the three methods, and then by Spearman's coefficient of rank correlation (r_s) from the static interaction analysis.

a. Amongst females' home-ranges
The ranges of females F5, F8, and F11 do not overlap with each other or with F6 and F7. The ranges are compacted together (Figures 4.12 and 4.13). Two resident female leopards (F6 and F7) in the Low Country had overlapping home-ranges. The high degree of overlap and frequency of joint use of these overlap areas could suggest, according to Sandell (1989), that essential resources may be concentrated

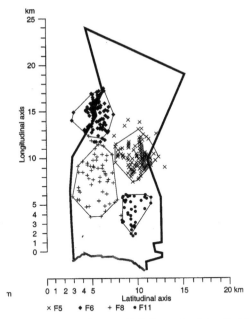

Figure 4.12 **Minimum convex polygon (95%) and plot of all fixes for four females (F5, F6, F8 and F11). For further details see legend in Figure 4.1**

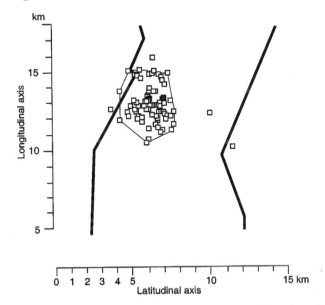

Figure 4.13 **Minimum convex polygon (95%) and plot of all fixes for female F7. For further details see legend in Figure 4.1**

in such areas. Estimates of biomass of natural prey in these areas (Mizutani 1995) support this suggestion. In the static interaction analysis, leopards F6 and F7 have the highest r_s value (–0.12 using all fixes), suggesting the possibility of attraction between these females. They appeared to be of different ages and could have been mother and daughter. With this exception, the ranges of females appear to have little or no overlap.

b. Amongst males' home-ranges
Resident adult males have big ranges, and the regularly used parts of these do not overlap but cover the ranges of several females. When the total range of male leopards is considered, some temporary overlapping was seen. All observed males used a narrow belt that runs north-west to south-east across the ranch. This common corridor (see Figures 4.14 and 4.15) covered five vegetation types occurring on the ranch. It covers the northern end of Lolldaiga mountains and an area of transition between the Low County and the Hills and Valley. If the food resources vary in space and time, the range must be larger to provide for the requirements of the animal at all times. This larger area may contain a surplus of food for most of the year; thus several animals can utilize the same area (the common corridor), and a system of overlapping ranges develops. Outside this corridor, all the home-ranges were specific to each adult male (Figures 4.14 and 4.15). The old male M4 had a comparatively small home-range. Leopard M3 was in its prime (and appeared to be the most dominant male on the ranch) and a few radio fixes (excluded by the 95% rule) indicated occasional very wide movements. The difference in movements between these two adult males may have been due to the difference in age and dominance rank or due to the difference in prey biomass within their home-ranges. The biomass of natural prey in M4's area, the Low Country (741 kg km^{-2}) was greater than in the Hills and Valley (170 kg km^{-2}, Mizutani 1995) in which most of the home-range of M3 occurred.

Subadult males present a different picture. When the 95% convex polygon of subadult M2 is drawn on the map (Figure 4.15), his movements appear to have been within those of other adult males and it looks as if his occupancy was overlapped by these adults, but the movements of M2 had been largely restricted to the 'common corridor'. Subadult male M9 had taken over M4's home-range in the Low Country after the death of the latter.

In the static interaction analysis, there is no overlap between males: the r_s values confirm that the manner in which male leopards occupied the areas was as if in 'repulsion', and the mean percentages of overlap ranged between 0% and 9%. The static interaction analysis using only fixes from the period during which both animals were radio-tracked concurrently reinforces the conclusion that the ranges of resident males did not overlap.

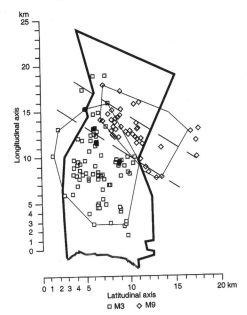

Figure 4.14   Minimum convex polygon (95%) and plot of all fixes for two males (M3 and M9). For further details see legend in Figure 4.1

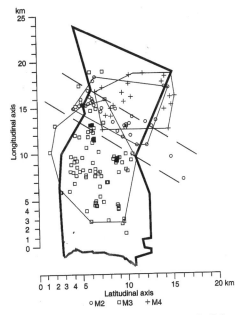

Figure 4.15   Minimum convex polygon (95%) and plot of all fixes for three males (M2, M3 and M4). For further details see legend in Figure 4.1

c. Between sexes

Taking F5 as an example, her home-range was not overlapped by that of any other *females* in all types of overlap matrix (adopting the convention that less than 10% overlap is ignored, see 'Methods'). Using the 85% polygon method, the overlapped area between F5 and *the male* M3, was 67% of F5's home-range and was 12% of M3's home-range. By the 90% harmonic mean method, it was 84% of F5's home-range and was 15% of M3's home-range. Using all fixes for static analysis, their calculated overlapped area was 21% of F5's homerange and 17% of M3's home-range. These calculations indicate a moderate degree of overlap between the two animals. However, when the fixes are used only from the period during which both leopards were radio-tracked concurrently, then only 2% of F5's home-range and 3% of M3's home-range were used in common. This means there was virtually no temporal overlap between them. The different results between the two types of static analysis suggest that, although the home-range of M3 overlapped largely on that of F5, in fact they avoided each other.

The average Spearman's correlation coefficient r_s value amongst all possible sets of individuals in the whole population was –0.72 (S.D.: 0.19, $n = 73$, using all fixes obtained from leopards). This suggests that, in the leopard population as a whole, individual leopards were avoiding each other but some degree of attraction was not excluded. The mean r_s value between females and males was also slightly larger than –0.73, below which the r_s value indicates that the shared area was 50% but contained only the least utilized parts of each range. It does not exclude the possibility of 'attraction' between the sexes. However, the r_s value derived from fixes taken when both animals were radio-tracked concurrently, indicates that in fact they avoided each other and they also avoided each other within the same sex. This is even more strongly indicated when fixes taken on the same days are examined (see Table 4.9).

Movements

a. Females

Neighbouring females appeared to avoid being near to one another; even F6 and F7, who had greatly overlapping home-ranges, appeared to space themselves apart since the dynamic interaction analysis showed the mean separation distance between them to be 2416 m (S.D.: 1396 m, $n = 45$). Two points emerge from the distributions; leopards F6 and F7, who were caught in a small area, appeared to be affiliative, while leopards F5, F7, F8 and F11, who were caught in different areas, seemed to be agonistic in their manner of occupying the range.

Female F6 with cubs had two sites where she was usually located, suggesting that the movements of adult female leopards are dependent on the mobility of their cubs. The movement and home-ranges of subadult leopards varied with age. Young female F11, who was partially independent, initially stayed within the homerange of her mother (F10) then could not be located for a while, but eventually returned to her natal area.

Table 4.9 Mean Spearman's correlation coefficients from static interaction analysis

Sex		Females			Males		
		All fixes	Concurrent fixes	Fixes from same days	All fixes	Concurrent fixes	Fixes from same days
Females	mean	-0.75	-0.67	-0.77	-0.68	-0.64	-0.75
	S.D.	0.21	0.25	0.23	0.19	0.22	0.11
	n	10	8	7	20	8	8
Males	mean	-0.68	-0.64	-0.75	-0.73	-0.81	-0.87
	S.D.	0.19	0.22	0.11	0.06	0.05	0.01
	n	20	8	8	6	4	2

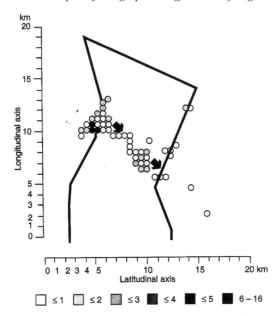

Figure 4.16 Grid-cell plot for subadult leopard M2 (0.25 km² cells with influence cells trimmed). For further details see legend in Figure 4.1.

b. Males
The results suggested that the movement of any particular male was determined by the movement of other leopards. After leopard M2 had moved to the middle and east of the Low Country, in the north part of the ranch, the resident leopard M3 transferred his activities to the Lolldaiga Mountains on the west side of the Low Country. During the same time, another male M4 was in residence in the north-east and the middle of the Low Country and leopard M2 moved on and disappeared to the east of the ranch. Later, leopard M4 was found dead outside the ranch to the east. Leopard M3 could not be located on the ranch for some time but later returned. Later a new leopard, M9, was caught on the east side of the ranch, where he remained for some time and then expanded his range into the north of the ranch.

The movements and home-ranges of male leopards appeared to be affected by the abundance of prey. In the Hills and Valley, where average prey biomass was a third of that in the Low Country, the home-range size of the male leopard M3 was 47.1% greater than the average home-range size for males in the Low Country.

c. Comparison between sexes of subadults
Figure 4.16 shows the home-range of the subadult male M2 by the grid-cell method. His range shifted from his natal range (west of the ranch, at Engwaki Rock where F6 was caught; she might be his mother), to the east of the ranch. The size of his home-

Table 4.10   Drift table for subadult female leopard F5

Survival 75 63 88 76 72 80 82 79 64 100 100 100 70
totals (%) 12 27 25 25 25 20 17 14 14 9   9   9 10 10

1	2	3	4	5	6	7	8	9	10	11	12	13	14
													3
												1	0
											0	0	0
										0	0	0	0
									0	0	0	0	0
								3	0	0	0	0	0
							0	0	0	0	0	0	0
						1	1	1	1	1	1	1	1
					2	1	1	1	1	1	1	1	1
				6	3	3	2	2	1	1	1	1	0
			3	1	0	0	0	0	0	0	0	0	0
		8	5	5	4	3	1	0	0	0	0	0	0
	18	10	10	7	6	6	6	4	3	3	3	3	3
12	9	7	7	6	5	3	3	3	3	3	3	3	2

57

Month	1	2	3	4	5	6	7	8	9	10	11	12	13	14
Fixes	18	34	11	16	22	8	4*	4*	6*	0	0†	0†	3	6

*Shows poor tracking in the month
†Shows no tracking attempted in the month

The drift table, a part of the grid-cell method, for female F5 is given above as an example of this method of presentation of results. The period represented extends over 14 months, given in the 'month' line (second from bottom). The first and last months correspond to December 1990 and January 1992, respectively. The bottom line shows the number of fixes recorded each month. These numbers are low for certain months in which only a limited number of days could be spent in the field, and in month 11 (Oct. 1991) and month 12 (Nov. 1991) no tracking was attempted. Nevertheless the table represents the period when F5 was intensively radio-tracked and while she was still subadult: 123 independent fixes were made and the maximum score in any one cell was 12. Total area was 98×500×500 = 2450 ha.

The programme starts (bottom left) by recording the number of grid cells in which fixes were located during month 1, which was 12, and looks at all subsequent months to see how many of these cells had fixes recorded from them (i.e. 'survive') – row across. In month 2, 18 new grid cells had fixes recorded from them and these gave the survival seen in the second row up, and so on. The total number of grid cells used each month is given at the top together with the percentage that survive from month-to-month. Thus, for each month it is possible to calculate the number of grid cells which were used in previous months. This allows one to determine the percentage survival of cells between months. If the home-range is stable and sufficient fixes are taken in each month, a high percentage survival is found between months. If the animal's range drifts (or indeed undergoes a sudden change), then there is a low percentage survival between months and new grid cells are being added to the animal's range in each month.

range estimated by the grid-cell method (12.75 km², see Table 4.6) was smaller than the results both from the minimum convex polygon method (maximum 69.97 km² and 90% peeled 31.02 km²) and from the harmonic mean method (90% isopleth 49.63 km²). A plot of home-range size against number of fixes shows it did not reach an asymptote and he never settled in the study area. He moved to the neighbouring ranch and eventually disappeared from there.

Results of drift analysis, in all four subadult leopards, F5, F11, M2, and M9 were examined in the way shown for F5 in Table 4.10. The percentage of cells that survived to subsequent months were higher in females than in males. The information that comes out of these tables is limited because the numbers of fixes are small. However, in general, females maintained their natal or core area, while males shifted or 'drifted' their ranges continuously. Subadult male leopard M9 periodically returned to his familiar home-range while leopard M2 moved gradually from his initial (natal) range at the western edge of the ranch to the east of the ranch. He moved out completely from the study area after 5 months.

d. Movements of resident adults

Resident males had the largest areas and moved rapidly from one end of their home-range to the other. Male leopards often made circuits, going around their homerange over several days, while females having smaller home-ranges normally took a couple of days. Adult male leopards moved greater distances than adult females. Female leopards appeared to be moving the minimum distances required to obtain prey, and to rear young, while for males, maintaining territory and locating mates probably accounted for the greater distances moved.

Discussion

This study impressed upon us the complexity of the territorial and ranging behaviour of leopards and our perception conforms with Bailey's (1993) conclusion that the land occupancy of leopards can be visualized as three layers of home-ranges. Within the system, the most important layer of home-ranges is that of the resident female leopards. The larger home-ranges of resident male leopards is superimposed on the mosaic of females' home-ranges. The third layer of home-ranges is occupied by transients that can be either young leopards who have not yet dispersed from their natal ranges or ones (either young or old) temporarily passing through the area to find vacancies. (Some observers would query whether sub-adults truly have home-ranges.)

Leopards are similar in size and life history to jaguars (*Panthera onca*) and mountain lions (*Felis concolor*). Comparing the home-ranges of these three species is particularly interesting (see Table 4.11). For this comparison, the home-ranges estimated by the minimum convex polygon method have been used because most studies present only this value. The minimum homerange size for leopards and jaguars seems to be about 10 km², while the home-range of the mountain lion is

Table 4.11   Comparison of home-range size (in km²) with other studies

Species	Study area	Home-range size		Methods	Sources
		total	*excluding forays*		
Leopard (*Panthera pardus*)	Lolldaiga Hills ranch, Kenya	9.7–109.8	7.0–43.1	radio-tracking	This study
	Tsavo NP, Kenya	11.5–120.6	9.1–63.4	radio-tracking	Hamilton (1976)
	Serengeti NP, Tanzania	15.9–17.8		radio-tracking	Bertram (1982)
		40.0–260.0	40.0–60.0	sightings	Schaller (1972)
		22.5–33.8		sightings	Cavallo (1990)
				spoor and sightings	Smith (1978)
	Matopos NP, Zimbabwe	10.0–19.0		radio-tracking	Norton and Henley (1987)
	Cape Province, South Africa	53.5–127.7	42.1–66.8	radio-tracking	Norton and Lawson (1985)
		444.0–670.0	388.0–487.0	radio-tracking	Le Roux and Skinner (1989)
	Londolozi Game Reserve, SA	33.0	23.0	radio-tracking	Bailey (1993)
	Kruger NP, SA	5.6–96.1		radio-tracking	Bothma and Le Riche (1984)
	Kalahari Desert, SA	800		radio-tracking	Stander (1994)
	Kaudom Game Reserve and Bushmanland, Namibia	101.0–285.0			
	Tai NP, West Africa	12.3		sightings	Hoppe-Dominik (1984)
		22.2–85.6		radio-tracking	Jenny (1996)
	Wilpattu NP, Sri Lanka	8.0–10.0		radio-tracking	Muckenhim and Eisenberg (1973)
	Royal Chitawan NP, Nepal	8		radio-tracking	Seidensticker (1976)
		8		radio-tracking	Sunquist (1983)
Jaguar (*Panthera onca*)	Cockscomb Basin, Belize	10.0–40.0		radio-tracking	Rabinowitz and Nottingham (1986)
	Pantanal Region, Brazil	21.0–76.0	97.7–168.4	radio-tracking	Crawshaw and Quigley (1991)
				radio-tracking and spoor	Schaller and Crawshaw (1980)
Mountain lion (*Felis concolor*)	Idaho Primitive Area, U.S.A.	173.0–453.0		radio-tracking	Seidensticker et al. (1973)

Table 4.12 Comparison of sizes of observed and expected metabolic home-range (in km²) for male leopards

Age class	Sample size	Peeled minimum convex polygon		Grid-cell		Peeled harmonic mean	
		observed	expected	observed	expected	observed	expected
Adult	2	37.13	27.44	18.75	29.67	73.17	33.69
Subadult	2	28.37	13.56	14.50	26.26	33.23	24.42
Whole population	4	32.75	22.40	16.25	28.20	53.2	28.76

Table 4.13 Comparison of mean size of home-range (km²) and home-range overlap with other studies

Species	Study area	Mean home-range size		Overlap			Sources
		female	male	female-female	male-female	male-male	
Leopard	Lolldaiga Hills Ranch, Kenya	**14.0***	**32.8***	both	overlap	both†	This study
	Tsavo NP, Kenya	14.1	36.3*		overlap		Hamilton (1976)
	Serengeti NP, Tanzania	15.9	**17.8**				Bertram (1982)
		40.0–60.0					Schaller (1972)
	Cape Province, SA	22.5	**33.8**		overlap		Cavallo (1990)
			49.5*			overlap	Norton and Henley (1987)
		487*	388*				Norton and Lawson (1985)
	Londolozi Game Res.	23.0*	33.0		overlap		Le Roux and Skinner (1989)
	Kruger NP, SA	15.1	**38.0***	overlap	overlap	overlap	Bailey (1993)
	Kalahari Desert, SA		800.0		overlap	overlap	Bothma and Le Riche (1984)
	Kaudom Game Reserve and Bushmanland, Namibia	127.8	216.5	overlap	overlap	overlap	Stander (1994)
	Wilpattu NP, Sri Lanka	<10		no overlap	overlap	no overlap	Muckenhirm and Eisenberg (1973)
	Royal Chitawan NP, Nepal	8	8 (young)		overlap		Seidensticker (1976)
							Sunquist (1983)
Jaguar	Cockscomb basin, Belize	10.5	33.4	no overlap	overlap	overlap	Rabinowitz and Nottingham (1986)
	Pantanal region, Brazil	**139.6***	**152.4***	overlap	overlap		Crawshaw and Quigley (1991)
		25.0–34.0	21.0–76.0	overlap	overlap		Schaller and Crawshaw (1980)

Note: Numbers in bold are mean home-range size including all age classes.
Numbers with * are home-range size excluding forays.
†In this study no overlap between home-ranges of resident adult males was observed.

much larger than the others. For the leopard, 10 km² appear to meet the minimum energy requirements. The maximum size of home-range for male leopards, estimated by excluding forays, was found to be several hundred square kilometres in three separate studies (see Table 4.13). This is greater than the maximum from this study (43 km²), which was exhibited by the male leopard M3.

Resident female leopards require access to high-quality habitat. Bailey (1993) found that females in poorer habitats generally had larger home-ranges than those in high-quality habitat; we found the same relationship in this study. Van Orsdol (1982) found similar results when he compared two prides of African lions in the Queen Elizabeth National Park, Uganda. Furthermore, Van Orsdol, Hanby and Bygott (1985) found that the range size of the lions was correlated with lean-season prey biomass, and not with good-season prey biomass. In an example from another species, the bobcat (*Felis rufus*), Litvaitis, Sherburne and Bissonette (1986) found that the average home-range of resident male bobcats (95.7 km²) was three times as large as that of resident females (31.2 km²), and the size of home-range was correlated with the body mass of bobcat. Metabolic home-range size (km²/kg$^{0.75}$ body mass) of bobcat was inversely correlated with estimated hare density.

The size of the home-range of leopards is influenced by the following factors; energy requirements; prey distribution and density; reproductive requirements; and intraspecific relations. The maximum size of home-ranges of resident male leopards is probably determined by the size of the females' home-ranges rather than prey availability. In this study, the mean size (regularly used) of a female's home-range by the minimum convex polygon method was 14.0 km² and the mean size of a male's home-range was 32.8 km². Of leopards who were successfully established in resident home-ranges, this gives a ratio of one male to 2.3 females. Since food ranges are minimized whereas mating ranges are expected to be maximized, male ranges should be larger than predicted by energy requirements. If it is assumed that the range sizes of females are determined by food abundance, that in turn meets the energy requirement, then size of the metabolic home-range for male leopards is given in the following equation:

$$R_{male} = R_{female} \times \frac{M_{male}^{0.75}}{M_{female}^{0.75}}$$

where R represents size of metabolic home-range and M represents body mass.

The expected metabolic home-ranges for this study are shown in Table 4.12. Predicted ranges for males, based on the body masses of leopards, are 1.60 (S.D.: 0.00, $n = 3$) times the female range size, whereas the observed ranges are 2.08 (S.D.: 1.05, $n = 3$) times larger than corresponding female ranges. However, the observed male ranges are not significantly larger than expected on the basis of energy requirements (Wilcoxon matched-pairs test; $Z = -1.826$, $P = 0.068$, $n = 4$). This is contrary to the

Table 14.4   Age of leopards before independence, at dispersal and at puberty

	Age of leopards (in months)	Sources
Nutritional independence	12–18	Turnbull-Kemp (1967)
		Eisenberg and Lockhart (1972)
		Muckenhirn and Eisenberg (1973)
		Hamilton (1976)
		Bertram (1978)
		Sunquist (1983)
		Le Roux and Skinner (1989)
		Bailey (1993)
Dispersal	30	Hamilton (1976)
	30–36	Bertram (1978)
	22	Schaller (1972)
	24–36	Muckenhirn and Eisenberg (1973)
	14	Le Roux and Skinner (1989)
Sexual maturity	24–35	Eaton (1977)

view expressed by Bailey (1974), following his study of bobcats, that males occupy proportionally larger ranges as a result of their polygynous reproductive strategy.

Comparison of home-range overlap is made in Table 4.13. Whilst overlapping ranges are easy to detect, it is more difficult to prove that ranges are exclusive. Either there must be a high level of confidence that all animals within an area are radio-collared, or data must be acquired on several animals with adjacent ranges. In this study, with one exception, home-ranges of the female leopards did not overlap and their movements indicated that the home-ranges of resident adult females were effectively exclusive on Lolldaiga Hills ranch. Between resident adult males in this study, there was no overlap in their home-range. This falls into the same pattern of other large solitary cats, in which resident adult males maintain exclusive ranges, showing little overlap with adjacent resident males. For ranges to be exclusive, the food resource must be so evenly distributed and stable that the area encompassed is just large enough to support the animal during the most critical period of the year. The more dominant a male is, the more profitable it is for him to roam over large areas to maximize his reproductive success, since he, being dominant, may have more chance to mate with other females. In such a situation it is impossible for other subordinate males to have exclusive ranges, hence overlap of home-ranges occurs. Maintaining exclusive ranges for males should be the best tactic when females are dense and evenly distributed.

The age of dispersing leopards appears quite variable and is probably related to the availability of resources and competition with resident leopards (Table 4.14). Dispersal may be delayed, especially if adjacent habitats are already occupied by resident leopards and there is no vacant range (as perhaps for F6 and M2). Mothers may share the home-range (as might have been the case for F6 and F7) and allow offspring to stay until resources become available elsewhere in order to ensure their survival (as was seen for F10 and F11). In solitary mammals, females tend to be philopatric; remaining in their natal home-ranges throughout their lives and having tolerant relationships with female kin (Waser and Jones 1983). If co-operative traits are to develop, Armitage (1986) suggested that they should occur among members of the sedentary sex – which is the female in leopards. A female's reproductive success depends largely on obtaining sufficient food resources (Trivers 1972). Males, on the other hand, are seldom philopatric and typically disperse from their natal home-ranges around sexual maturity (Pusey and Packer 1987). For males more than females, the cost of dispersal may be outweighed by increased opportunities to mate with a greater number of non-relatives. Though data do not yet exist for most felid species, it can be expected that solitary felids will show similar female philopatry.

Subadult female leopards in this study seem to be more philopatric than subadult males. Therefore, dispersing subadult males are important for leopard populations in order to ensure that inbreeding is kept to a minimum. On the other hand, if subadult males can mature in the area while successfully avoiding the resident males, they may increase their chances of taking over resident status when a resident male dies or is injured (as occurred when M4 was replaced by M9). The extent of the home-range among resident males appeared to be based on prior use. In south-western Cape Province (Norton and Henley 1987), a younger male leopard apparently displaced an older, probably resident, male in poor condition. The older male eventually abandoned his area, became a stock raider, and was later killed by a farmer well outside his previous range. The young male took over the range of the old one.

Our results suggest that leopards may be correctly called 'solitary', but as Leyhausen (1965) and Linn (1984) have emphasized, solitary mammals are by no means asocial. Instead, solitary behaviour is to be contrasted with co-operative behaviour. The main factors promoting solitary living are probably prey characteristics and hunting mode. Predators that generally take prey much smaller than themselves can almost always subdue the prey alone and consume the whole prey rather quickly. If the prey biomass is adequate to meet the requirements of a female rearing cubs while they are dependent on her, it is an advantage for the female to be solitary to monopolize whole carcasses to ensure food for her cubs. The frequency with which social interactions among leopards are seen and described is thus important in understanding their social organization. Comparative data reveal that leopard, mountain lion (*Felis concolor*), and tiger are highly solitary. Other workers have reported sociality in tigers and mountain lions at kills; in our study, leopards were never seen to show such sociality and perhaps the leopard is the most solitary of this trio of species. The findings of other workers (Schaller 1972; Hamilton 1976; Bailey

1993; Stander 1994) support the assertion that leopards are highly solitary, but it is worth noting an incident observed by Leyhausen (1988) in Samburu National Park when he saw a male leopard join a female and a half-grown cub, play with the cub for a long time, and then depart leading the two others away in single file.

The higher the density of leopards in an area, the more interactions within the leopard community might occur. An occasion has been reported when five different leopards were seen to come sequentially to feed at a bait during the course of one night on one of the ranches in Laikipia, Kenya (Mr C. Francombe, pers. comm.). Associations of two leopards were noted by us both from spoor investigations and from radio-tracking. On two occasions, two leopards travelled together along a road. In the first it may have been F5 and a male, and in the second, F10 walked with M1 or M3. On two occasions, F10 and F11 (females that were mother and young daughter) were seen by night guards to come to a boma together where they killed a sheep. Once while radio-tracking at night, F6 and F7 were located approximately 500 m apart. Leopards F5 and M9 were radio-tracked within 500 m of each other for three consecutive days; this female F5 was probably on heat and this reflected courtship by M9.

Aggressive encounters between male leopards of the kind reported by Hamilton (1976), or fighting among leopards, were never observed on the ranch. During this study, a large male cub (M12) was killed in the Ol Jogi Game Reserve by an older male: they fought over a female on heat. Bailey (1993) suggested that, as subadult males were able to remain in an adult male's homerange without apparent conflict, they probably did not become, or were not capable of becoming, established residents in occupied areas. He thought that violent conflicts between male leopards occurred primarily when a new male was attempting to become established in an area.

On the Lolldaiga Hills, leopards seemed to know where their neighbours were and could avoid them or associate with them. In stable leopard populations, individuals probably become familiar with each other and soon become aware if a neighbouring resident dies or a new individual arrives in the area. After a resident male (M4) died, a new, previously uncaptured male (M9) was captured at the edge of M4's home-range. An old male leopard (M13) was caught in a trap, in which M3 had been caught 7 days before, at the centre of the ranch. M13 appeared to move in the middle part of the ranch, within the home-range of M3, and they were sometimes found to be very close (800 m apart) in a valley. After finding the two males near together, on the following day, we found M3 in the site where M13 had been found on the previous day. But we have no evidence that they ever met up. Two weeks later, M13 was found dead on a neighbouring ranch, through some misadventure, in the east slope of Microwave Ridge. Old male M13 might have been a transient male pushed from a neighbouring ranch into the Lolldaiga Hills where he could not establish himself and went to the east of the ranch.

We have come to think of leopards as having a 'dispersed' or 'attenuated' social structure; what Leyhausen (1988) termed a 'neighbourhood system'. They are aware of their positions in a network of contacts, are alert to intruders and may investigate vacated areas "as if in an attempt to encounter again the stimuli produced by neighbours" (Calhoun and Webb 1953).

Acknowledgements

We are grateful to the Office of the President of Kenya for permission to carry out research. We have had the continuous co-operation of the Kenya Wildlife Services. Support has been received from: the Leverhulme Trust, Nissan Motor Co., The Toyota Foundation, Olympus Optical Co., The Elsa Wild Animal Appeal, Bonar (East Africa), D. T. Dobie Ltd., and the Daiwa Anglo-Japanese Foundation. We would like to thank the owners of Lolldaiga Hills ranch, particularly Dr Mizutani's husband, Robert Wells, for permission to study on their land and for all the assistance they have given. We thank neighbouring ranches for their co-operation. The Department of Zoology, Cambridge has provided every facility. We thank referees for valuable and constructive criticisms, particularly Ian Linn for his incisive comments on methodology and concepts of home-range.

References

Ahn, P.M. and Geiger, L.C. (1987). *Soils of Laikipia District, Kenya*. Department of Soil survey, Government of Kenya.

Armitage, K.B. (1986). Marmot polygyny revisited determinants of male and female reproductive strategies. In *Ecological Aspect of Social Evolution*: 303–331. Rubinstein, D.I. and Wrangham, R.W. (eds). Princeton: Princeton University Press.

Bailey, T.N. (1974). Social organisation in a bobcat population. *J. Wildl. Manage.* 38: 435–446.

Bailey, T.N. (1993). *The African Leopard. Ecology and Behaviour of a Solitary Felid*. New York: Columbia University Press.

Baker, R.R. (1978). *The Evolutionary Ecology of Animal Migration*. London: Hodder and Stoughton.

Bertram, B. (1978). *Pride of Lions*. London: J.M. Dent and Sons.

Bertram, B.C.R. (1982). Leopard ecology as studied by radio tracking. *Symp. zool. Soc. Lond.* No. 49: 341–352.

Bothma, J. du P. and Le Riche, E.A.N. (1984). Aspects of the ecology and behaviour of the leopard (*Panthera pardus*) in the Kalahari desert. *Koedoe* (Suppl.) 27: 259–279.

Breitenmoser, U., Kaczenski, P., Dötterer, M., Breitenmoser-Würster, C. Capt, S., Bernhart, F. and Liberek, M. (1993). Spatial organization and recruitment of lynx (*Lynx lynx*) in a re-introduced population in the Swiss Jura Mountains. *J. Zool. (Lond.)* 231: 449–464.

Brown, J.L. and Orians, G.H. (1970). Spacing patterns in mobile animals. *Annu. Rev. Ecol. Syst.* 1: 239–262.

Burt, W.H. (1943). Territoriality and home-range concepts as applied to mammals. *J. Mammal.* 24: 346–352.

Calhoun, J. B. and Webb, W. L. (1953). Induced emigrations among small mammals. *Science N.Y.* 117: 385–390.

Cavallo, J.A. (1990). Cat in the human cradle. *Nat. Hist.* 2: 52–61.

Crawshaw, P.G., Jr and Quigley, H.B. (1991). Jaguar spacing, activity and habitat use in a seasonally flooded environment in Brazil. *J. Zool. (Lond.)* 223: 357–370.

Davies, N.B. (1978). Ecological questions about territorial behaviour. In *Behavioural ecology: an evolutionary approach*: 317– 350. Krebs, J.R. and Davies, N.B. (eds). Oxford: Blackwell Scientific Publications.

Dixon, K.R. and Chapman, J. (1980). Harmonic mean measure of animal activity areas. *Ecology* 61: 1040–1044.

Doncaster, C.P. (1990). Non-parametric estimates of interaction from radio-tracking data. *J. Theor. Biol.* 143: 431–443.

Doncaster, C.P. and Macdonald, D.W. (1991). Drifting territoriality in the red fox, *Vulpes vulpes. J. Anim. Ecol.* 60: 423–439.

Eaton, R.L. (1977). Reproductive biology of the leopard. *Zool. Garden* 47 (5): 329–351.

Edwards, D.C. and Bogdan, A.V. (1951). *Important Grass Plants of Kenya*. Nairobi: Sir Isaac Pitman & Sons Ltd.

Eisenberg, J.F. and Lockhart, M. (1972). An ecological reconnaissance of the Wilpattu National Park, Ceylon. *Smithson. Contrib. Zool.* 101: 1–56.

Hackman, B.D. (1988). *Geology of the Baringo–Laikipia Area*. Report No. 104. Ministry of Environment and Natural Resources, Mines and Geology Department, Nairobi, Kenya.

Hackman, B.D., Charsley, T.J., Kagasi, J., Key, R.M., Siambi, W.S. and Wilkinson, A. F. (1989). *Geology of the Isiolo Area*. Report No. 103, Ministry of Environment and Natural Resources, Mines and Geology Department. Nairobi, Kenya.

Hamilton, P.H. (1976). *The movements of leopards in Tsavo National Park, Kenya as determined by radio tracking*. MSc thesis, University of Nairobi.

Harris, S., Cresswell, W. J., Forde, P. G., Trewhella, W. J., Woollard, T. and Wray, S. (1990). Home-range analysis using radio-tracking data – a review of problems and techniques particularly as applied to the study of mammals. *Mammal Rev.* 20 (2/3): 97–123.

Heady, H.F. (1960). *Range Management in East Africa*. Nairobi: Kenya Agriculture and Forestry Research Organization cooperating with the United States Educational Commission in the United Kingdom.

Hoppe-Dominik, B. (1984). Etude du spectre des proies de la panthère *Panthera pardus* dans le Parc National de Tái en Côte d'Ivoire. *Mammalia* 48 (4): 477–487.

Jenny, D. (1996). Spatial organization of leopards *Panthera pardus* in Tai National Park, Ivory Coast: Is rainforest habitat a 'tropical haven'? *J. Zool. (Lond.)* 240: 427–440.

Jewell, P.A. (1966). The concept of home-range in mammals. *Sym. zool. Soc. Lond.* No. 18: 85–109.

Kenward, R. (1987). *Wildlife Radio Tagging. Equipment, Field Techniques and Data Analysis.* London: Academic Press.

Kenward, R. (1990). *RANGES IV.* Software for analysing animal location data. Inst. Terrestrial Ecol., Wareham, U.K.

Kitchener, A. (1991). *The Natural History of the Wild Cats.* London: Christopher Helm, A. and C. Black.

Kruuk, H. (1972). *The Spotted Hyaena.* Chicago: University of Chicago Press.

Lair, H. (1987). Estimating the location of the focal centre in red squirrel home ranges. *Ecology* 60: 1092–1101.

Le Roux, P.G. and Skinner, J.D. (1989). A note on the ecology of the leopard (*Panthera pardus* L.) in the Londolozi Game Reserve, South Africa. *Afr. J. Ecol.* 27: 167–171.

Leyhausen, P. (1965). The communal organization of solitary mammals. *Symp. Zool. Soc. Lond.* 14: 249–263.

Leyhausen, P. (1988). The tame and the wild – another Just-So Story. In *The Domestic Cat*: 57–66. Turner, D.C. and Bateson, P. Cambridge: Cambridge University Press.

Linn, I. (1984). Home ranges and social systems in solitary mammals. *Acta Zool. Fenn.* 171: 245–249. *Home Range of Leopards* 285

Linn, I. and Key, G. (1996). Use of space by the African ground squirrel *Xerus erythropus. Mammal Rev.* 26: 9–26.

Litvaitis, J.A., Sherburne, J.A. and Bissonette, J.A. (1986). Bobcat habitat use and home-range size in relation to prey density. *J. Wildl. Manage.* 50: 110–117.

Mizutani, F. (1993). Home range of leopards and their impact on livestock on Kenyan ranches. *Symp. Zool. Soc. Lond.* No. 65: 425–439.

Mizutani, F. (1995). *The Ecology of Leopards and their Impact on Livestock Ranches in Kenya.* Dissert. for DPhil, University of Cambridge.

Mohr, C.O. (1947). Table of equivalent populations of North American small mammals. *Am. Midl. Nat.* 37: 223–249.

Muckenhirn, N. and Eisenberg, J.F. (1973). Home ranges and predation in the Ceylon leopard. In *The World's Cats* 1: 142– 175. Eaton, R.L. (ed.). World Wildlife Safari, Winston, Oregon.

Norton, P.M. and Henley, S.R. (1987). Home range and movements of male leopards in the Cedarberg wilderness area, Cape Province. *S.A.J. Wildl. Res.* 17 (2): 41–48.

Norton, P.M. and Lawson, A.B. (1985). Radio tracking of leopards and caracals in the Stellenbosch area, Cape Province. *S.A.J. Wildl. Res.* 15: 17–24.

Pollock, J.I. (1975). *The Social Behaviour and Ecology of Indri Indri.* PhD Dissert. University of London.

Pratt, D.J. and Gwynne, M.D. (1977). *Rangeland and Management of Ecology in East Africa.* London: Hodder and Stoughton.

Pusey, A.E. and Packer, C. (1987). The evolution of sex-biased dispersal in lions. *Behaviour* 101: 275–310.

Rabinowitz, A.R. and Nottingham, B.G., Jr (1986). Ecology and behaviour of the Jaguar (*Panthera onca*) in Belize, Central America. *J. Zool. (Lond.) (A)* 210: 149–159.

Samuel, M.D., Pierce, D.J. and Garton, E.O. (1985). Identifying areas of concentrated use within the home range. *J. Anim. Ecol.* 54: 711–719.

Sandell, M. (1989). The mating tactics and spacing patterns of solitary carnivores. In *Carnivore Behaviour, Ecology and Evolution*: 164–182. Gittleman, J. L. (ed.). London: Chapman and Hall.

Schaller, G.B. (1972). *The Serengeti Lion*. Chicago: University of Chicago Press.

Schaller, G.B. and Crawshaw, P.G. (1980). Movement patterns of jaguar. *Biotropica* 12: 161–168.

Seidensticker, J.C. (1976). On the ecological separation between tigers and leopards. *Biotropica* 8: 225–234.

Seidensticker, J.C., Hornocker, M.G., Wiles, W.V. and Messick, J.P. (1973). Mountain lion social organisation in the Idaho Primitive Area. *Wildl. Monogr.* 35: 1–60.

Smith, R.M. (1978). Movement patterns and feeding behaviour of the leopard in Rhodes Matopos National Park, Rhodesia. *Carnivore* 1: 58–69.

Spencer, W.D. and Barrett, R.H. (1984). An evaluation of the harmonic mean measure for defining carnivore activity areas. *Acta Zool. Fenn.* 171: 225–259.

Stander, P.E. (1994). *Ecology and Hunting Behaviour of Lions and Leopards*. Dissert. DPhil, University of Cambridge.

Sunquist, M.E. (1981). The social organisation of tigers (*Panthera tigris*) in Royal Chitawan National Park, Nepal. *Smithson. Contrib. Zool.* No. 336.

Sunquist, M.E. (1983). Dispersal of three radiotagged leopards. *J. Mammal.* 64(2): 337–341.

Swihart, R.K. and Slade, N.A. (1985). Testing for independence of observations in animal movements. *Ecology* 66: 1176–1184.

Todd, I. (1993). *Wildtrak. Non-parametric Home-range Analysis for the Macintosh. User's Guide*. Oxford: ISIS Innovation Ltd., University of Oxford.

Trivers, R.L. (1972). Parental investment and sexual selection. In *Sexual Selection and the Descent of Man*: 139–179. B. Campbell (ed.). Chicago: Aldine.

Turnbull-Kemp, P. (1967). *The Leopard*. Cape Town: Howard Timmins.

Van Orsdol, K.G. (1982). Ranges and food habits of lions in Ruwenzori National Park, Uganda. *Symp. Zool. Soc. Lond.* No. 49: 325–340.

Van Orsdol, K.G., Hanby, J.P. and Bygott, J.D. (1985). Ecological correlates of lion social organisation (*Panthera leo*). *J. Zool. (Lond.)* 206: 97–112.

Waser, P.M. and Jones, W.T. (1983). Natural philopatry among solitary mammals. *Q. Rev. Biol.* 58: 355–380.

White, C.G and Garrott, R.A. (1991). *Analysis of Wildlife Radiotracking Data*. San Diego: Academic Press. 286 F. Mizutani and P. A. Jewell .

Chapter 5

Notes on the Geometry of Crime

Patricia L. Brantingham and Paul J. Brantingham

Spatial patterning of crime has long been observed. Guerry (1833) noted conviction rate differences between the departments of France early in the nineteenth century. Tobias (1972: 122–147) has lately described fine differences in the distribution of criminal residences and crimes in Victorian London and Manchester. Burt (1925), Shaw and McKay (1969), and many other criminal ecologists (see Voss and Petersen 1971) reported the spatial patterning of criminal residence, while Brearly (1932), Reckless (1933), Schmid (1960a, 1960b), Shannon (1954), Harries (1971), and others reported the spatial patterning of criminal events.

Though observations of patterning abound, explanations have, until recently, tended to the simplistic. Most explanations have centered on areal correlations between crime phenomena and other social phenomena (Plint 1851; Shaw and McKay 1969; Bagley 1965; Turner 1969b) in an attempt to describe variations in motivations to commit crime. Implicit in most such attempts at explanation is the assumption that variations in motivation lead directly to variations in spatial patterning. Under such an assumption, the spatial pattern itself is merely derivative and of little scientific interest. Wolfgang (1966: 120), for instance, in his classic study of homicide in Philadelphia, argued that the spatial pattern of offenses was of no importance, and was of local interest only to police; and the *Journal of Criminal Law and Criminology* has declined to print crime occurrence maps in the interest of saving space (see, for example, Bullock 1955: 567).

Within the last ten years, the discipline of criminology has begun to attract scholars of diverse background. Environmental psychologists, geographers, and urban planners have joined sociologists, lawyers, and clinical psychologists in studying crime. With an increase in the diversity of research orientations has come a renaissance of interest in the spatial patterning of crime. With growing interest in the patterning of crime has come an interest in how the distribution of opportunities for criminal acts influences the actual commission of crimes. (Jeffery 1977; Mayhew et al. 1976; Brantingham and Brantingham 1975, 1977).

Much current work on crime patterning assumes (explicitly or implicitly) an opportunity/motivation interaction rubric for explaining observed crime (see Jeffery 1977; Baldwin and Bottoms 1976; Brantingham and Brantingham 1978; Carter and Hill 1980, Mayhew et al. 1976). This chapter will build on the current trend and propose a theoretical model for looking at crime as it occurs in urban space. The model will use concepts of *opportunity* and *motivation* and will tie these together with concepts of mobility and *perception*.[1]

We have previously proposed a model for crime site selection which can be described by the following propositions (Brantingham and Brantingham 1978):

(1) Individuals exist who are motivated to commit specific offenses.

(a)   The sources of motivation are diverse. Different etiological models or theories may appropriately be invoked to explain the motivation of different individuals or groups.
(b)   The strength of such motivation varies.
(c)   The character of such motivation varies from affective to instrumental.

(2) Given the motivation of an individual to commit an offense, the actual commission of an offense is the end result of a multistaged decision process which seeks out and identifies, within the general environment, a target or victim positioned in time and space.

(a)   In the case of high affect motivation, the decision process will probably involve a minimal number of stages.
(b)   In the case of high instrumental motivation, the decision process locating a target or victim may include many stages and much careful searching.

(3) The environment emits many signals, or cues, about its physical, spatial, cultural, legal, and psychological characteristics.

(a)   These cues can vary from generalized to detailed.

(4) An individual who is motivated to commit a crime uses cues (either learned through experience or learned through social transmission) from the environment to locate and identify targets or victims.
(5) As experiential knowledge grows, an individual who is motivated to commit a crime learns which individual cues, clusters of cues, and sequences of cues are associated with "good" victims or targets. These cues, cue clusters, and cue sequences can be considered a template which is used in victim or target selection. Potential victims or targets are compared to the template and either rejected or accepted depending on the congruence.

(a)   The process of template construction and the search process may be consciously conducted, or these processes may occur in an unconscious,

---

1   The term perception is used here to include cognition or structuring of visual images. Geographers and planners generally use the term perception to mean cognition. Psychologists usually separate the two terms. This chapter uses the terminology of geographers and planners.

cybernetic fashion so that the individual cannot articulate how they are done.

(6) Once the template is established, it becomes relatively fixed and influences future search behavior, thereby becoming self-reinforcing.

(7) Because of the multiplicity of targets and victims; many potential crime selection templates could be constructed. But because the spatial and temporal distribution of offenders, targets, and victims is not regular, but clustered or patterned, and because human environmental perception has some universal properties, individual templates have similarities which can be identified.

These propositions are not spatially specific. They posit that criminals engage in a search behavior which may vary in intensity, and that criminals use previous knowledge to evaluate and select targets. The propositions do not describe the spatial characteristics of the search patterns or the selection patterns. The model presented in this chapter will attempt to articulate these general propositions *spatially*.

In presenting the spatial model, simple cases will be presented first. These initial cases, with simple initial conditions or simplifying assumptions, will be transformed into more realistic situations in stepwise fashion. The cases will describe the search areas of criminals under varying spatial distributions of criminals and victims or targets within varying hypothetical urban forms. The theoretical cases will be built up using what, empirically, is known about the spatial distribution of crime, what is known about criminal and noncriminal spatial behavior, and inductive relationships.

Case 1: Basic Search Area for Individual Offender

Initial conditions:

   (a) single, individual criminal
   (b) uniform distribution of potential targets
   (c) the criminal based in a single home location.

Empirical work in criminology has repeatedly demonstrated that most offenders commit a large number of their offenses "close" to home. What is "close" varies by offense and city, but in all offenses which have been studied, it has been found that crimes usually occur only a short distance from the home of the offender, or, put slightly differently, the average crime trip is short. Bullock (1955: 571) showed that 40 percent of all Houston homicides in 1945–1949 occurred within one city block of the offender's residence and 74 percent occurred within two miles. Pokorny (1965) found similar patterns in homicides in Houston in 1958–1961. Capone and Nichols (1976) report such a pattern for robberies in Dade County, Florida in 1971. Amir (1971) found such a pattern for rape in Philadelphia. Baldwin and Bottoms (1976: 78–98) found this pattern for larceny, breaking offenses, and taking and driving away offenses in Sheffield. The pattern varies somewhat by offense. Crimes against the person such as homicide, assault, and rape occur "closer" to home with fewer long journeys to a crime site, while property crimes such as larceny and burglary occur further from offenders' homes with more long crime trips (White 1932; Reiss 1967; Pyle 1974; Baldwin and Bottoms 1976). But, overall, there is a decrease in crime as distance increases.

Such a phenomenon, the reduction of activity or interaction as distance increases, has been repeatedly observed in spatial behavior of all types and can be generically referred to as "distance decay." Shopping pattern, personal social interactions, telephone calls, migration, and even criminal behavior appear to cluster around home or base locations (see Lowe and Moryadas 1975; Haggett 1965). Capone and Nichols (1976) fit robbery to a distance decay function. Smith (1976) fits crime trips in Rochester, New York, to a gravity potential function.

A rationale for such a pattern is easy to construct. It takes time, money, and effort to overcome distance. If any of these factors is constrained, then close locations have inherent advantages over distant locations. In addition, in any movement in space away from a home base, the close locations will be seen more frequently. Consequently, more information will be available about locations close to the home base than about locations far away. As criminals search for targets, they are likely to be able to find an area which emits cues associated with a "good" target when the "good" crime area is close to the home base. Information flows should bias search behavior toward previously known areas.

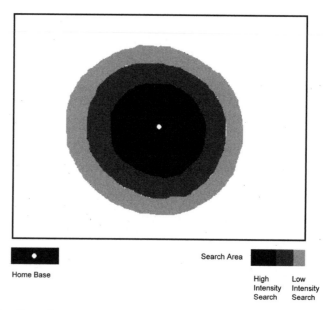

Figure 5.1   **Search area for individual offender**

In the hypothetical case presented here, it is assumed that there is only one criminal, based at one home location, and that potential targets are distributed evenly in space. In such an idealized situation, the expected target area would be a circular field and the probability of any particular potential target becoming an actual target would decrease as the distance from the home base increased (see Figure 5.1). In fact, the decline away from home might be stepwise, dependent on a number of distance thresholds.

Before considering more realistic initial conditions, this most basic case must be modified slightly. In their search behavior criminals are looking for "good" victims or targets. Part of what makes a victim or target "good" or "bad" is availability, potential payoff, and the risk of apprehension or confrontation associated with it (Reppetto 1974: 14–17, 28–29; Letkemann 1973: 137–157; Waller and Okihiro 1978). Information about potential victims and targets is probably spatially biased toward the home base, but information is also spatially biased for the other people who live close to the criminal's home base. While criminals know more of the area close to home and are more likely to locate a target easily, they are also more likely to *be* known and increase their risks close to home. One would expect that there would be an area right around the home base where offenses would become less likely (see Figure 5.2). This small zone of relatively decreased activity was reported by Turner (1969a) in his study of Philadelphia delinquents. In that study, a distance decay model developed from a peak about a city block distant from home with a zone of very little delinquent activity within a city block of home. (Homicide might be expected to be an exception to this case 1 variant: it is an explosive crime which occurs in the home or its immediate vicinity with little or no victim search behavior by the killer. Note, however, that homicide differs from other crimes in that it has a high discovery and clearance rate – a pattern consistent with the risk inherent in criminal activity too close to home.)

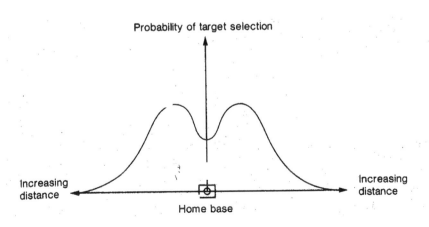

Figure 5.2   Modified search area for individual offender (cross-section view)

LIVERPOOL JOHN MOORES UNIVERSITY
LEARNING SERVICES

Case 2: Basic Search Area for a Cluster of Criminals

Initial conditions:

(a) cluster of offenders
(b) uniform distribution of targets
(c) offenders working from home location.

One recurring spatial fact in criminology is that criminals, both adult and juvenile, are often spatially clustered. Petrovich (1971: 243–244) describes the spatial clustering of criminal residences in Paris in the last half of the eighteenth century. Inciardi (1978: 32–37) describes the development of criminal districts in New York City during the colonial period and then during the first half of the nineteenth century. Tobias (1972: 130–135, 142–144) describes the criminal "rookeries" of London and Manchester in the middle of the nineteenth century. Shaw and McKay (1969) describe the criminal areas of Chicago and other major American cities during the 1920s and 1930s. Morris (1958) describes the delinquency areas of Croydon, an industrial suburb of London, in the 1950s. Baldwin and Bottoms (1976) describe the offender areas of Sheffield in the 1960s. In all cases, it is clear the criminal residences cluster together. In fact, much research in criminological motivation has really involved correlating criminal residence with sociodemographic areal characteristics (Voss and Petersen 1971).

The clustering of criminals is just a special case of clusterings of human groups in space. Urban areas can be viewed as a mosaic of clusters of people – clusters which are measurably, internally homogeneous on social, economic, and demographic characteristics (Timms 1971). Criminals have also been shown to be disproportionately represented in certain subpopulations which can be identified along sociodemographic dimensions such as wealth, age, sex, and ethnicity. Consequently, criminal residences usually cluster within certain restricted urban areas.

When the search area of a single criminal is generalized to a search area for a cluster of criminals, new criminal search patterns emerge (see Figure 5.3). The specifics of the search pattern will depend on how potential offenders cluster.

Case 3: Complex Search Area for One Individual Offender

Initial conditions:

(a) one individual offender
(b) uniform distribution of potential targets,
(c) offender is no longer tied solely to a home base, but works, or goes to school, and shops in other parts of the urban area.

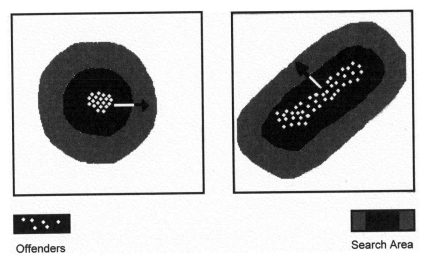

Offenders　　　　　　　　　　　　　　　　　Search Area

Figure 5.3   Search area for clustered offenders

One of the striking things about criminals, often forgotten, is that most of them behave as ordinary people most of the time. Most offenders are not tied exclusively to some home base, but, like other people, are mobile. They move about the city. They develop information about other parts of an urban area through working (even sporadically), traveling to school, shopping, or seeking out entertainment and recreation. Criminals will develop an action space[2] based on both their criminal *and* their innocent activities. Their actions help form an "awareness space," the parts of the city they have some knowledge about. Information about the urban area will be distorted by movement patterns.[3] Criminals can thus be said to possess a nonuniform information base defined by their awareness space.

Given a uniform distribution of targets, and a nonuniform information base, criminals will probably commit most of their offenses close to home, work, shopping, their usual entertainment areas, or along paths between home, shopping, work, and entertainment areas: in general, offenses should occur within the criminal's awareness space. It seems unlikely that they will stray into unknown areas of a city.

In fact, research into specific crimes has demonstrated that most property offenders ply their trade in lower and working class areas which are probably not far from home or other well-known nodes. Reppetto's (1974) sample of Boston burglars operated in neighborhoods they knew despite the fact that they identified other types of areas as having better targets. Rengert (1975) found that Philadelphia burglars committed most offenses close to home or in the central business district and speculated that

---

2   For a general description of action spaces, see Horton and Reynolds (1971).

3   For discussion of information biases of urban residents, see, generally, Appleyard (1969), Klein (1967), Saarinen (1969), or Porteous (1977).

differences in the spatial clustering of male and female burglaries might be explained by action space differentials produced by socially defined differences in mobility patterns. A West German study has shown that many out-of-town burglars commit their offenses on or very near the major arterial highways, while locally resident burglars commit their offenses throughout the town (Fink 1969). Clinard and Abbott (1973: 37) examined a sample of property offenders in Kampala and found offense patterns consistent with an awareness space model: 23 percent of the offenders had stolen from employers, 26 percent had stolen from friends or neighbors, 28 percent from strangers, 4 percent had stolen from stores, only 2 percent had stolen from relatives.

Direct evidence for the patterning of crime around the nodes and the paths between them that form offenders' action spaces is found in two more recent studies. Porteous's study (1977: 253) of the Burnside gang in Saanich, British Columbia, found that the activity space defined by home, school, work, shopping and recreation areas contained most of the gang's delinquent acts. Rengert and Wasilchick's (1980) research with burglars in Delaware County, Pennsylvania (a suburb of Philadelphia) showed a very strong relationship between crime location and principal pathways from home to work and from home to recreation locations.

The type of awareness space, and, consequently, action space, that a criminal develops is likely to be slightly different in general characteristics from the awareness space of most other urban residents. In common with other people, the criminal's awareness space is likely to be dominated by major nodes in his field of mobility: home, shopping areas, school or workplace, entertainment centers. But, since a criminal, particularly a property offender, is often actively engaged in a target search process, we might expect that his awareness space would expand from the nodes themselves (and the paths between them) to include, at least, the fringes of residential and commercial areas found along the paths and close to the nodes. Studies of burglary and robbery in Detroit (Luedtke and Associates 1970: 30) and of robbery in Oakland (Angel 1968; Wilcox 1973) have described such a diffusion effect reaching outward about two blocks into residential areas from major shopping centers, commercial strips along major highways, major industrial and other employment and entertainment centers.

The awareness space and action space of offenders should vary with age just as the awareness and action spaces of most urban residents vary by age. Chapin and Brent (1969) surveyed people in 43 metropolitan areas. The old, those with young children, women, and those who were unemployed had more limited action spaces and spent more time at home. Young, unattached people spent the most time away from home. Similarly, cognitive maps of urban areas seem to vary by age, sex, and race (Everitt and Cadwallader 1972; Orleans and Schmidt 1972). Women, who are often tied to home, and the very young and the old have more limited cognitive maps than males and working aged people. It was also found that cognitive maps varied by socioeconomic status (Orleans 1973). Inhabitants of poorer areas of the city had more limited cognitive maps of the larger urban area than people from affluent areas.

Criminological findings consistent with these deductions on age have been reported by Baldwin and Bottoms (1976) for offenders in Sheffield, and by Reppetto (1974) for burglars in Boston. Rengert (1975) reports differentials in male and female burglar behavior in Philadelphia which are consistent with expectations. Reppetto's findings are consistent with expectations on racial differences, but Baldwin and Bottom's findings are only partially consistent with respect to socioeconomic status expectations.

Finally, the awareness space of the offender, and his cognitive map, probably varies with the actual urban form of the city. It has been proposed that awareness spaces are primarily based on nodes centered at home, work or school, shopping locations, recreational areas, and the paths connecting these. In an urban area where shopping, recreation, and work locations are dispersed, awareness spaces should tend to be larger. In urban areas where these activities are concentrated, awareness spaces should be spatially restricted. For all people, even criminals, much of any city is really unknown territory which either does not exist (cognitively) at all, or is populated with the terrors of the unfamiliar.

Since awareness spaces are dominated by regular activities and movement between these activities, it seems reasonable to assume that the form of movement between activities will influence the level of awareness. In an urban area dominated by fixed rail mass transit, awareness spaces should, primarily, be nodal with less cognitive emphasis on path elements. We might expect criminal activity to be greater near major nodes in the transportation network. In urban areas which are serviced by bus transit or automobiles, we might expect criminal activity to be more linear, stretched out along the major transportation paths between nodes. This pattern should be especially strong in urban areas which have a few major transportation arteries which could be expected to be a part of many criminals' awareness spaces.

The crime pattern expected from the search activities of a single criminal operating within a normal awareness space, assuming a uniform distribution of targets or victims, is shown by Figure 5.4.

Case 4: Complex Search Area for Multiple Offenders

Initial conditions:

(a) multiple offenders
(b) uniform distribution of targets
(c) home, work or school, shopping, and entertainment bases.

The pattern described in the third case can be generalized to a cluster of offenders by overlaying, conceptually, the individual patterns. Home locations are likely to be spatially clustered (see Shaw and McKay 1969; Voss and Petersen 1971). Work, shopping, and entertainment locations may be more dispersed depending on the structure of individual urban areas. The crime patterns should relate to shopping and

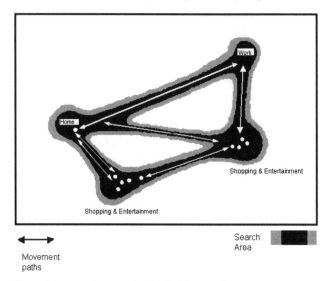

Figure 5.4   Complex search area for individual offender

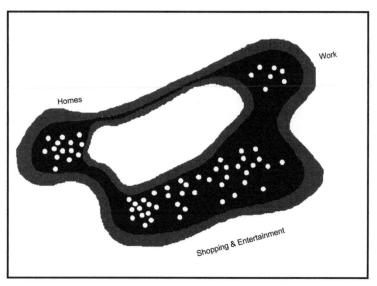

Figure 5.5   Complex search area for cluster of offenders

entertainment centers used by the crime prone population, not the total shopping and entertainment complex of the urban area (see Figure 5.5). In addition, since much criminal activity, especially among juveniles, is group based, there should be some communality in the overlaying.

The traces of this hypothesized composite search pattern can be seen in much empirical criminology. Probably the best example is by Porteous (1977), who studied the Burnside gang in Saanich, a suburb of Victoria, British Columbia. He found that the home residences, schools, and meeting places (entertainment locations) of the gang members formed the core area (some 1.5 miles in diameter) for the gang's activities and that 80 percent of the gang's delinquent acts occurred within this core area. Morris (1958) found that juveniles in Croydon, England, committed the largest proportion of their offenses in the shopping areas they normally frequented. Wilcox's (1973) study of robbery in Oakland might also fit the pattern, as she found that the overwhelming majority of offenses occurred in or near low-cost entertainment areas.

Case 5: Selective Search Area for Multiple Offenders

Initial conditions:

(a) multiple offenders distributed uniformly in the urban area
(b) nonuniform distribution of potential targets
(c) offender based in a single location.

The first four cases assumed that there was a uniform distribution of targets. This obviously is not the condition of the real world. Targets or potential victims are very unevenly distributed across space and time. For example, street robbery requires the presence of victims on the street. Certain parts of cities (at certain times of day) have many pedestrians. In other parts of cities and at other times of day, the streets may be deserted.

Robbery targets are spatially and temporally clustered. As another example, auto theft obviously requires that the offender locate an automobile in time and space. Clearly automobiles are unevenly distributed in space and the distribution of them changes radically between working and nonworking hours. As Sarah Boggs (1965) has demonstrated, and subsequent studies in opportunity have reaffirmed (for example, Mayhew et al. 1976), the gross availability of targets influences the pattern of crime occurrence.

Consider then, the simplest situation with a nonuniform distribution of targets, but with a uniform distribution of offenders. In this situation we would expect that offenses would vary with the concentration of targets (see Figure 5.6).

Linking this nonuniform distribution of targets with what is known about distance decay spatial behavior and the bias in spatial knowledge to places close to home, work, or recreation areas, we would expect that potential offenders living far away from the clustering of targets would be less likely to actually commit offenses.

This pattern is consistently reported in the criminological literature. Ernest W. Burgess (1916) reported it in the delinquency patterns of Lawrence, Kansas, before World War I. He found "geographical ... proximity to the business street" to be the

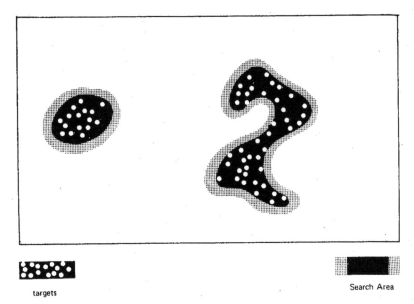

targets   Search Area

Figure 5.6   Search area with nonuniform distribution of targets and uniform distribution of offenders

critical determinant of why the children of one ward had very high delinquency rates while the children of other wards, similar on sociodemographic and economic measures, had low delinquency rates. Thrasher (1927), in the largest study of juvenile gangs ever undertaken, argued that the physical environment and especially the residential proximity to opportunities for theft were major determinants of a gang's criminal activity. Shaw and McKay (1929, 1931, 1969) reported proximity to criminal opportunities as critical determinants of areal delinquency rates in a series of studies covering some six decades of data in Chicago. In their report to the National Commission of Law Observance, for instance, Shaw and McKay (1931: 68) argued that "in general, proximity to industry and commerce is an index of the areas of Chicago in which high rates of delinquents are found."[4] Lander (1954) found high delinquency residence rates related to commercial land use concentrations, but not to industrial concentrations. Most graphic, perhaps, is Tobias's (1972) mapping of Mayhew's nineteenth century reports on London rookeries. All of the rookeries were strategically located on the boundary of the City of London, in proximity to several sets of criminal opportunity.

---

4   Peculiarly, they denied that this consistently observed fact could have any analytic importance. This refusal to treat empirical findings as having direct value is considered by Brantingham and Jeffery in the Afterword.

Case 6: Selective Search area for a Single Offender

Initial conditions:

(a) single offender
(b) nonuniform distribution of potential targets
(c) home, work or school, shopping, and recreational bases.

As was pointed out in Case 2, offenders are not uniformly distributed in urban space. Part of the variation may be the result of an apparent higher motivation to commit crimes within selected socioeconomic groups (see Hindelang 1978).

Part of the variation may be the result of knowledge of and access to potentially "good" targets or victims. The commission of a crime requires that a motivated individual come in contact with a potential target or victim. Using the terminology developed in the preceding descriptive cases, the criminal's "awareness space" must include targets which he considers "good."

Those parts of the urban area that the offender knows fairly well and is likely to travel through represent a "potential" space for criminal activity. A criminal's search for targets is likely to be biased toward his habitual awareness space, particularly, as is described in the propositions at the beginning of the chapter, toward those subareas within the awareness space which are perceived as "good" target areas. One characteristic of a good target area is the availability of targets. Thus, a criminal will probably be spatially biased toward seeking targets in the subarea of his action space which contains a clustering of targets, a choice of criminal opportunities (see Figure 5.7).

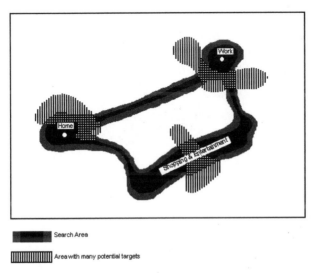

■■■■ Search Area

||||||||||| Area with many potential targets

Figure 5.7   Selective complex search area for individual offender

Another aspect of a good target area is low perceived risk. Except in the highest affect crimes, such as murder, the potential criminal searches for targets in situations where he feels "safe." The actual area of criminal activity is likely to be a subset of the intersection of the criminal's awareness space with the areas containing targets or victims: These will be the areas which fit the template of a good target area (see Figure 5.8).

Several recent studies in the crime prevention through environmental, design (CPTED) literature and in the spatial analysis of crime have reported results consistent with the idea that crimes are more likely to occur in subparts of a criminal's traditional awareness space which are perceived to be "safe" and which have ample targets. For example, the surge of branch bank robberies near major highways could be considered consistent with this pattern. The highways are likely to be pathways in the criminal's usual awareness space; and the banks are vulnerable. The criminal can escape quickly on the highway.

Similarly, the growth in convenience store robberies is also consistent with this pattern. As Dufala (1976) reported in his study of such robberies in Tallahassee, Florida, the stores which were near major roads and which had no surrounding evening business activity were most vulnerable. The nearness to the major roads placed the stores within the awareness spaces of many urban residents (the obvious marketing reason for their location). The stores also became part of the action spaces of robbers. If robbers are looking for low risk, it seems likely that stores near but

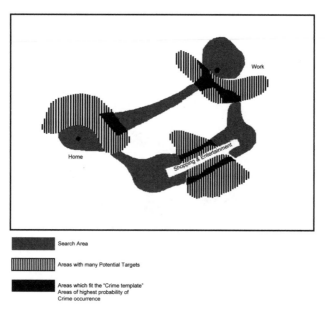

Figure 5.8   Selective crime occurrence area for individual offender

not on main roads will have lower risks than stores directly on main roads and will be more likely to be victimized. Those stores near the main road will be quieter, surrounded by fewer potential witnesses, have fewer people around who might intervene in the robbery.

Generally, remote, inaccessible locations or people in remote locations are not victimized. Such remoteness can be measured in various metrics.

Bevis and Nutter (1977), for instance, have shown that differential accessibility produced by differences in the permeability of the street network affects the burglary rates of neighborhoods in Minneapolis. Neighborhoods rendered inaccessible by the complexity of the street system had lower rates than those which were easily accessible. Crime occurs near areas of activity, along transportation paths or in residential areas close to where criminals live.

Case 7: Selective Search Area for Multiple Offenders

Initial conditions:

(a) multiple offenders
(b) nonuniform distribution of potential targets
(c) home, work or school, shopping and recreation bases.

Case 6 represented the hypothetical pattern for a single offender. The pattern for all offenders can be constructed by simultaneously considering the individual patterns. Those areas within the general urban space which are part of the most individual selective crime occurrence areas will have the most numerous crimes (see Figure 5.9).

Evidence for Case 7 is found in Rengert's (1972) study of the distribution of arson and vandalism in Philadelphia. Considering a model which took into account areal opportunities, areal risks (in terms of relative police efficiency), relative aggregate familiarity with areas, and accessibility of the police districts of Philadelphia, he was able to explain 73 percent of the observed variance in the spatial distribution of these crimes.

Case 8: Dynamic Search Area for a Single Offender

Initial conditions:

(a) single offender
(b) nonuniform distribution of potential offenders
(c) home, work or school, shopping and recreation bases.

Principles of Geographical Offender Profiling

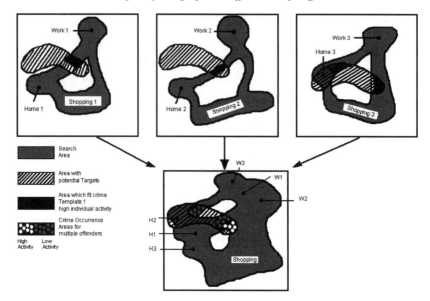

Figure 5.9

The previous two cases identified subareas within a criminal's awareness space where crimes are more likely to take place. It was assumed, implicitly, that the awareness spaces of individuals in general, and criminals in particular, are fixed over time. A more reasonable assumption would be that the awareness space is dynamic and can change over time. In terms of the general propositions presented at the beginning of this chapter, a "new" or "novice" criminal begins with an awareness space developed through noncriminal activities. When the novice criminal begins to search out victims or targets, he probably uses cues learned from friends who may have committed crimes (Letkemann 1973: 117–136; Mack 1964: 51), cues learned from the media (note the imitative crimes which have followed "caper" dramas on American television), and generalizations from previously learned feelings of security. The novice probably looks for targets within his awareness space and may even search fringe areas. He is unlikely to penetrate into totally foreign areas where he will feel uncomfortable or stand out as different or not belonging (Brantingham and Brantingham 1975; Reppetto 1974; Newman 1972; compare, Sacks 1972). Over time, if the novice continues to commit offenses, his awareness space is likely to accumulate more detailed information about the areas in which he has searched and found good targets. Over time the criminal is also likely to expand his awareness space to include areas which were adjacent to his prenovice awareness space (see Figure 5.10).

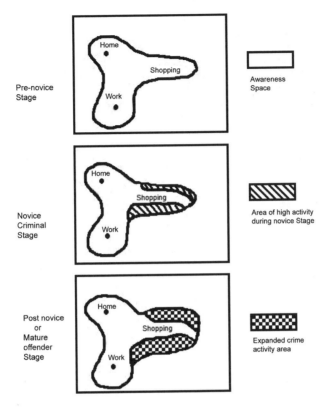

Figure 5.10 Maturation of crime search area

Case 9: Dynamic Search Area for Multiple Offenders

Initial conditions:

(a) multiple offenders
(b) nonuniform distribution of targets or victims
(c) home, work or school, shopping and recreation bases.

As in the other generalizations from individual patterns to patterns for multiple offenders, the individual patterns can be overlaid. In discussing dynamic search areas, it should be mentioned that it is likely that information will flow between offenders and that an individual's awareness space is likely to be modified by what he learns from other offenders. The interaction by communication of knowledge between offenders has been discussed in the learning of criminal behavior and skills which is supposed to occur in prison (Letkemann 1973; Mack 1963). It seems likely that information about "good" target areas diffuses within criminal social networks (Shover 1972a; Mack 1963). Over time, the awareness spaces of criminals who have common social contacts are likely to converge, at least the subpart of the awareness spaces which identify good target areas (see Figure 5.11). This convergence should result in more clustered crime patterns.

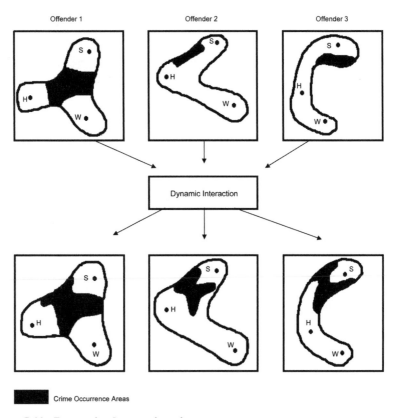

Figure 5.11   Dynamic changes in crime occurrence area

Summary

The hypothetical cases presented above were an attempt to articulate, spatially, the target selection behavior of criminals. Basically, it has been argued that the spatial patterning of crime in a particular urban area depends on:

(1) the spatial distribution of potential offenders;
(2) the spatial distribution of potential targets;
(3) the general awareness spaces of potential offenders;
(4) whether the awareness space includes potentially "good" targets in perceived "good" crime areas; and
(5) the dynamic interchange of information between potential offenders which may modify their awareness spaces.

It has been argued that the patterning of crime, and even the volume of crime, depends on motivation and opportunity, *and* mobility and perception. Crime occurrence is not the direct, unmediated result of motivation. Crime is a dependent phenomenon modified by urban form and general patterns of perception or cognition.

Consequences

Using the hypothetical cases as a starting platform, it is possible, deductively, to arrive at some general statements about crime patterns and to explain certain empirically reported patterns which previously had been unexplained.

(1) Older cities with a generally concentric zonal form, and with a dense core, will have a crime pattern which clusters toward the core. There should be a relatively steep crime gradient.
In a city with a concentric zone form there is a central business district surrounded by a zone-in-transition which is, in turn, surrounded by residential areas of increasing cost. In such a city, the socioeconomic groups with the highest incidence of criminal behavior are likely to live in or near the zone-in-transition. Entertainment and work opportunities are likely to be close to the homes of potential offenders. Commercial and industrial targets will be close to the residences of potential criminals. There is also likely to be foot traffic in the core areas. All of these conditions provide targets for crime. Employing concepts of "distance decay," crime should be highest toward the core and around the zone-in-transition, and decrease away from the zone-in-transition. This, of course, is the classic pattern reported by the Chicago School ecologists.

(2) Newer cities with a mosaic urban form will have a more dispersed crime pattern, with less concentration of crime than in older, denser cities.
With a mosaic urban form, concentrations of potential criminals will be dispersed in clusters throughout the urban area. Entertainment centers and work locations are likely to be separated from the residential areas where many potential criminals live. The potential offenders of a mosaic city are likely to have larger awareness spaces than potential offenders in a concentric zone city because they must move more extensively in order to reach work, shopping and entertainment locations. With larger awareness spaces, the potential offenders of a mosaic city will have a

broader target search area and will be likely to find targets in more places, producing a dispersed crime pattern. This is the pattern reported in post-World War II studies in cities affected by dispersed public housing policies or by rapid development keyed to the transport potentials of the automobile.

(3) New cities with dispersed shopping and much strip commercial development have a higher potential for property crime.
Looking back to the hypothetical cases describing the distribution of targets, dispersed shopping and strip development put retail and commercial business into the awareness spaces of more individuals and within close reach of more people. Such easier access, which is the obvious marketing rationale for dispersing commercial activity, should make property offenses more frequent. An individual who is weakly motivated to commit a commercial property offense might be deterred if he had to walk two miles to find a target, but might not be deterred if he only had to walk two blocks.

The relative desirability of various combinations of travel mode and travel time is, of course, open to empirical investigation. Reppetto's (1974) Boston burglars expressed specific time-trouble-distance limits to their journeys to crime. But for illustrative purposes, consider a clustered commercial shopping area which is roughly circular with a radius of one-half mile. Suppose that the average juvenile will travel about one-half mile to commit a property offense such as theft or burglary (Figure 5.12). The donut-shaped area one-half mile wide is the feeder area providing potential offenders to the central commercial area. This feeder area is 2.35 square miles. If the same amount of commercial activity were converted into strip development one-sixteenth of a mile wide, it would produce a strip 12.56 miles long (Figure 5.12). Using the same basic idea that a juvenile will travel up to one-half mile to commit a property offense, the strip commercial area will have a feeder area 13.4 square miles in area. This strip feeder area is 5.7 times larger than the feeder area for the cluster development. Assuming that the two feeder areas are similar demographically, and have similar densities, the stores in the hypothetical strip development will suffer exposure to a far larger number of potential offenders and will be at much greater risk of becoming a target.

(4) Development of major transportation arteries leads to a concentration of criminal events close to the highways, particularly near major intersections.
Major transportation arteries are likely to become part of the awareness space of many urban residents, including potential criminals. To use Kevin Lynch's terminology (1960), the transportation arteries become paths. Major intersections are likely to become nodal points. We have argued in this chapter that a criminal's search area begins within his awareness space. Paths and nodes become reasonable starting points in such a search.

Areas close to major paths and intersections have other attractions for instrumental type offenses such as robbery or burglary. Robbers and burglars look for targets

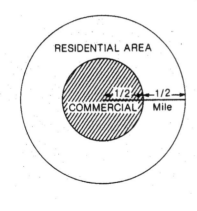

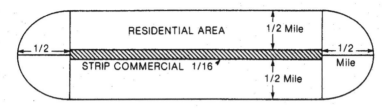

Figure 5.12   Feeder areas for commercial activities

within "safe" crime areas. Major transportation arteries, if the criminal has a car, offer easy escape.

Because of easy access and availability to customers, stores and services locate along the traffic arteries and at nodes. Such stores and services are potential targets.

The areas adjacent to major transportation arteries are likely to have a disproportionate number of potential targets, be perceived as relatively "safe" crime search areas, and be part of many offenders' awareness spaces. All this should lead to higher crime rates near major arteries, particularly near nodal points on arteries (see Fink 1969; Wilcox 1973; Luedtke & Associates 1970).

(5) Areas with grid networks, in general, have higher potential crime rates than areas with organic street layouts.

In order for a crime to occur, the criminal has to locate a target or victim in his awareness space. A criminal's awareness space will change with new information and as the result of searching. The expansion of an awareness space will most probably occur in a connected fashion; the borders or edges of currently known areas will be explored first. In exploring new areas, the potential offender will find it easier to penetrate areas with predictable road networks. Areas with grid street layouts are more predictable than areas with winding roads, cul-de-sacs, or dead ends.

Criminal behavior in searching new areas is *spatially* similar to other urban residents. Since residential areas with more organic street layouts and cul-de-sacs and dead ends are more difficult to use as through paths, these residential areas are less likely to experience much through traffic. Nonresidents are less likely to be found in these areas, therefore they are more likely to be identified by residents when present. Because nonresidents are more easily identifiable, and because they may become lost or disoriented, offenders are less likely to expand their search areas very far into nongrid residential areas (see Bevis and Nutter 1977).

(6) Older cities with dispersed low income housing and public transit are likely to have a concentration of crime around the core, and nodes of higher crime around the low income housing areas.

This statement about crime patterns is really just a corollary to the first statement which described crime gradients in the "zonal" city. Because of public policy in many countries, particularly Britain, subsidized low income housing has been dispersed in many older cities. Given that, historically, more criminals have been found in low income groups (a point reaffirmed by Hindelang's 1978 cross-analysis of arrest, victimization, and self-report data), this dispersal will have an obvious impact on crime patterns. In older cities with a dominant core, the awareness spaces of criminals living in the low income housing areas will include their home area and the core area. Their search for targets will be biased towards these areas. Such a pattern of crime was found by Morris (1958) in Croydon, and Baldwin and Bottoms in Sheffield (1976), and was reported by McKay in the post-World War II data for Chicago in the revised edition of the Shaw and McKay classic, *Juvenile Delinquency and Urban Areas* (1969).

(7) The shifting of work areas out of core areas into fringe areas of a city will tend to increase crime in suburban areas.

In many growing urban areas industrial and wholesale trade operations are increasing in urban fringe areas, or in the outer ring of urban areas, and decreasing in the urban core. The shift away from the core is partly the result of the industrial move to one-floor plants which obviously require the larger blocks of land which are available at lower cost in fringe areas and partly the result of improved urban highway systems which decrease the accessibility advantage of central core locations.

Whatever the reasons for the shift, the movement of work locations to the urban fringe should influence crime patterns. Because journey-to-work patterns will change, awareness spaces will change for those criminals who work (regularly or occasionally). Those fringe and suburban work locations and suburban residential and commercial areas along the paths to and from work areas will become part of the awareness spaces of employed criminals and may even become part of the awareness spaces of nonworking criminals who communicate with workers.

In addition, the movement of industrial and wholesale trade changes the opportunity structure, putting more targets within the reach of those people who live in suburban areas and may be motivated to commit property offenses.

(8) Major entertainment complexes such as sports arenas are likely to produce localized associated increases in crime. If these complexes are near residential areas with many potential offenders, the associated crime should increase disproportionately.

Major entertainment complexes are likely to become part of the awareness space of most urban residents. These complexes also produce temporally concentrated clusters of victims and targets when activities are going on. Thus, a concentration of targets is likely to occur within the awareness space of many criminals.

If, in addition, the entertainment complexes are located near residential areas with many people who are motivated to commit crimes, the easy accessibility and the strength of the awareness space of residents should increase associated crime even more.

(9) Cities with a core "red light district" are likely to have concentrations of crime in those areas. However, dispersing the activities which cluster in a "red light district" will not necessarily decrease the total amount of crime, though the spatial patterning of crime should change.

Historically, cities have always had "red light districts," areas where prostitution, gambling, and bars concentrate. These areas attract potential victims and potential offenders. In fact, in these areas the offender and victim distinction can become blurred. In the case of murder and assault, the victim precipitation literature shows how easily the victim might have been the offender (Vetter and Silverman 1978: 76). In street robbery, the victim may become an offender on another day.

City administrators try to control such areas through traditional means such as enforcing criminal code violations, passing municipal ordinances controlling businesses, and increasing police presence. In some cities the activities in the district are broken up, often to appear in a more dispersed pattern in other parts of the city. Reckless (1933) documented such a dispersal of the Chicago red light district in 1912 and noted the migration of the vice area from the urban core to the suburban fringe.

The dispersal of the red light activities may increase or decrease the amount of crime. Whether crime increases or decreases depends on the distribution of targets after the dispersal and how the awareness spaces of potential criminals change. If the breakup of a red light district results in a total decrease in red light activities and the remaining activities become part of the awareness spaces of fewer potential criminals (or patrons in general), then the total amount of crime may decrease. However, the breaking up of a red light district may backfire on city administrators. New areas may pick up the red light businesses, the awareness spaces of the former patrons and criminals who "worked" the old red light district will change. For some, new areas with increased red light activities will be incorporated into their awareness spaces. Potential criminals will be attracted into previously unknown parts of the city. If these previously unknown parts of the city have many good targets or victims, then crime may increase. Reckless (1933) recorded an increase in crime in the Chicago suburbs, together with an overall decrease in metropolitan levels of crime as some red light businesses were driven outside Chicago proper, while others folded after the 1912 clean-up. More recently, Harries (1976: 384) has reported that urban renewal in Lawton, Oklahoma, destroyed the city's compact vice area and dispersed the businesses throughout the suburbs, creating a tough law enforcement problem and an incredibly high crime rate.

Conclusion

In conclusion, it has been argued in this chapter that crime occurrence is not the direct result of motivation, but is mediated by perceived opportunity. This, in turn, is influenced by the actual distribution of opportunities, urban form, and mobility. It has been argued that criminals are not random in their behavior and that by exploring urban structure and how people interact with the urban spatial structure, it should be possible to predict the spatial distribution of crime and explain some of the variation in volume of crime between urban areas and between cities.

References

Amir, M. (1971). *Patterns in Forcible Rape*. Chicago: University of Chicago Press.

Bagley, C. (1965). Juvenile delinquency in Exeter: An ecological and comparative study. *Urban Studies*, 2, 33–50.

Angel, S. (1968). *Discouraging Crime through City Planning*. Berkeley, CA: Centre for Planning and Development Research.

Baldwin, J. and Bottoms, A.E. (1976). *The Urban Criminal. A Study in Sheffield*. London: Tavistock Publications.

Bevis, C. and Nutter, J. (1977). Changing street layouts to reduce residential burglary. Annual Meeting of the American Society of Criminology, Atlanta.

Boggs, S. (1965). Urban crime patterns. *American Sociological Review*, 30(6), 899–908.

Brantingham, P.L. and Brantingham, P.J. (1975). Spatial patterning of burglary. *Howard Journal of Penology and Crime Prevention*, 14, 11–24.

Brantingham, P.L. and Brantingham, P.J. (1977). Housing patterns and burglary in a medium-sized American city. In J.F. Scott and S. Dinitz (eds), *Criminal Justice Planning*, (pp. 63–74). New York; Praeger.

Brantingham, P.L. and Brantingham P.J. (1978). A theoretical model of crime site selection. In M.Krohn and R. L. Akers (eds), *Crime, Law and Sanction*, (pp.105–118). Beverly Hills: Sage Publications.

Brearley, H.C. (1932). *Homicide in the United States*. Chapel Hill: University of North Carolina Press.

Bullock, H.A. (1955). Urban homicide in theory and fact. *Journal of Criminal Law, Criminology and Police Science*, 45(5), 565–575.

Burgess, E.W. (1916). Juvenile delinquency in a small city. *Journal of the American Institute of Criminal Law and Criminology*, 6, 724–728.

Burt, C. (1925). *The Young Delinquent*. London: Appleton.

Capone, D.C. and Nichols, W.W. (1976). Urban Structure and criminal mobility. *American Behavioral Scientist*, 20, 199–214.

Carter, R.L. and Hill, K.Q. (1975). *The Criminal's Image of the City*. New York: Pergamon.

Chapin, F.S. and Brent, R.K. (1969). Human activity systems in the metropolitan United States. *Environment and Behavior*, 1, 107–130.

Clinard, M.B. and Abbott, D.J. (1973). *Crime in Developing Countries: A Comparative Perspective*. New York: John Wiley & Sons.

Everitt, J. and Cadwallader, M. (1972). The home area concept in urban analysis. In J. Mitchell (Ed), *Delinquency, Crime and Society*. Chicago: University of Chicago Press.

Fink, G. (1969). Einsbruchstatorte vornehmlich an einfallstrassen? *Kriminalstik*, 23, 358–360.

Haggett, P. (1965). *Locational Analysis in Human Geography*. London: Edward Arnold.

Harries, K.D. (1971). The geography of American crime 1968. *The Journal of Geography*, 70, 204–213.

Hindelang, M.J. (1978). Race and involvement in common law personal crimes. *American Sociological Review*, 43, 93–109.

Inciardi, J.A. (1978). Reflections on crime: An introduction to criminology and criminal justice. New York: Holt, Rinehart and Winston.

Jeffery, C.R. (1965). Criminal behavior and learning theory. *Journal of Criminal Law, Criminology and Police Science*, 56, 294.

Lander, B. (1954). *Towards and Understanding of Juvenile Delinquency*. New York: Columbia University Press.

Letkemann, P. (1973). *Crime As Work*. Englewood Cliffs, NJ: Prentice-Hall.

Lowe, J.C. and Morydas, S. (1975). *The Geography of Movement*. Boston, MA: Houghton-Mifflin.

Luedtke, G. and Associates. (1970). *Crime and the Physical City: Neighbourhood Design Techniques for Crime Reduction*. Springfield, VA: National Technical Information Service.

Lynch, K. (1960). *The Image of the City*. Cambridge, MA: MIT Press.

Mack, J. (1964). Full-time miscreants: Delinquent neighbourhoods and criminal networks. *British Journal of Sociology*, 15, 38–53.

Mayhew, P.M., Clarke, R.V.G, Sturman, A. and Hough, J.M. (1976). Crime as opportunity. *Home Office Research Study No. 34*. London: HMSO.

Morris, T. (1958). *The Criminal Area: A Study in Social Ecology*. London: Routledge and Kegan Paul.

Newman, O. (1971). *Defensible Space*. New York: Macmillan.

Petrovich, P. (1971). Recherches sur la criminalite a Paris dans la seconde moitie du XVIII siecle. In A. Abbiateci et al. (eds), *Crimes et Criminalite en France sous l'Ancien Regione 17–18 siecles*. Paris: Librarie Armand Colin.

Plint, T. (1851). *Crime in England.* London: Charles Gilpin.

Pokorny, A. (1965). A comparison of homicides in two cities. *Journal of Criminal Law, Criminology, and Police Science,* 56: 479–487.

Porteous, J.D. (1977). *Environment and Behaviour: Planning and Everyday Urban Life.* Reading, MA: Addison-Wesley.

Pyle, G.F. (1974). *The Spatial Dynamics of Crime.* Department of Geography Research Paper No. 159. Chicago: The University of Chicago.

Orleans, P. (1973). Differential Cognition of Urban Residents: Effects of Social Scales on Mapping. In R.M. Downs and D. Stea (eds), *Image and Environment* (pp. 115–130). Chicago: Aldine.

Orleans, P. and Schmidt, S. (1972). Mapping the City: Environmental Cognition of Urban Residents. In W.J. Mitchell (Ed), *Environmental Design Research and Practice.* Los Angeles: University of California.

Reckless, W.C. (1933). *Vice in Chicago.* Chicago: University of Chicago Press.

Reiss, A. (1971). *Place of Residence of Arrested Persons compared with Place where the Offense was Charged in Arrest.* A Report to President's Commission on Law Enforcement and Administration of Justice.

Rengert, G.F. (1972). Spatial aspects of criminal behaviour: a suggested approach. Paper read at East Lakes Division, Association of American Geographers annual meeting. Department of Geography, Temple University.

Rengert, G.F. (1975). Some effects of being female on criminal spatial behavior. *The Pennsylvania Geographer,* 13(2), 10–18.

Rengert, G.F. and Wasilchick, J. (1980). Residential burglary: The awareness and use of extended space. Paper read at American Society of Criminology annual meeting, San Francisco.

Repetto, T.A. (1974). *Residential Crime.* Cambridge, MA: Ballinger.

Sacks, H. (1972). Notes on police assessment of moral character. In D.Sudnow (ed), *Studies in Social Interaction,* (pp. 280–293). New York: Free Press.

Schmid, C. (1960a). Urban crime areas, part 1. *American Sociological Review,* 25, 527–543.

Schmid, C. (1960b). Urban crime areas, part 2. *American Sociological Review,* 25, 655–678.

Shannon, L.W. (1954). The spatial distribution of criminal offences by states. *Journal of Criminal Law, Criminology and Police Sciences,* 45, 264–273.

Shaw, C.R. (1929). *Delinquency Areas.* Chicago: University of Chicago Press.

Shaw, C.R. and McKay, H.D. (1931). *Social Factors in Juvenile Delinquency.* Washington, D.C: Government Printing Office.

Shaw, C.R. and McKay, H.D. (1969). *Juvenile Delinquency and Urban Areas (Revised Edition).* Chicago: Chicago University Press.

Shover, N.E. (1972). Structures and careers in burglary. *Journal of Criminal Law, Criminology and Police Science,* 63, 540–549.

Smith, T.S. (1976). Inverse distance variations for the flow of crime in urban areas. *Social Forces,* 25(4), 804–815.

Thrasher, F.M. (1963). *The Gang.* Chicago: University of Chicago Press. Originally published in 1927.

Timms, D.W.G. (1971). *The Urban Mosaic: Towards a Theory of Residential Differentiation.* Cambridge: Cambridge University Press.

Tobias, J.J. (1972). *Urban Crime in Victorian England.* New York: Schocken Books. (Revised version of *Crime and Industrial Society in the 19th Century,* 1967).

Turner, S. (1969). Delinquency and distance. In Sellin, T. and Wolfgang, M.E. (eds). *Delinquency: Selected Studies* (pp. 11–26). New York: John Wiley & Sons.

Turner, S. (1969b). The ecology of delinquency. In Sellin, T. and Wolfgang, M.E. (eds). *Delinquency: Selected Studies.* New York: John Wiley & Sons.

Vetter, H.J. and Silverman, I.J. (1978). *The Nature of Crime.* Philadelphia: W.B. Saunders Company.

Voss, H.L. and Petersen, D.M. (1971). *Ecology, Crime and Delinquency.* New York: Appleton.

Waller, I. and Okihiro, N. (1978). Burglary and the public: A victimological approach to criminal justice. Paper presented at the annual meeting of the American Society of Criminology, Chicago, November.

White, R.C. (1932). The relation of felonies to environmental factors in Indianapolis. *Social Forces,* 10(4), 498–509.

Wilcox, S. (1973). *The Geography of Robbery.* The Prevention and Control of Robbery 3. Davis, CA: The Centre of Administration of Criminal Justice, University of California.

PART 2
Offenders' Geography

Chapter 6

Delinquency and Distance

Stanley Turner

A number of interesting questions arise when one considers the matter of the relationship between the place where a delinquent lives and the place where he commits his violation of the law. How far does the delinquent live from where his offense takes place? Does the type of his offense affect that distance? And finally, does the presence of an accomplice have any effect on this relationship? It would also be interesting to compare the replies to these questions with findings of studies of distance involving adult offenders and their offenses and with studies where distance has been examined in relation to the selection of marriage partners, migration, removals, etc. This article will focus on all of these matters, using information available for certain types of delinquent events included in the research reported by Sellin and Wolfgang in their book, *The Measurement of Delinquency*. The events chosen were those in which offenses resulted in bodily injury to victims and/or the loss or damage to property; they represented a ten percent sample of delinquent events known to the police of Philadelphia in 1960. We shall refer to these events as index events because they were the ones which furnished the basis for the index of delinquency contributed by the authors mentioned.

The first question considered was: how far away does the offender live from the scene of his offense? To answer this question the location of each offense was pinpointed on a map of Philadelphia approximately ten feet long; then the residence of each offender was plotted and the "taxicab" distance from the offense to the residence was measured by using a map measure (watch pattern) . Index events were selected because:

> Index offenses have a "real location", that is, they occur at an obvious location. Many nonindex offenses have a vague location; truancy, possession of burglary tools, runaway, intoxication, incorrigibility, for instance, all have a diffuse or continuous location. Index offenses involve physical injury, theft, or property damage and can almost always he pinpointed.[1]

Index offenses were selected as more reliable indicators of changes in the extent of delinquency. It was felt that using them would present a more stable picture of the relation between delinquency and distance.

---

1   Some exceptions can occur. For instance, police may discover a juvenile riding a bike which the offender admits that he stole but will not disclose the place from which he stole it.

Certain alternative ways of measuring distance exist but were rejected.

1. Measuring the distance from where the offense occurred to some fixed point such as the center of the city.[2]
2. Measuring the distance from the offender's residence to the victim's residence.
3. Measuring the distance from the offense to the victim's residence.[3]

Method 1 was rejected since it assumes a point that is somewhat arbitrary (the "center" of the city, for instance) or has no relevance to the offender. Whatever influences the distances that offenders go, it is not a matter of distance from a common fixed point.

Methods 2 and 3 are of use only when the victim and the offender meet, as in homicide. But in most index crimes this is not true. Or in some crimes there is no specific victim at a specific residence. Damage to city property, embezzlement in a large corporation, etc., would all be index crimes, but with no specific residence for the victim.

Similarly, there are various methods of measuring the distance from the offense to the residence of the offender.

1. Measure the beeline distance from the offense to the offender's residence.
2. Measure the distance from the center of the census tract of occurrence to the center of the census tract of residence.

The first method understates the true distance by a roughly calculable amount. The second method introduces a more complicated bias. Any offense occurring in the same census tract of residence is given a distance of zero; thus, whether an offense gets assigned a score of zero depends in part on how far the offender travels and how large the census tract is. Furthermore, the size of a census tract is inversely related to its population.

For these reasons we decided to use the more arduous method of taking the minimal estimated route from the offense to the offender's residence. Distance was read off the measuring wheel to the nearest unit and transcribed onto a card with certain other information.

Removal of Bias from the Data

Two biases were detected in the data: first, the sample was a ten percent systematic sample of offenses and in every offense that was selected, all offenders were used.

---

2   R. Clyde White, "The relation of felonies to environmental factors in Indianapolis," *Social Forces*, 10 (4), 498–509.

3   Henry Allen Bullock, "Urban homicide in theory and fact," *Journal of Criminal Law, Criminology and Police Science,* 45, 565–575, (January–February 1955).

This means that the sample was a cluster sample of offenders, not a systematic sample. The residence of one offender is correlated with the residence of the other offenders in the offense: if one offender is so many units away from the offense, all are. For this reason, the decision was made to use the average distance of all offenders in an offense. Thus, one and only one distance figure was used for each offense: the arithmetic mean of all offenders participating in the offense.

The second bias was introduced by the device used to measure distance. The map measure is a device that looks like a pocket watch with a small wheel at the bottom. The wheel skims along the surface of the map and causes three hands under its glass face to turn. These three hands measure inches, feet, and tens of feet. The raw data obtained front this wheel displayed heaping at multiples of two. This was probably due to the tendency to round numbers off to the nearest even digit. To eliminate this bias, we gathered the data into groups five units in size. Thus, instead of having units of length equal to 125 feet, we presented the data in units of 615 feet (5 times 123). The raw data appear in Figure 6.1. The same data are presented but, instead, cumulated percentage of cases as a function of distance is presented in Figure 6.2. These figures show that the median distance traveled was 3.5 units (about 40% of a mile) , three quarters of the offenses took place within one mile, and the range was from, zero units to 23 miles (198 units) . Two main facts stand out:

1. Most offenders live a short distance from their offenses.
2. The proportion wanes with distance.

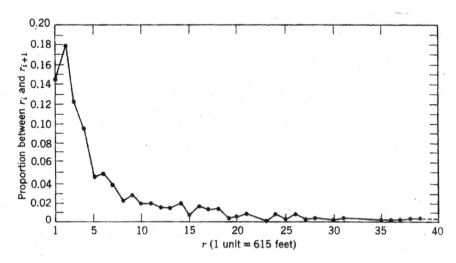

Figure 6.1   Proportion of index offenses occurring between r_i and r_{i+1} (distance between place of residence and place of occurrence in units of 615 feet). Last 5 percent of cases not graphed. Farthest value = 198 units

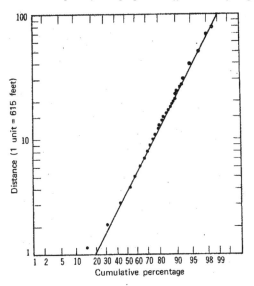

Figure 6.2   **The cumulative percentage of index offenses occurring at a given distance (values plotted on log-normal paper)**

Discussion

The data thus far presented overlook one fact. As the distance increases, larger and larger amounts of area are included. Thus, going out one unit of distance from a point includes all the area swept out by a radius one unit in length; but going out two units from the same point sweeps out much more than twice as much area. This implies that one should divide the proportion of events that take place so many units from a point by the area included. That is

$$Y_i = \frac{\Sigma P(r_i)}{\pi r^2_i}$$

Where $P(r_i)$ = the proportion of cases in a circle r units in radius and Y_t is the cumulative proportion of events per unit area.[4] The data are presented in Table 6.1.

---

4   Another and perhaps better way of presenting these data would be to divide r into a number of nonoverlapping intervals such that a significant number of events occur in each interval. Divide the number of events in the interval by the area relevant to the interval. Thus, if Δr_i is a band and r is the midpoint of Δr then $2\pi r \Delta r$ is the width of the band. Y_i in this case would relate to the probability per unit area and be plotted against r. This way would have the property of additivity, that is, the probability of an event falling in either of two areas would be the sure of their respective probabilities.

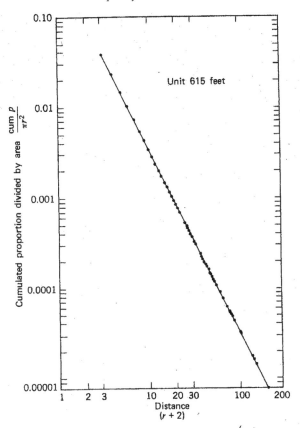

Figure 6.3 Cumulated proportion of index offenses at a given distance divided by area and plotted against that distance plus 2 units

An analysis of Table 4.1 shows that the relation between the cumulative proportion of index offenses per unit area and distance is almost linear except for distances a very short way from the offender's residence. This can be corrected by plotting the offenses not against r but against $r + k$ units of distance. In this case, k is estimated by trial and error at roughly two units. Thus the cumulative proportion of events per unit is plotted not against r but against $r + 2$. The results of these corrections are shown in Figure 6.3. Here the plot is essentially linear on log-log paper. The interpretation of k is similar to the threshold in psychological experimentation. The offender tends to commit offenses nearer to his residence, and his tendency wanes as distance increases. However, very close to his residence, say a block or two, he is less likely to commit as many offenses as we would expect. Some additional comment on this will follow.

Table 6.1   Frequency and distance

r	f	cum f	P	cum P	cum $\frac{P}{\pi r^2}$
1.1	73	73	.145	.145	.0383
2.1	90	163	.179	.325	.0234
3.1	62	225	.123	.448	.0148
4.1	49	274	.098	.546	.0103
5.1	24	298	.048	.594	.00726
6.1	25	323	.050	.643	.00550
7.1	20	343	.040	.683	.00431
8.1	12	355	.024	.707	.00343
9.1	14	369	.028	.735	.00282
10.1	10	397	.020	.755	.00236
11.1	10	389	.020	.775	.00200
12.1	8	397	.016	.791	.00172
13.1	8	405	.016	.806	.00150
14.1	10	415	.020	.827	.00132
15.1	4	419	.008	.835	.00116
16.1	8	427	.016	.851	.00104
17.1	7	434	.014	.864	.000941
18.1	7	441	.014	.878	.000854
19.1	2	443	.004	.882	.000770
20.1	3	446	.006	.888	.000700
21.1	4	450	.008	.896	.000641
22.1	1	451	.002	.898	.000536
23.1	4	455	.008	.906	.000497
24.1	2	457	.004	.910	.000460
26.1	4	461	.008	.918	.000429
27.1	2	463	.004	.922	.000400
28.1	2	465	.004	.926	.000373
29.1	1	466	.002	.928	.000326
31.1	2	468	.004	.932	.00307
35.1	1	469	.002	.934	.000241
36.1	1	470	.002	.936	.000229
37.1	1	471	.002	.938	.000217
38.1	2	473	.004	.942	.00207
39.1	2	475	.004	.946	.00197
40.1	1	476	.002	.948	.000188
41.1	2	478	.004	.952	.000179
43.1	1	479	.002	.954	.000164
45.1	1	480	.002	.956	.000150

Continued

Table 6.1 (continued)

r	f	cum f	P	cum P	cum P / πr^2
46.1	1	481	.002	.958	.000144
47.1	1	482	.002	.960	.000138
48.1	2	484	.004	.964	.000133
49.1	1	485	.002	.966	.000128
50.1	1	486	.002	.968	_000123
53.1	1	487	.002 ,	.970	.000110
54.1	1	488	.002	.973	.000106
58.1	i	489	.002	.974	.0000919
63.1	1	490	.002	.976	.0000780
70.1	1	491	.002	.978	.0000634
74.1	1	492	.002	.980	.0000568
76.1	1	493	.002	.982	.0000540
77.1	1	494	.002	.984	.0000527
79.1	1	495	.002	.986	.0000502
84.1	1	496	.002	.988	.0000445
98.1	1	497	.002	.990	.0000327
99.1	1	498	.002	.992	.0000322
133.1	1	499	.002	.994	.0000179
138.1	1	500	.002	.996	.0000166
146.1	1	501	.002	.998	.0000148
198.1	1	502	.002	1.000	.00000811
Total		502	1.000	1.000	

Internal Comparisons

The data were broken down and plotted separately in two ways.

1. Offender was alone versus offender having one or more accomplices.
2. The offenses involved bodily injury or, lacking bodily injury, involved property theft or, lacking both injury and theft, involved property damage; all index offenses must have at least one of these features.

Table 6.2 shows the results of this procedure and the same data are plotted in Figure 6.4.

There is little difference among any of the groups plotted except that the size of the constant added to the independent variable is larger in some cases than in others. Figure 6.5 may clarify this.

Table 6.2   Partial table of cumulative proportion of offenses at a given distance by offense type and by offender alone or offender with accomplices)

	Bodily Injury Offenses				Alone		
r	cum f	cum P	$\dfrac{\text{cum } P}{r^2}$	r	cum f	cum P	$\dfrac{\text{cum } P}{r^2}$
1.1	229	.200	.0526	1.1	49	.184	.0485
3.1	81	.559	.0185	3.1	138	.519	.0172
10.1	119	.821	.0026	10.1	213	.801	.00250
31.1	137	.945	.000311	31.1	250	.940	.000309
98.1	145	1.000	.0000331	99.1	263	.989	.0000320
				198.1	266	1.000	.00000811

	Thefts				Accomplice		
r	cum f	cum P	$\dfrac{\text{cum } P}{r^2}$	r	cum f	cum P	$\dfrac{\text{cum } P}{r^2}$
1.1	31	.108	.0285	1.1	24	.102	.0268
3.1	110	.385	.0127	3.1	, 87	.369	.0122
10.1	201	. 704	.00219	10.1	166	.704	.00219
30.1	260	.909	.000319	30.1	218	.924	.000325
98.1	282	.986	.0000326	98.1	235	.996	.0000329
198.1	286	1.000	.00000811	138.1	236	1.000	.0000167

	Damage				All Offenses		
r	cum f	cum P	$\dfrac{\text{cum } P}{r^2}$	r	cum f	cum P	$\dfrac{\text{cum } P}{r^2}$
1.1	13	.183	.0482	1.1	73	.145	.0383
3.1	34	.479	.0159	3.1	225	.449	.0148
10.1	59	.831	.00259	10.1	379	.755	.00236
24.1	70	.986	.000540	20.1	466	.928	.000326
53.1	71	1.000	.000113	98.1	497	.990	.0060327
				198.1	502	1.000	.0000081 I

Figure 6.5 illustrates one possible interpretation: in many crimes the offender runs some risk of identification. In fact, in crimes against the person the victim is frequently known to the juvenile. The largest additive constant is in the offense lacking physical injury but involving theft. In these cases the offender goes somewhat farther

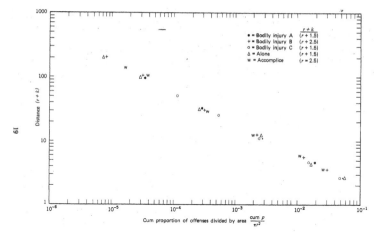

Figure 6.4   **Cumulative proportion of offenses at given distances by offense type and by presence or absence of accomplices**

away than in others, perhaps in order to find a victim unknown to him. Additionally, in some cases, what the offender steals may be identifiable. Large items such as bicycles and autos seem to fall into this category, If the offender intends to steal a bicycle and use it himself, a wise rule would be to steal it outside the radius in which he intends to use it.

When the offender is accompanied by an accomplice, they both tend to live near each other. If the above reasoning about the threshold of distance is true, then when they are together the threshold should be somewhat greater than in the case of a single offender. This is illustrated in the second case in Figure 6.5.

Comparisons with Other Studies

In order to compare the present study to other forms of distance studies so as to find out if distance and criminality might differ from distance and other social events, data were taken largely from an article by Gunnar Boalt and Carl-Gunnar Janson.[5]

The results of plotting these studies are shown in Figure 6.6 and Tables 6.3, 6.4 and 6.5.

These studies show a good deal of similarity to the present study when presented in the form used. In fact, what may be the explanation is the geometry of the situation rather than the sociology.

---

5   Distance and Social Relations, *Acta Sociologica*, 2(2), pp. 73–97, 1957.

DELINQUENCY AND DISTANCE

Offender Alone

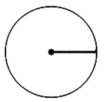

Rule: Go out from residence a distance to avoid identification

Offender with Accomplices

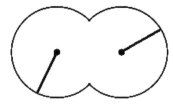

Rule: Same

Offender Steals a Vehicle

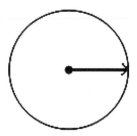

Rule: Go out from residence a distance *r* which is greater
than the distance in which you intend to use the vehicle.

Figure 6.5   Delinquency and distance

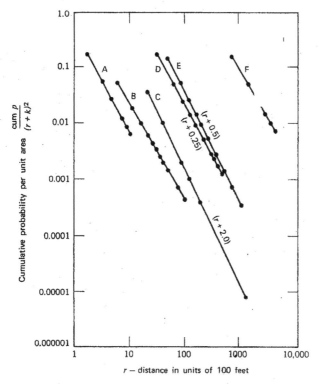

Key	Study	Distance between	Place	Date	N	Unit
A	Dodd	Tellers and hearers of a slogan	C – ville	WW II	125	50 Yds
B	Bossard	Pairs of marriage license applicants	Philadelphia	1951	5000	1 block
C	Present	Delinquents residence and offense location	Philadelphia	1960	502	615 ft
D	Bullock	Residence of murderer and offense location	Houston	1945 – 9	489	0.5 mile
E	Stouffer	Removals from 12 census tracts	Cleveland	1933 – 5	12,292	3000 ft
F	Bergsten	City of residence and birthplace	Va̎ x jo̎	1940	15,609	20 lm

Figure 6.6 **Cumulative probability of events per unit area plotted against distance for various studies**

Table 6.3   Frequency and Cumulative Probabilities per Unit Area of Various Events

Stouffer (Unit 3000 ft)			*Bergsten (Unit 20 km)*			*Dodd (Unit 50 yards)*		
r	f	$\dfrac{cum\ P}{r^2}$	r	f	$\dfrac{cum\ P}{r^2}$	r	f	$\dfrac{cum\ P}{r^2}$
1	5,585	.145	1	8,870	.181	1	67	.171
2	2,471	.0521	2	1,730	.0540	2	23	.0573
3	1,313	.0269	3	1,064	.0264	3	12	.0289
4	737	.0164	4	470	.0155	4	10	.0178
5	431	.0109	5	717	.0105	5	4	.01188
7	5`17	.00585	6	347	.00748	6	5	.00856
10	475	.00299				7	4	.00650
15	532	.00139						
20	174	.000793		15,609			125	
31	37	.000331						
	12,292							

Removals in Cleveland, Ohio, from 1933–1935, for Whites in 12 census tracts. Cited in Boalt and C. Janson, *op. cit.*

Distance from residence (Växjö, Sweden) to birthplace.

Bergsten: Sydsvenske Födelseortsfält (birthplace areas in southern Sweden), Lund 1951, *op. cit.*, pp. 65–66.

Cited in *Distance and Social Relations*, G. Baolt and C. Janson, pp. 73–97.

Dodd, S.C., "Testing Message Diffusion in Controlled Experiments: Charting the Distance and Time Factors in the Interactance Hypothesis," *Amer. Soc. Review*, 18, 410–416, (1953).

Distance between tellers and hearers place of residence for 125 pairs of persons in "c-ville."

Table 6.4   Bossard Unit = 1 Block (500 Feet)

	1885–1886		1905		1915		1951	
r	*f*	$\dfrac{cum\ P}{r^2}$	*f*	$\dfrac{cum\ P}{r^2}$	*f*	$\dfrac{cum\ P}{r^2}$	*f*	$\dfrac{cum\ P}{r^2}$
1	1063	.0677	220	.0141	373	.0237	859	.547
2	264	.0211	239	.00730	201	.00914	304	.185
3	187	.0107	264	.00511	207	.00552	210	.00971
4	178	.00673	230	.00379	226	.00401	155	.00608
5	196	.00481	180	.00288	176	.00301	151	.00428
6	187	.00367	190	.00234	175	.00240	119	.00336
7	147	.00288	190	.00196	163	.00198	91	.00258
8	139	.00235	137	.00164	130	.00161	80	.00206
9	134	.00196	128	.00140	120	.00139	68	.00168
10	117	.00166	142	.00122	124	.00121	79	.00141
15	463	.000870	469	.000676	396	.000649	284	.000707
20	290	.000536	321	.000431	279	.000409	197	.000429
N = 5000		5000	5000		5000			

[a]Distance between residences of first 5000 pairs of persons obtaining marriage licenses in Philadelphia 1885–86, 1905, 1915 and 1951.
[b]J.H.S. Bossard, "Residential Propinquity as a Factor in Marriage Selection," *Amer. J. Sociology*, 38, 214–224 (1932).
[c]R. Abrams, "Residential Propinquity as a Factor in Marriage Selection": Fifty Year Trends in Philadelphia, *Amer. Soc. Review*, 8, 288–294 (1943). Both cited in Boalt and Janson, *op. cit.*

We propose that the general equation describing distance and delinquency (and a number of other social events as well) is a power function of distance with a negative exponent. That is

$$Y_i = a\,(r_i + k)^{-b}$$

where Y_i is the cumulated proportion of events per unit area, a is a scale factor relating to the unit of measure of distance, r is the distance, k is a constant estimated from the data and is very small with respect to the range of r. In our present study, the values for all cases combined are

$$Y_i = 0.33\,(r_i + 2)^{-2}$$

and Figure 6.7 shows how well the data points fit the above equation.

Table 6.5   Bullock (Unit 0.5 Mile)

r	Assailant Victim Percent	Assailant Victim $\dfrac{cum\ P}{r^2}$	Assailant Offense Percent	Assailant Offense $\dfrac{cum\ P}{r^2}$	Victim Offense Percent	Victim Offense $\dfrac{cum\ P}{r^2}$
1	46.7	.149	57.0	.181	61.0	.194
2	10.8	.0458	10.0	.0533	14.3	.0599
3	5.8	.0224	5.0	.0255	8.2	.0295
4	6.9	.0140	2.2	.0148	3.9	.0174
5	4.1	.00946	2.8	.00980	2.8	.0115
6	1.1	.00667	1.5	.00694	1.1	.00807
7	3.0	.00509	2.8	.00528	2.6	.00610
8	2.8	.00404	1.7	.00413	1.5	.00474
9	1.1	.00323	1.3	.00331	1.3	.00380
10	1.1	.00265	0.4	.00270	0.6	.00310
11	0.2	.00220	0.2	.00223	0.6	.00256
12	1.5	.00188	0.6	.00189	0.2	.00217
13	0.9	.00162	0.6	.00140	0.4	.00186
14	0.4	.00140	0.2		0.4	.00161
?	13.6		13.7		1.1	
	100.00		100.00		100.00	

[a] H.A. Bullock, *op. cit.,* pp. 565–575.
[b] Distance between residence of assailant and residence of victim, residence of assailant and place of occurrence, and residence of victim and place of occurrence for 489 criminal homicides in Houston, Texas, 1945–1949.

Summary

The delinquent offender resides close to the location of his offense. This is true in spite of the type of offense committed or the presence or absence of accomplices. However, there does appear to be a falling off within a block of his residence particularly for certain types of offenses (identifiable property thefts?)

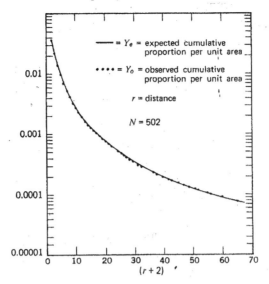

Figure 6.7

Summary

If the delinquent lives close to his offense, there would be little difference between defining a high delinquency area in terms of offender's residence or offense location. A program designed to lower the number of delinquents in an area could reasonably expect a drop in the number of delinquencies in that area. And ecological studies of high delinquency areas can thus have some measure of confidence that the social characteristics of the high offense areas actually refer to the offenders who committed the offenses.

However, there is certainly more to crime and distance than this study indicates: certain types of offenses might not obey the above equation – for example, white-collar crime and professional crime. However, it might be that such offenses merely involve a larger threshold value (k in the above equation).

Chapter 7

Crime and Mobility: An Empirical Study

William M. Rhodes and Catherine Conly*

Introduction

This research is organized around the concept of a "criminal commute," a theoretical construct in which offenders with diverse motivations to commit crimes are seen to select crime sites of varying distances from their home bases. The term "commute" is employed because of an assumed similarity between the purposeful travel decisions made by urban commuters on their way to jobs, shopping, and recreation, and decisions made by many offenders during their searches for crime targets.

In the section that follows, we review literature relevant to the criminal commute and develop a model used to specify a formal hypothesis that can be subjected to statistical testing. This is followed by a section on the data base and the empirical techniques used to test this hypothesis. In succeeding sections, the length of the criminal commute is tested for its correlation with the characteristics of the offender, the victim, the offense, areas where criminals live, and areas where they commit their crimes.

The Criminal Commute: A Theoretical Perspective

A theoretical model of criminal choice is sketched in this section. In this model, the offender's socioeconomic situation and motivations are assumed important to the propensity to crime. But equal in importance to motivation to break the law is the opportunity to do so successfully. In this regard, the accessibility of "good" targets takes on importance, and criminal decisions are seen as resulting from an interaction between motivation and opportunity.

An important ingredient of the model we use is a theory of how potential offenders learn about available targets. The assumption is made that offenders, like noncriminals, obtain environmental cues from trips for work, school, shopping, and recreation in a subspace of the urban landscape. Like noncriminals, offenders use

*This project was funded by the Ford Foundation and the District of Columbia Office of Criminal Justice Plans and Analysis (OOJPandA 78-07-24). The complete study can be found in Rhodes, Conly, and Schacter (1980). We greatly appreciate the thoughtful comments of Brian Forst, Courtney Knauth, and Marcus Felson.

these environmental cues to construct "cognate maps" of the urban area. But whereas noncriminals presumably use their cognate maps in making day-to-day decisions about legitimate activities, offenders can be presumed to use theirs to choose the locations of illegitimate ones. An important purpose of this research is to investigate the criminal trips made by urban offenders, on the assumption that these trips are influenced by characteristics of the urban landscape.[1]

Other researchers have investigated aspects of the criminal commute, finding, for instance, that property offenders tend to travel farther than offenders committing crimes against persons (Blumin 1973; Repetto 1974; Capone and Nichols 1976; Smith 1976) and that for property offenses longer trips tend to net a greater "return" than do shorter trips (Pyle 1974; Reppetto 1974).[2] Unfortunately, most researchers have stopped with empirical generalities, seldom attempting to offer formal models suitable to deriving specific testable hypotheses.[3] One notable exception has been the work of Paul and Patricia Brantingham on the geography of crime (1978, 1981).

The Brantinghams developed a model in which the concepts of opportunity and motivation are integrated with concepts of mobility and perception. First, they assume the existence of diverse motivations among criminals, using no single theory to explain criminal behavior. Motivations are, however, characterized as varying between *affective* and *instrumental*. That is, an offender seeks a degree of immediate gratification from the offense (rape is an example of an affective offense) or a degree of deferred gratification (burglary, in which goods must be fenced, is an example of an instrumental offense).

Second, the Brantinghams assume that, given the offender's motivation, the actual commission of the offense is the end result of a multistage decision process in which the offender seeks out crime victims. The extent of this search varies, of course. In

---

1   Since drafting this chapter, we have become aware of a study with a similar frame of reference, but a different empirical approach: George F. Rengert and John Wasilchick, "Residential burglary: The awareness and use of extended space," a paper presented at the Annual Meeting of the American Society of Criminology, San Francisco, November 1980.

2   Capone and Nichols (1976) provide a representative exploration for these patterns:

> Robbery trips declined with increasing distance from the origin node because offenders tend to commit crimes in areas about which they have knowledge; armed and unarmed trip distances differed significantly because of the robbery and the planned nature and common use of a vehicle in armed robbery; and the average distance of robbery trips varied according to the type of premise because different types of premises yield different returns and present different risks, influencing an offender to travel greater distances if the potential return is attractive and/or the probability of being apprehended is minimized.

3   There are exceptions. Lawrence Cohen and Marcus Felson (1979) employ a "routine activity approach" to explain the "convergence in space and time of likely offenders, suitable targets and the absence of capable guardians against crime." They focus on more global concerns than does this study and emphasize the roles of victims, an area that is underemphasized in our approach.

the case of highly affective motivation or spontaneous offenses, the search may be limited. In instrumental motivation or planned offenses, it may be more extensive. Third, the Brantinghams adopt a social-psychological view in postulating how this search might be conducted. The urban environment "emits many signals, or cues, about its physical, spatial, cultural, legal, and psychological characteristics." Some of these cues indicate good targets; others indicate the contrary. These cues are learned, both from direct experience and from interactions with others.

The assumption that criminals acquire criminal skills and attitudes through social interaction and personal observation has a long and honored history in the criminological literature (Sutherland and Cressey 1970; Matza 1969; Jeffery 1965; Akers 1973). The Brantinghams elaborate the social-learning paradigm by emphasizing that the physical as well as the social environment gives off multiple cues. For instance, both potential and active offenders observe how the criminal justice system treats other offenders in their immediate communities. They observe the response of citizens in reporting crimes, of the police in handling calls for assistance, and of the courts in punishing offenders. They also learn how one is expected to act to fit into given neighborhoods and social contexts. Most important for this analysis, offenders observe potential targets and victims. From this view, acquirng skills and knowledge necessary for committing a crime is a continual process for individuals with the requisite motivation.

One implication of the Brantinghams' theory is that offenders will more frequently commit offenses in the neighborhoods around their own domiciles, since these are areas they know best. As a result, the distribution of travel should be concentrated at short distances, and there should be a comparatively smaller proportion of long trips.

A second implication of the Brantinghams' model is that the distance traveled by an offender will depend on the offense he commits. It is more likely that crime sites will be sought out for planned, instrumental offenses and that offenses that are spontaneous and affective will occur where they are the most convenient for the offender. We would expect that the distances traveled to commit instrumental offenses, such as burglary, would be greater than the distances traveled to commit more affective offenses, like rape.

A third assumption consistent with the above model is that offenders are "clustered" in certain areas of the city. This notion has withstood historical scrutiny (Guerry 1833; Tobias 1972; Burt 1925; Shaw and McKay 1969; Baldwin and Bottoms 1976) and – whether based on ecological correlations[4] or individual offender addresses (Shaw and McKay 1969; White 1932; Bullock 1955; Capone and Nichols 1976) – seems

---

4　The seminal work in this area is that of Shaw and McKay (1969). Since World War II, the classical ecological approach has fallen into disrepute (Berry and Kasarda 1977). Shaw and McKay's work has also been subjected to criticism (Voss and Petersen 1971; Baldwin and Bottoms 1976). Recent work in this area has been statistically sophisticated, generally "explaining" crime rates by the use of variables representing "anomie" and "economic factors" (Lander 1954; Polk 1957–1958; Bordua 1958–1959; Chilton 1964; Schmid 1960a, 1960b). These studies were criticized by Hirschi and Selvin (1967), but some of these data have been

to indicate that cities have areas with concentrations of criminals. This is not to say that the socioeconomic conditions associated with certain areas that house offenders necessarily cause crime. On the contrary, neighborhoods with similar economic and social compositions can produce markedly different offender rates (Baldwin and Bottoms 1976). But the notion of criminal clusterings is consistent with the learning theory aspects of the Brantinghams' approach.

The notion that certain areas of the city serve as magnets for crime, depending on their intrinsic attractiveness and accessibility as targets, is also consistent with the learning theory paradigm; targets of the lowest attractive power (offering low gain for the offender and carrying a high risk of apprehension and high costs for committing an offense) would be unlikely to experience many criminal events. Targets of the next highest order will experience only local offenses (that is, a relatively higher concentration of unplanned/affective crimes). Areas with the "best" targets will have neighborhood spillover effects, attracting both the local offender and the instrumental/planned offender from nonlocal areas.

It is very important in this study to distinguish between two aspects of attractiveness, which we have labeled *target attractiveness* and *spatial attractiveness*. As mentioned, some areas of a city provide good crime targets-high gain to the offender, a low investment (in terms of tools and other costs of "doing business"), and a low risk of apprehension. Areas that offer targets especially high on a hypothetical scale of these criteria are high in terms of target attractiveness. However, an urban area will not be heavily victimized – even if it is high in target attractiveness – if it is so situated spatially that its target vulnerability is not apparent to potential offenders. This notion of relative vulnerability is related to the theoretical construct of a cognate map. Urban areas that are fairly isolated from the everyday activities of potential offenders, and consequently of little salience to their mental maps of the city, will be said to be low on a hypothetical scale measuring spatial attractiveness. In contrast, areas that are more familiar to potential offenders are high on the spatial attractiveness scale.

This distinction between target and spatial attractiveness affords a two-dimensional view of the appeal as targets of areas within a city. Areas high in both target and spatial attractiveness can be expected to have high victimization rates relative to areas low in either dimension.

In order to operationalize the theoretical construct of spatial attractiveness, we have found it useful in our model to distinguish between urban areas that are private and those that are public. Single-family residential areas illustrate territories presumed to be private. Residential areas offer few attractions for most outsiders, including prospective offenders, and thus nonresidents are unlikely to develop accurate cognate maps of these areas. Shopping centers and commercial areas are examples of more public territories. Such areas are more likely to attract outsiders,

---

reanalyzed by Chilton and Dussich (1974). These authors report a strong correlation between two factors identified as a dependent variable. Two excellent recent studies in the genre are Pyle (1974) and Baldwin and Bottoms (1976).

including prospective criminals. As a result, offenders may build detailed cognate maps of these areas and call on these maps when selecting targets.

The above implications of the Brantinghams' model, that offenses are concentrated around offenders' domiciles, that distance traveled to commit a crime varies with the type of offense, that offender residences are clustered in certain areas of the city, and that potential targets vary according to target and spatial attractiveness, suggest some testable hypotheses. One of several that was tested in our original study is discussed here:

> The distance that an offender travels to commit his crime depends on the individual characteristics of the offender, of the immediate environment in which he lives, and of the larger area that surrounds it, as well as on the type of crime that he commits and the type and location of potential targets.

An offender's individual characteristics may have an impact on how far he travels to commit his offense. Unfortunately, our theory is imprecise as to which of many personal factors might matter and how they would influence the decision.

It is also difficult to make predictions about the relationship between an offender's "immediate environment" – the few blocks around his home – and the distance he travels. While he is undoubtedly very familiar with the area, he is also likely to be well known. So regardless of how good the targets are in the immediate vicinity of his home, he may choose to travel away from home to commit his crimes, hoping to reduce his risk of detection.

Our model offers more guidance when it comes to the influence of "surrounding areas," which we define as areas that are several blocks away from the offender's residence but close enough to be traversed regularly during his everyday activities. Some surrounding areas can be characterized as private, especially those heavily used for single-family residences, and to a lesser extent, those used for multiple-family dwellings. Since offenders are unlikely to be attracted to areas with predominantly private land-use patterns for legitimate purposes, they are not likely to develop cognate maps of them and consequently are not apt to choose targets from within these private areas. These isolated areas might as a result be very low on the spatial attractiveness dimension. Other surrounding areas are more oriented to public use – particularly those used for commercial purposes, but also those that are industrial – and criminals are likely to familiarize themselves with such environments. Unlike isolated areas, these relatively public areas would be high on the spatial attractiveness dimension. We would expect offenders to travel into these public areas to commit their crimes.

The type of crime committed also probably influences the distance traveled. This research concentrates on three offenses: rape, robbery, and burglary. These crimes have distinctively different targets; they seem to require different criminal skills, and it would appear that they have differing instrumental-affective attributes. Residential and commercial burglary is an offense against property. Interpersonal contact is not anticipated by the burglar. The crime is essentially that of entering a facility surreptitiously, locating valuables, escaping, and marketing (if necessary) whatever is stolen. In contrast, robbery is a mixed offense against both property and persons. It requires a somewhat different set of skills. The offender must be able to control his victim, but he need not have the skills to dispose of the property stolen, which is generally in the form of cash. Forcible rape is an offense against persons. It requires skills in rigorously controlling (and sometimes setting up) a victim. The three offenses differ according to motivation. There is evidence that robbery is a somewhat more affective (as well as unplanned) offense than burglary. Rape, of course, is extreme as an affective offense.

A second hypothesis[5] tested in our original study and discussed in this chapter is as follows:

> The distance traveled to commit an offense will be positively associated with the magnitude of the offense, especially as the latter pertains to the offender's gain from committing the crime, and the degree of planning associated with longer trips will be reflected in the characteristics of the targets hit.

Offenses committed within an offender's neighborhood are expected to be more situationally induced than those committed outside it. The time and expense associated with a trip are investments; they are more likely to be made after the offender has planned his activity (though exceptions exist, such as offenses committed during the evening around the bar districts). Additionally, offenders who are traveling outside their immediate neighborhoods into surrounding neighborhoods with which they are less familiar may be demonstrating a greater willingness to take risks. For these reasons, the distance traveled is expected to indicate the degree of planning.

Land Use in the District of Columbia

The data used to construct our units of urban space came from MAGIS, an automated land-use file for the District of Columbia that contains information on a sub-block basis, by lots.[6] Data about offenders and offenses came from PROMIS.[7]

Because offender and offense addresses from PROMIS case files could not be correlated with MAGIS lot-level data, it was necessary for us to aggregate the MAGIS data into larger areal units called squares. Technically, a square is a

---

5   In our original study, we examined two other hypotheses, one related to recidivism and one related to disparity in justice administration.

6   MAGIS is an automated system of information pertaining to land-use patterns and social-economic conditions in the District of Columbia. The file was assembled through a cooperative venture of the District of Columbia Office of Planning and Development and the D.C. Department of Housing and Community Development.

7   PROMIS is an acronym for Prosecutor's Management Information System, a computerized information system maintained by the Office of the United States Attorney for the District of Columbia.

Table 7.1   Variables created for "squares" from MAGIS data

(All variables represent either aggregate percentages or weighted means of all properties or lots within a given square)

1. *Area*	The sum of the land areas of all lots within a square.
2. *Assessed Value*	Market value per square foot.
3. *Improvement Value*	Improvement value per square foot.
4. *Street Rate*	Mean of adjusted street rates of all lots within a square.
5. *Residential Multiple*	Percentage of land area within square classified as being used for single family occupancy.
6. *Residential Multiple*	Percentage of land area classified as being used for multiple family occupancy.
7. *Temporary Lodging*	Percentage of land area classified as being used for transient residential lodgers, including hotels, motels, private clubs, tourist homes, or dormitories.
8. *Small Business*	Percentage of land area classified as being used by small commercial businesses, including small stores, restaurants, barber or beauty shops, supermarkets, small offices, banks, and other miscellaneous.
9. *Large Business*	Percentage of land area classified as being used by large businesses, including department stores, shopping malls, large offices, or planned commercial developments.
10. *Parking*	Percentage of land area classified as being used by parking garages, parking lots, or vehicular service stations.
11. *Recreational*	Percentage of land area classified as being used for entertainment, theaters, or restaurants.
12. *Industrial*	Percentage of land area classified as being used for industrial purposes, including raw material handling, manufacturing, or warehousing.
13. *Special Purpose*	Percentage of land area classified for special purposes, including religious, medical, educational, public service, embassies, museums and libraries, and recreational.
14. *Latest Year Built*	Most recent year that a structure was built within square
15. *Latest Sale Date*	Most recent date of property sale within square.
16. *Construction*	Yes/no variable indicating whether at least one construction permit was granted within square during 1974.
17. *Demolition*	Yes/no variable indicating whether at least one demolition permit was granted within square during 1974.
18. *Condemnation*	Yes/no variable indicating whether any property or structure within square was condemned.

geographic unit defined by the D.C. Office of Planning and Development, and while it is not identical to a city block, it can be thought of as a city block for present purposes. We aggregated this lot-level data in terms of the variables described in Table 7.1. The variables "Assessed Value" through "Special Purpose" (1–14) are the weighted averages across the lots contained in the square.[8] About 30 percent of the lots had no known land use (an empty lot designation) and entered the calculations as zero values. Most of these appeared to be used by the federal government.[9] For the remaining variables (15–18), "Latest Year Built" is the most recent year that any residence was built on the square, and "Construction," "Demolition," and "Condemnation" indicate whether there was a permit for construction, a permit for demolition, or a condemnation order for any of the lots contained within a square.

When this data base was assembled, principal component factor analysis (with a varimax rotation) was used to identify seven factors that entered into the subsequent analysis. Each summary factor is closely related to one or more of the original eighteen variables. For example, Large Business is strongly associated with lots that are zoned for either large business or special purposes. It also tends to comprise lots that have high assessment and improvement values. In addition to Large Business, six other summary factors were derived: Single Residential, Transitional, Industrial, Multiple Residential, Small Business, and Mixed. Due to failure to recognize a coding idiosyncrasy in the MAGIS file, no factor associated with federal government land use was used in the analysis.

Table 7.2 shows how these summary factors are related to the original variables. A plus sign indicates a positive relationship, as reflected in a factor score in excess of .50. A minus sign indicates a negative correlation, meaning a factor score less than −.50.

While offender and offense addresses could have been analyzed at the square level, we did not feel that this degree of resolution would adequately reflect our notions of immediate environment and surrounding area. To further aggregate these data, we began with the surveyor's map of the District of Columbia, imposing on it a grid of 900 equal-sized blocks that fell within the geographic boundaries of the District of Columbia.

We next determined the addresses for every offender in our data base. By locating an offender's address within a block, we were able to identify the immediate environment where the offender lived. Each immediate environment, or block, had an area of about five surveyor's squares per block. The land-use variables characterizing an immediate environment are the weighted means of each of the seven factor

---

8   Let $V_{i,j,k}$ represent the ith variable in the j_{th} lot of the k_{th} square. Let L_{ik} equal the land area of the j_{th} lot of the k_{th} square. Then the square level of value for the k_{th} square is:

9   It was impossible to cross-tabulate the incidence of "empty lots" with the codes for "tax exemption due to government use," thus establishing that the empty lots were used for government purposes.

Table 7.2   Relationship between the factor scores and the original land use variables

Original Land-Use Variables	Large Business	Single Residential	Transitional	Industrial	Multiple Residential	Small Business	Mixed
Improvement Value	+						
Assessed Value	+						
Large Business	+						
Special Purpose	+						
Residential Single		+					
Sale Date		+					
Temporary Lodging			+				
Construction			+				
Demolition			+				
Industrial				+			
Area				+			
Residential Multiple					+		
Year Built						+	
Small Business						+	
Recreational							+
Condemnation							−
Parking							
Street Rate							

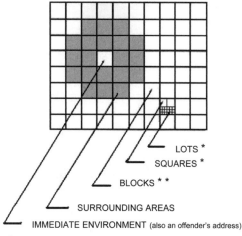

LOTS *
SQUARES *
BLOCKS * *
SURROUNDING AREAS
IMMEDIATE ENVIRONMENT (also an offender's address)

* As designated in surveyor's map of The District of Columbia
* * Designated for purposes of this study

Figure 7.1   Relationships between lots, squares, immediate neighborhoods, and surrounding neighborhoods

scores across all the squares within it.[10] Next, we identified the area surrounding the offender's immediate environment. This surrounding area consisted of all blocks that were no more than two blocks away from the immediate environment. The surrounding area thus consists of about .56 square miles of land mass. The summary factors used to characterize a surrounding area are the simple averages of the summary factors for those blocks of which it is composed. Figure 7.1 depicts the relationships among lots, squares, immediate environments, and surrounding areas. Similar calculations were made for areas where offenders committed their crimes.

In order to determine offender and offense addresses, we extracted a sample of arrested offenders from PROMIS for 1974. Our sample consisted of 796 burglars, 832 robbers, and 430 rapists, determined by the offense cited at arrest by the police officer. If robbery, rape, or burglary were among the offenses cited in up to four charges, the offender was included in the data base.

There are limitations to drawing overall conclusions about offense and offender locations from PROMIS data. First, the sample was weighted toward offenders with lengthier records, and presumably these tend to be older criminals who are

---

10   Let V_{ijk} represent the ith variable in the jth square of the kth immediate environment. Let L_{jk} equal the land area of the jth square in the kth immediate environment.

likely to differ from the general population of offenders in numerous respects.[11] Additionally, PROMIS excludes juvenile offenders unless processed as adults, further skewing the sample toward older individuals.

Second, data were frequently missing. Offenders who either resided or committed their offenses outside the District of Columbia were excluded from the analysis. In the former instance, the characteristics of the offender's residence were unknown because the residence was not identifiable in MAGIS; in the latter, the offense did not enter PROMIS because it was committed outside the jurisdiction of the U.S. Attorney for the District of Columbia. Sometimes, too, an address could not be located within the District. In other instances, the address was known but could not be matched with the MAGIS file. The attrition in data was 14 percent for burglary, 22 percent for robbery, and 25 percent for rape.

Third, these data were derived from the offenses committed by people who were *caught* and who may differ from the total population of offenders in unknown ways, including, perhaps, their skill at committing crimes and avoiding arrest.

Still, the remaining data do allow us to draw reasonable, if qualified, inferences about the areas where known offenders live and where they are known to commit their offenses.

The Criminal Commute: Distance Traveled and Characteristics of Offender, Victim, and Offense

Once we recorded the addresses where offenders lived and at which they committed their offenses, it was possible to compute the distance between the two points. In discussing this distance, it is convenient to report the findings as if the offender commenced his trip at home and ended it at the crime site, with no intermediate stops. This assumption need not be taken literally. Rather, it serves as a heuristic device enabling us to quantify how far away from home the offender committed his crime:

Data coders were given two methods to calculate these distances. *Line distances* were recorded as the straight line mileage between offender residence and the place of offense. *Wheel distances* were recorded as the distance that an offender would have to travel by car to arrive at his target. Given the geography of the District of

---

11 The computerized cases of offenders in each offense group were sorted in ascending order according to their police identification numbers. This meant that offenders with the most extensive records appeared at the top of the coding list and were coded first. The initial expectation was that all offenders who committed robbery, burglary, or rape in 1974 would be coded in the MAGIS exercise. Unfortunately, due to time and money constraints, an all-inclusive coding effort was possible only for the small sample of those who committed rape. Realizing that it would not be possible to code all cases after one-half of the coding had been completed, we supplemented the sample of older offenders with a random sample of those younger, less criminally experienced offenders who remained.

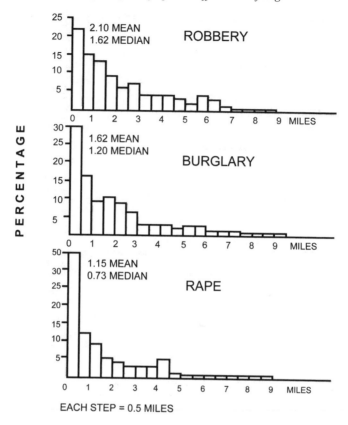

Figure 7.2   Distributions of travel distances for three offenses

Columbia, especially its array of parks and railroad lines and the barrier created by the Anacostia River, wheel distance appeared to be the more appropriate measurement. Additionally, empirical analysis showed a stronger relationship between wheel distance and variables of interest. Consequently, we will use it as our basis of measurement.

With regard to wheel distance, patterns were discovered that were similar to the "decay" function uncovered by earlier researchers. In Figure 7.2, a step diagram is used to summarize the distribution of distance traveled, using half-mile increments. It is evident from these diagrams that, among our arrestees, robbers do the most commuting to their offenses, traveling an average of 2.10 miles. Burglars travel slightly less, averaging about 1.62 miles, and rapists travel considerably less, averaging about 1.15 miles, or only about half what robbers average. Another way to view these distributions is to note the high concentration of offenses that occur around the offender's home. Almost half the rapes occur within one-half mile of the offender's home; this falls to 30 percent for burglaries and to less than 25 percent for robberies.

Although distances traveled may differ for offenders who were not caught, these findings are consistent with the hypothesis that offenders victimize areas they know best, concentrating on targets within their immediate environments and surrounding areas. Of course, the findings are also consistent with the explanation that closer targets are more frequently hit simply because the costs of seeking out the victim and traveling to his location are less. The findings also support the hypothesis that more situationally induced crimes, like rape, occur closer to home, while offenses involving more planning (burglary and robbery) result in more travel.

There is more that can be asked about these trips. For instance, we can compare the average factor score values[12] for blocks that were victimized in terms of each of our three selected offenses, with the average factor score values for all blocks

Table 7.3   Summary measures of the immediate and surrounding neighborhood of the offense

	D.C. Average	Rape	Robbery	Burglary
Immediate Environments				
Large Business	−.05	−.04	.25	.12
Single Residential	.08	−.03	−.04	−.04
Transitional	−.04	.29	.60	.51
Industrial	.33	.03	−.00	.01
Multiple Residential	.18	.35	.24	.25
Small Business	.20	.12	.15	.10
Mixed	−.01	−.31	−.34	−.38
Surrounding Areas				
Large Business	−.05	.07	.31	.18
Single Residential	.08	−.02	−.08	−.07
Transitional	−.03	.23	.37	.31
Industrial	.33	.08	.11	.11
Multiple Residential	.18	.22	.19	.16
Small Business	.20	.11	.10	.09
Mixed	−.02	−.23	−.28	−.28
N. of Observations	905	321	651	688

Table 7.4 Comparison of offender and offense neighborhoods

	Rape			Robbery			Burglary		
	Offender		Offense	Offender		Offense	Offender		Offense
Immediate Environments (target attractiveness)									
Large Business	-.13	*	-.04	-.16	*	.25	-.11	*	.12
Single Residential	.11	*	-.03	.10	*	-.04	.16	*	-.04
Transitional	.16	*	.29	.16	*	.60	.28	*	.51
Industrial	.04		.03	-.01		-.00	-.02		.01
Multiple Residential	.38		.35	.39	*	.24	.30		.25
Small Business	.05		.12	.01	*	.15	-.03	*	.10
Mixed	-.34		-.31	-.38		-.34	-.52	*	-.38
Surrounding Areas (spatial attractiveness)									
Large Business	.06	*	.07	-.09	*	.31	-.03	*	.18
Single Residential	.02		-.02	-.01		-.08	-.02	*	-.07
Transitional	.18		.23	.16	*	.37	.25	*	.31
Industrial	.06		.08	.03		.11	.05		.11
Multiple Residential	.24	.	.22	.21		.19	.17		.16
Small Business	.10		.11	.07		.10	.08		.09
Mixed	-.25		-.23	-.29		-.28	-.32	*	-.28
N. of Observations	315		313	632		640	674		61

Note: *Indicates a statistically significant difference at .05 level of confidence.

in D.C. This comparison should provide some clues about the land-use patterns of urban areas that cause these areas to be crime targets. We can also compare the average factor score values for blocks that were victimized with the average factor score values for blocks where offenders reside. This contrast should provide some hints about the flow of offenders between urban areas. These comparisons are drawn below.

From Table 7.3, it appears that the factor scores of areas known to be victimized by crime differ from averages of the factor scores for all blocks in D.C. Using both immediate environments of the crime and surrounding areas as units of reference, it appears that victimized areas are more transitional, more heavily used for business and special purposes, and less heavily used for small business purposes and private single-family homes than are the average D.C. immediate and surrounding areas. Before inferring from these findings that areas with these characteristics offer targets and attract offenders, however, it must be considered that a high victimization rate may simply imply proximity to a large concentration of offenders.

A more meaningful way to look at the data in Table 7.3 is to compare the summary measures of areas where offenders live with the summary measures of areas where crimes are committed. This is done in Table 7.4. In drawing this comparison, we are especially interested in differences in summary variables between areas that surround crime targets and areas that surround offender addresses. To the extent that these differences arise, we can take them to explain – why offenders travel away from their home bases to commit an offense. We will say that the uncovered differences imply information about a target area's *spatial attractiveness.* To a lesser extent, we are also interested in differences in summary variables between the offender's immediate environment (the block where he lives) and the offense's immediate environment (the block where the offense occurred). Although the theoretical linkages are weaker, we believe that differences between the crime site and the offender's home represent aspects of *target attractiveness,* that is, types of land use that make a block a "good" target rather than just a visible one.

Focusing first on target attractiveness, it seems from the comparison of factor scores for offender and offense immediate areas that offenders victimize transitional areas-that is, those that have a high proportion of temporary lodgings, construction, and demolition. The correlation is strongest for robbery and burglary, but still very significant for rape. Business areas also seem to offer targets. Victimization of these areas appears to be heavy for robbers and burglars, but only marginal for rapists.

Some immediate neighborhoods appear to be notable for not offering targets, particularly those high in single-family residences. Offenders tend to victimize areas with lower concentrations of single-family homes, and although the effect seems to

---

12 To compute the averages for all of D.C., we counted every block in the data base once. To calculate the average for offense locations, a block was counted as many times as offenses occurred within it. Thus, blocks with no offenses did not enter the calculations. Likewise, to calculate the average for offender addresses, a block was counted as many times as it had offender addresses.

be somewhat weaker, areas of lesser concentrations of multiple-family residences. There is no evidence that industrial areas offer especially good (or poor) targets.

Thus, it might be concluded that in ranking areas in terms of target attractiveness, transitional and commercial areas should be placed high on the list. Residential areas rank low, and industrial areas fall somewhere in between. It is not surprising that the rankings appear to be stronger for robbery and burglary than for rape, given the largely affective, spontaneous nature of the latter.

Taking spatial attractiveness as the focus, it appears from the correlations in Table 7.4 that areas with concentrations of large businesses serve as magnets that attract offenders. The same can be said of transitional areas and industrial areas. In contrast to large business areas, surrounding areas with greater than average concentrations of small businesses do not seem to have great spatial attractiveness. Other urban spaces that appear not to draw offenders seeking targets are residential areas, both those devoted to single-family and multiple housing. Single-family land use is especially significant in this regard.

These findings can be given numerous interpretations, including some that are consistent with the theoretical perspective adopted in this study. There seems a persistent tendency for offenders to move into public areas to commit their offenses (although the targets themselves need not be "public"). Thus we see distinct patterns of movement into large business districts, transitional areas, and industrial areas, and somewhat less movement into small business districts. Large business districts, small business districts, and industrial areas are open to the public. Multiple-residential areas are semipublic, and there is less reason for nonresidents to be there, even though nonresidents might often be indistinguishable from residents and thus be able to hunt for targets. The areas that are the most private are those with high concentrations of single-family dwellings, which do not attract offenders.

For the most part, offenders commit their crimes in the vicinity of their domiciles. But when they do travel, they seem to commit their crimes in areas that are public in nature, a pattern consistent with the theory that the offender formulates a cognate map of the areas he visits and commits his offenses within those areas.

Having drawn the above conclusions from simple comparisons of the differences between the neighborhoods where offenses occur and offenders live, we must alert the reader to one important caveat. As would be expected, for any of our summary land-use variables, the values for the immediate and surrounding area are always highly collinear, with a correlation coefficient that is generally in excess of .80. This collinearity makes it difficult to disentangle the effects of target and spatial attractiveness. For instance, a variable-take Small Business as an example – may contribute to an area's target attractiveness but not to its spatial attractiveness. Nevertheless, because of the strong correlation between Small Business when measured on the immediate and surrounding area levels, it might appear from Table 7.4 that its presence in an area contributes to both spatial and target attractiveness.

As a precaution against drawing spurious conclusions, a multivariate analysis was employed. Variables relating to the immediate neighborhood were held constant, while variables relating to the surrounding area were examined (and vice versa). This technique also allowed us to control for the proximity of attractive targets to offender residences, which is an important control since, all else being equal, offenders travel short distances to commit offenses. This multivariate technique and the results from its application are discussed next.

Distance Traveled and Offender Neighborhoods

A multivariate technique was used to examine whether wheel distance varied according to the seven land-use characteristics of the offender's immediate or surrounding area. In addition, some variables that our complete analysis showed to be at least marginally correlated ($P < .05$) with distance traveled were incorporated in this model, including:

(1) The offender's age, coded as YOUNG (under 21) or OLD (over 35);
(2) The time the offense was committed, with NIGHT signifying that it occurred between 8 p.m. and 8 a.m.;
(3) The use of a gun, knife, or club (coded WEAPON);
(4) The relationship between the offender and the victim, coded PERSON, where STRANGER means that the victim was neither a friend nor relative and INSTITUTION indicates that the offender victimized an establishment rather than an individual (with a residual category used for unknown victim types);
(5) An offender's known heroin use as reported by the arresting officer (HEROIN);
(6) Number of previous arrests (PREV ARRESTS), truncated at five; and
(7) The fact that an offender was not a permanent resident of Washington, D.C. (TRAN).

Immediate Environments

The factor scores associated with the block where the offender lived seemed to have little explanatory power regarding the distance he traveled to commit his offense. While some of the regression parameters are marginally significant at .10, those scores are small given the large sample size, and their directions fail to suggest any obvious relationships.

Surrounding Areas

In contrast, summary variables related to the surrounding area seem to provide the statistical model with much of its explanatory capability. Distance traveled seems to be positively related to the extent to which the offender's surrounding area consists of single-family dwellings, multiple dwellings, and small businesses; it

Table 7.5   Regression results on distance traveled

	(1)[a]	(2)[b]	(3)[c]	(4)[d]	(5)[e]
Robbery					
Single Residential	+	+	+	+	+
Multiple Residential	+	+	+	+	0
Small Business	+	+	+	+	0
Large Business	0	0	0	0	0
Mixed	0	0	0	0	0
Transitional	−	−	−	−	−
Industrial	−	−	−	−	0
Burglary					
Single Residential	+	0	+	+	0
Multiple Residential	+	0	+	+	+
Small Business	+	+	+	+	0
Large Business	0	0	0	+	0
Mixed	0	0	−	−	0
Transitional	−	−	−	−	−
Industrial	−	−	−	−	−
Rape					
Single Residential	+	+	+	+	0
Multiple Residential	0	0	0	0	0
Small Business	0	0	0	0	0
Large Business	0	0	0	0	0
Mixed	0	0	0	0	0
Transitional	0	0	−	−	0
Industrial	0	0	0	0	0

a. Immediate and surrounding neighborhood variables (least squares regression).
b. Variables in column 1, estimated by tobit.
c. Variables in column 1 and 2 plus offense and offender variables (offender's age, time offense committed, weapon, relationship between offender and victim, heroin use, number of previous arrests, and fact that offender was non D.C. resident), estimated by OLS.
d. Same variables as to column 3, estimated by tobit.
e. Same variables as in column 3 and 4, estimated by probit.

Table 7.6   Regression results on wheel distance for robbery, burglary, and rape taken as a group (OLS regression)

	Coefficient	*Standard Error*
Constant	1.62	
Immediate Neighborhood		
Large Business	.044	.15
Single Residential	.19*	.12
Transitional	−.20	.11
Industrial	.29 * *	.11
Multiple Residential	−.057	.08
Small Business	.18	.12
Mixed	.16*	.09
Surrounding Neighborhood		
Large Business	.32	.25
Single Residential	.68**	.20
Transitional	−1.50**	.27
Industrial	.69**	.23
Multiple Residential	−.57**	.14
Small Business	.67**	.22
Mixed	−.48	.27
Non-neighborhood Variables		
Previous Arrest	.044	.023
Young	.30*	.023
Old	−.11	.13
Night	.15	.10
Weapon	−.17	.12
Transient	.090	.11
Stranger	.37 * *	.13
Institution	−.27	.18
Person	.22	.14
Heroin	.13	.17

Number of observations equals 1306; R^2 equals .17.
*Indicates statistical significance at .10 level of confidence.
**Indicates statistical significance at .05 level of confidence.

seems to be negatively related to the extent to which the surrounding neighborhood is characterized as transitional, industrial, and mixed. The extent to which the surrounding neighborhood was composed of large businesses and special purpose land use was not correlated with the distance traveled. Although of lesser interest for our concerns, it should be noted that distance traveled tends to increase (as would be expected) when the victim is a stranger, that younger offenders travel somewhat shorter distances than older offenders, and that offenders with criminal records travel somewhat farther than those offenders without records.

The results summarized above do not hold across all three offenses, although when they do hold for an offense they were robust when different statistical techniques were employed.

In Table 7.5, regression results are summarized for each of the three offenses. In column one, factor score variables were used in an ordinary least squares – regression. The same variables were used in the regression reported in column two, but the estimating technique was tobit. The offense and offender variables were added to regressions 3, 4, and 5, and the estimating techniques were OLS, tobit, and probit, respectively. A positive sign denotes a statistically significant positive correlation between the dependent and independent variables, and a minus sign indicates significant negative correlation. Zero indicates a lack of statistical significance, using a two-tailed test at the .10 level of confidence.

The statistical model explains little about the distances traveled by persons committing rape. There is some evidence of longer trips when the surrounding area is single-family residential and of shorter ones when it is transitional. Overall, however, no distinct patterns arise. In contrast, there are consistent patterns for robbery and burglary that, for the most part agree with the pattern uncovered in a regression that was done for all three offenses taken together (see Table 7.6).

Looking exclusively at robbers and burglars, we see that these offenders seem to travel longer distances when the surrounding area is either single or multiple family residential. This pattern was expected, given that these areas are likely to be private and therefore not part of an offender's personal cognate map; thus, they are low in spatial attractiveness and the offender appears to travel beyond them looking for targets. It also appears that offenders travel farther from their homes when the surrounding area is heavily used for small business purposes. This finding is contrary to the expectation that since small businesses are public, neighborhoods with concentrations of them would tend to attract criminals. Nevertheless, the correlation is consistent with the findings reported earlier, which led us to dispute any assertion that small businesses serve as crime magnets. The question remains as to why concentrations of small businesses fail to attract offenders when individual small businesses themselves are targets.

To the extent that a surrounding area is transitional or industrial, offenders travel shorter distances, with those distances being especially abbreviated for transitional neighborhoods. These findings could be explained by the public nature, and hence spatial attractiveness, of both these areas. The large effect of transitional areas could be further explained by the especially good targets they contain.

Even though areas of large business and special land-use concentrations were shown earlier both to offer good targets and to serve as magnets for offenders, no statistically significant relationship was uncovered between this land use and length of journey. This lack of statistical significance might be interpreted to mean that a surrounding area of heavily concentrated large business causes offenders to travel moderate distances. That is, offenders living near business and commercial areas travel into those areas to commit their offenses, while offenders who live near transitional neighborhoods stay near home to commit most of theirs, and offenders who live near predominantly residential areas travel farther than individuals who do not live near such areas.

In our regression analysis, the statistical significance of the coefficient associated with industrial areas is marginal. This may indicate that industrial areas are between transitional areas and large business areas in terms of spatial attractiveness.

Conclusions

In summary, it appears that offenders travel beyond the areas of the lowest attractive power, residential neighborhoods, looking for targets a considerable distance from home. This finding is consistent with the theory that the private nature of these areas retards the development of cognate maps by potential offenders, which tends to insulate targets surrounded by private residential land use.

Surrounding areas used for small business purposes have the same effect: offenders bypass such areas in favor of distant targets. One explanation may be that small business areas are incorrectly thought of as public. Instead, they may serve very local interests – as scatterings of stores in relatively self-contained neighborhoods generally do – and may remain closed to potential offenders.

Large business areas are intermediate on the scale of attractiveness. To the extent that a surrounding neighborhood is engaged in large business uses, the neighborhood tends to attract offenders into itself. Once there, offenders victimize both the large businesses and surrounding targets. Industrial areas act somewhat like both large business and transitional areas. To the extent that the surrounding area is characterized as transitional, offenders stay close to home. Apparently this is because transitional areas have high appeal both as targets and in terms of spatial attraction.

References

Akers, R. (1973). *Deviant Behavior: A Social Learning Approach*. Belmont, CA: Wadsworth.

Baldwin, J. and Bottoms, A.E. (1976). *The Urban Criminal. A Study in Sheffield*. London: Tavistock Publications.

Blumin, D. (1973). *Victims: A Study of Crime in a Boston Housing Project*. Boston: City of Boston, Mayor's Safe Street Act, Advisory Committee.

Brantingham, P.L. and Brantingham P.J. (1981). Notes on the geometry of crime. In Brantingham, P.J. and Brantingham P.L. (eds), *Environmental Criminology* (pp. 27–54). Beverly Hills: Sage Publications.

Brantingham, P.L. and Brantingham P.J. (1978). A theoretical model of crime site selection. In M. Krohn and R. L. Akers (eds), *Crime, Law and Sanction*, (pp. 105–118). Beverly Hills: Sage Publications.

Bullock, H.A. (1955). Urban homicide in theory and fact. *Journal of Criminal Law, Criminology and Police Science,* 45(5), 565–575.

Burt, C. (1925). *The Young Delinquent*. London: Appleton.

Capone, D.C.; Nichols, W.W. (1975). Crime and distance: An analysis of offender behavior in space. *Proceedings of the Association of American Geographers,* 7, 45–49.

Capone, D. and Nicholas, W.W. (1976). Urban structure and criminal mobility. *American Behavioral Scientist,* 20, 199–213.

Guerry, A.M. (1833). *Essai sur la Statistique Morale de la France*. Paris: Crochard.

Jeffery, C.R. (1965). Criminal behavior and learning theory. *Journal of Criminal Law, Criminology and Police Science*, 56, 294.

Matza, D. (1969). *Becoming Deviant*. Englewood Cliffs, NJ: Prentice-Hall.

Pyle, G.F. et al. (1974). *The Spatial Dynamics of Crime*. Department of Geography Research Paper No. 159. Chicago: The University of Chicago.

Repetto, T.A. (1974). *Residential Crime*. Cambridge, MA: Ballinger.

Shaw, C.R. and McKay, H.D. (1931). *Social Factors in Juvenile Delinquency*. Washington, D.C: Government Printing Office.

Sutherland, E. and Cressey, D. (1970). *Criminology (8th Edition)*. Philadelphia: J.B. Lippincott.

Tobias, J.J. (1972). *Urban Crime in Victorian England*. New York: Schocken Books. (Revised version of *Crime and Industrial Society in the 19th Century,* 1967).

White, R.C. (1932). The relation of felonies to environmental factors in Indianapolis. *Social Forces*, 10(4), 498–509.

Chapter 8

Place, Space, and Police Investigations: Hunting Serial Violent Criminals

D. Kim Rossmo

Introduction

A focus of any police investigation is the crime scene and its evidentiary contents. What is often overlooked, however, is a geographic perspective on the actions preceding the offense: the spatial behavior that led to the crime scene. For any violent crime to occur there must have been an intersection in both time and place between the victim and offender. How did this happen? What were the antecedents? What do the spatial elements of the crime tell us about the offender and his or her actions? What are the hunting patterns of predatory offenders? These questions are particularly relevant in cases of serial murder, rape and arson.

Environmental criminology and routine activity theory provide a general framework for addressing these questions. In addition, the model of crime-site selection developed by Brantingham and Brantingham (1981) suggests a specific approach for determining the most probable location of offender residence in cases of serial violent crimes. Research in this area represents a practical application of criminological theory to the real world of police investigation, which not only can contribute useful information to law enforcement agencies but may also open up possibilities for new and innovative investigative methodologies.

The nature of serial violent crime creates unique problems for law enforcement, requiring special police responses and investigative strategies. Klockars (1983) asserts that there are only three ways to solve a crime: (1) a confession, (2) a witness and (3) physical evidence. Traditionally, the search for witnesses, suspects and evidence has followed a path, originating from the victim and the crime scene outward. Most homicides, for example, are cleared for the simple reason that they involve people who know each other, and the process of offender identification is often only one of suspect elimination.

Such obvious connections rarely exist in cases of stranger crimes. The lack of any relationship between the victims and the offender makes these crimes difficult to solve. In conducting these types of investigations working outward from the victim is a difficult task. The alternative, then, is to work inward, trying to establish some type of link between potential suspects and the victim or crime scene. This process requires the delineation of a likely group of potential suspects; such efforts, however, can produce lists often numbering into the thousands, causing problems with information overload. In the still unsolved Seattle-area Green River Killer case, for example, 18,000 suspect names have been collected. But as of February 1992, the police have only had the time and resources to investigate some 12,000 of these (Montgomery 1992). The Yorkshire Ripper case had, by the time it was solved, 268,000 names in the nominal index (Doney 1990).

Clues derived from crime location and place can be of significant assistance to law enforcement in the investigation of repetitive offenses. The probable spatial behavior of the offender can be derived from information contained in the known crime site locations (e.g., encounter/apprehension sites, murder scenes, body/property dump sites), their geographic connections, and the characteristics and demography of the surrounding neighborhoods. Determining the probability of the offender residing in various areas, and displaying those results through the use of choropleth or isopleth maps, can assist police efforts to apprehend criminals. This information allows police departments to focus their investigative activities, geographically prioritize suspects and concentrate saturation or directed patrolling efforts in those zones where the criminal predator is most likely to be active. Such investigative approaches have been termed geographic profiling (Rossmo 1995) or geoforensic analysis (Newton and Newton 1985).

Environmental Criminology

Traditionally, the main interest of criminology has been the offender, and much effort has gone into studying offender backgrounds, peer influences, criminal careers and deterrence. This focus has tended to ignore the other components of crime – the victim, the criminal law and the crime. The crime setting or place, the "where and when" of the criminal act, makes up what Brantingham and Brantingham (1981) call the fourth dimension of crime – the primary concern of environmental criminology. "Environmental criminologists set out to use the geographic imagination in concert with the sociological imagination to describe, understand, and control criminal events" (Brantingham and Brantingham 1981:21). The roots of this perspective lie in human ecology, Jeffery's bio-social learning approach and Hirschi's social control theory (Brantingham and Brantingham 1981; Void and Bernard 1986).

Research in this area has taken a broad approach by including in its analyses operational, perceptual, behavioral, physical, social, psychological, legal, cultural, and geographic settings. These works range from micro to meso to macrospatial levels of analytic focus. One of environmental criminology's major interests, the study of the dimensions of crime at the microspatial level, has often led to useful findings in the area of crime prevention (see, for example, Clarke 1992). Other projects have included the analyses of: crime trips (Rhodes and Conly 1981); efforts to understand target and victim selections through opportunities for crime (Brantingham and Brantingham 1981); crime prevention initiatives, notably crime prevention through environmental design (Jeffery 1977; Wood 1981); proposals for rapid transit security (Felson 1989); patterns of fugitive migration (Rossmo 1987); and other methods (see Clarke 1992). The spatial relationship between the offender's home and his or her crimes is an underlying theme in much of this work. Is it possible to "invert" this research and use the locations of a series of crimes to suggest where an offender might reside? By reversing the reasoning and logic of these theoretical models, it may be feasible to predict the most probable location of a criminal's residence. Such a result would allow the principles of environmental criminology and the geography of crime to be practically applied to the police investigative process.

Geography and Crime Investigation

While police officers are intuitively aware of the influence of place on crime, they sometimes are unaware of the different ways in which geography can assist their work. In spite of this general lack of understanding, however, there are some specific examples of the use of geographic principles by the police in efforts to investigate crimes and apprehend suspects.

Some police dog handlers, for instance, have noted patterns in the escape routes and movements of offenders fleeing from the scenes of their crimes (Eden 1985). This predictability in the movements of those under stress has been observed in both actual trackings of suspects and experimental reenactments using police dog quarries. Fleeing criminals tend to turn to the left if they are right-handed, move to the right upon encountering obstacles, discard evidentiary items to their right and stay near the outside walls when hiding in large buildings (Eden 1985). Different patterns are found when conducting passive tracks for missing persons. Lost subjects tend to bear to the right in their wanderings, and men seem to favor downhill paths while women and children choose uphill routes (Eden 1985).

Senior Superintendent Arvind Verma describes how the Indian Police Service in the Bihar province have used a form of geographical analysis in the investigation of certain types of crimes. *Dacoities* are robberies with violence involving gangs of five or more offenders. This type of criminal act dates back to 500 BC and usually occurs in the countryside. The lack of anonymity in a rural setting requires the *dacoity* gang to attack villages other than their own, and then only during those nights when the moon is new. There is usually little or no artificial lighting in rural India, and the lunar dark phase is a period of almost complete blackness that provides cover for such criminal activities.

Upon being notified of a *dacoity*, the police will first determine the length of time between the occurrence of the crime and first light. Knowing the average speed that a person can travel cross-country on foot then allows the police to calculate a distance radius, centered on the crime site, which determines a circle within which the home village of the *dacoity* members most probably lies. There are few vehicles and if the criminals are not home by daylight, they run the risk of being observed by farmers who begin to work the fields at dawn.

The villages located within this circle can then be narrowed down by eliminating those of the same caste as the victim village, as "brother" is not likely to harm "brother." And, if a sufficiently detailed description of the criminals can be obtained, dress, modus operandi and other details can help determine the caste of the gang, allowing the police to concentrate further on the appropriate villages. Patrols can then speed to these places and attempt to intercept the *dacoity* members, or to proceed to investigate known criminal offenders residing in the area.

In an effort to focus the Hillside Strangler investigation, the Los Angeles, CA Police Department (LAPD) attempted to determine the most likely location of the scene of the homicides. The police knew where the victims had been apprehended and where their bodies had been dumped, and the distances between these two points (Gates and Shah 1992). The LAPD computer analysts viewed the problem in terms of Venn diagrams, with the center of each circle representing victim availability, the circumference representing offender capacity and the radius representing offender ability (Holt 1993).

Vectors drawn from the point where the victims were abducted to the location where their bodies were found were added together to produce a common radius, which defined a circle encompassing an area of just over three square miles. The LAPD saturated this zone with 200 police officers in an attempt to find the murderers. While they were not successful, it is possible that the heavy police presence inhibited the killers, and prompted murderer Kenneth Bianchi's move from Los Angeles to Bellingham, WA. The center of this zone, the LAPD later found out, was not far from co-murderer Angelo Buono's automobile upholstery shop-cum-residence (Gates and Shah 1992).

Geographic techniques were also used in the Yorkshire Ripper investigation. With the murders still unsolved after five and one-half years, Her Majesty's Inspector of Constabulary Lawrence Byford implemented a case review process (Kind 1987a). Detectives had become divided over the issue of the killer's residence. One school of thought, led by the chief investigating officer, believed that the Ripper was from the Sunderland area, while other investigators thought he was a local man. After an intensive investigative review, the Byford advisory team came to the latter conclusion.

To help test this deduction, they applied two "navigational metrical tests" to the spatial and temporal data associated with the crimes (Kind 1987a: 388–390). The first test involved the calculation of the center of gravity (spatial mean) for the 17 crimes (13 murders and four assaults) believed to be linked to the Yorkshire Ripper. The second test consisted of plotting time of offense against length of day (approximated by month of year). The rationale behind this approach had its basis in the theory that the killer would not be willing to attack late at night if his return journey to home was too far.

The first navigational test resulted in the finding that the center of gravity for the Ripper attacks lay near Bradford. The second test determined that the later attacks were those located in the West Yorkshire cities of Leeds and Bradford. Both tests therefore supported the team's original hypothesis that the killer was a local man. Peter William Sutcliffe, who resided in the district of Heaton in the city of Bradford, was arrested three weeks later by a patrol constable and sergeant in Sheffield.

Newton and Newton (1985) applied what they termed geoforensic analysis to a series of unsolved female homicides that occurred in Fort Worth, TX from 1983 to 1985. They found that localized serial murder or rape tends to form place-time patterns different from those seen in "normal" criminal violence. The unsolved Fort Worth murders were analyzed by employing both quantitative (areal associations, crime site connections, centrographic analysis), and qualitative (landscape analysis) techniques.

Newton and Swoope (1987) also utilized geoforensic techniques in a retrospective analysis of the Hillside Strangler case. Different geographic centers were calculated from the coordinates of the locations of various types of crime sites. They discriminated between points of fatal encounter, body or car dump sites and victim's residences, and found that the geographic center of the body dump sites most accurately predicted the location of the residence of murderer Angelo Buono. A search radius (circumscribing an area around the geographic center in which the killers were thought to most likely be found) was also calculated, the range of which decreased with the addition of the spatial information provided by each new murder.

Criminal Geographic Targeting

The locations where crimes happen are not completely random, but instead often have a degree of underlying spatial structure. As chaotic as they may sometimes appear to be, there is often a rationality influencing the geography of their occurrence. Routine activity theory suggests that crimes tend to occur in those locations where suitable (in terms of profit and risk) victims are encountered by motivated offenders as both move through their daily activities (Clarke and Felson. 1993; Cornish and Clarke 1986; Felson 1986, 1987). As offenders travel among their homes, workplaces, and social activity sites, their activity space (composed of these locations and their connecting paths) describes an awareness space that forms part of a larger mental map – an "image of the city" built upon experience and knowledge.

Within a person's activity space is usually an anchor point or base, the single most important place in their spatial life. For the vast majority of people this is their residence. For others, however, the anchor point may be elsewhere, such as the work site or a close friend's home. It should be remembered that some street criminals do not have a permanent residence and may base their activities out of a bar, pool hall or some other such social activity location (Rengert 1990). They might also be homeless, living on the street, or may be transient or mobile to such a degree that they lack any real form of anchor point.

Brantingham and Brantingham (1981) suggest that the process of criminal target selection is a dynamic one. Crimes occur in those locations where suitable targets are overlapped by the offender's awareness space. Offenders may then move outward in their search for additional targets, their interactions decreasing with distance. Search pattern probabilities can thus be modeled by a distance-decay function that show an inverse relationship between the level of interactions and the distance from the locations and routes that comprise the activity space. There may also be a "buffer zone" centered around the criminal's home, within which the offender sees targets as being too risky to victimize because of their proximity to his or her residence (cf. Newton and Swoope 1987).

The Brantingham and Brantingham (1981) model predicts, for the simplest case, that the residence of the offender would lie at the center of the crime pattern and therefore could be approximated by the spatial mean. The intricacy of most activity spaces, however, suggests that more complex patterns may be appropriate. Rengert (1991) proposes four hypothetical spatial patterns that could be used to describe the geography of crime sites: (1) a uniform pattern with no distance-decay influence; (2) a bull's-eye pattern with spatial clustering, exhibiting distance-decay, centered around the offender's primary anchor point; (3) a bimodal pattern with crime clusters centered around two anchor points; and (4) a teardrop pattern with a directional bias oriented toward a secondary anchor point.

Situations can also be distorted by a variety of other real world factors – movement often follows street grids, traffic flows can distort mobility patterns, variations exist in zoning and land use, and crime locations may cluster depending upon the nature of the target backdrop (i.e., the spatial distribution of targets or victims). The spatial mean is therefore limited in its ability to pinpoint criminal residence.

However, combining centrographic principles and journey to crime research in a manner informed by environmental criminological theory can produce a viable method for predicting the location of offender residence from crime site coordinates. One such effort is criminal geographic targeting (CGT), a computerized geographic profiling technique used in police investigations of complex serial crimes (Rossmo 1993). By examining the spatial data connected to a series of crime sites, the CGT model generates a three-dimensional surface, the "height" of which represents the relative probability that a given point is the residence or workplace of the offender.

Criminal geographic targeting is based on the Brantingham and Brantingham (1981) model for crime site selection and on the routine activities approach (Felson 1986). It uses a distance-decay function $f(d)$ that simulates journey to crime behavior. A probability value $f(d_i)$ is assigned to each point (x, y), located at distance d from crime site i. The final probability value for a point (x, y), representing the likelihood that the offender lives at that location, is determined by adding together the n values derived at that point from the n different crime sites.

The use of CGT in actual police investigations – and tests of the model on solved cases of serial murder, rape and arson – have produced promising results, usually locating the offender's residence in the top 5% or less of the total hunting area. The model is based on a four-step process:

(1) Map boundaries delineating the offender's hunting area are first established using the locations of the crimes and standard procedures for addressing edge effects.

(2) Manhattan distances (i.e., orthogonal distances measured along the street grid) from every "point" on the map, the number of which is determined by the measurement resolution of the x and y scales, to each crime location are then calculated.

(3) Next, these Manhattan distances are used as independent variable values in a function that produces a number that: (a) if the point lies outside the buffer zone, becomes smaller the longer the distance, following some form of distance-decay; or (b) if the point lies inside the buffer zone, becomes larger the longer the distance. Numbers are computed from this function for each of the crime locations. For example, if there are 12 crime locations, each point on the map will have 12 numbers associated with it.

(4) Finally, these multiple numbers are multiplied together to produce a single score for each map point. The higher the resultant score, the greater the probability that the point contains the offender's residence.[1]

---

1. The function is of the form:

$$P_{ij} = \prod_{c=1}^{T} k \left[\emptyset / \left(|x_i - x_c| + |y_j - y_c| \right)^f + (1 - \emptyset)(B^{g-f})/(2B - |x_i - x_c| - |y_j - y_c|)^g \right]$$

where:

$$|x_i - x_c| + |y_j - y_c| > B \supset \emptyset = 1$$
$$|x_i - x_c| + |y_j - y_c| \leq B \supset \emptyset = 0$$

and:

P_{ij} is the resultant probability for point ij:
k is an empirically determined constant;
B is the radius of the buffer zone;
T is the total number of crime sites;
f is an empirically determined exponent;
g is an empirically determined exponent;
x_i, y_j are the coordinates of point ij; and
x_c, y_c are the coordinates of the cth crime site location.

When the probabilities are calculated for every point on the map, the end result is a three-dimensional probability surface that can be represented by an isopleth map. Figure 8.1 shows an example of such a surface derived from the crime locations of a serial rapist in San Diego, CA (LeBeau 1992). An isopleth graph shows the value of one variable (in this instance, probability scores) as a function of two other variables (in this instance, north-south and east-west distances). Continuous lines mark out areas of equal probability much as contour lines mark out areas of equal altitude on a relief map. Alternatively, if viewed from above, the probability surface can be depicted by a two-dimensional choropleth map (Harries 1990). In the latter case, the result can be overlaid on a city map of the involved area, and specific streets or blocks prioritized according to the associated values shown on the CGT choropleth probability map (see Figure 8.2; this is a hypothetical case involving a crime series in the District of Columbia).

Any methodology, whether investigative or scientific, should meet three important criteria: validity, reliability and utility. The CGT model works on the assumption that a relationship, modeled on some form of distance decay function, exists between crime location and offender residence. The process can be thought of as a mathematical method for assigning a series of scores to the various points on a map that represents the serial offender's hunting area. Since the model cannot locate the residence of a criminal that lies outside of the boundaries of the hunting area map, it is necessary to limit the process to non-commuting offenders.

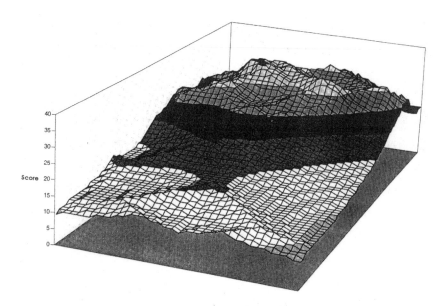

Figure 8.1   Three-dimensional isopleth map of San Diego serial rapist (LeBeau 1992)

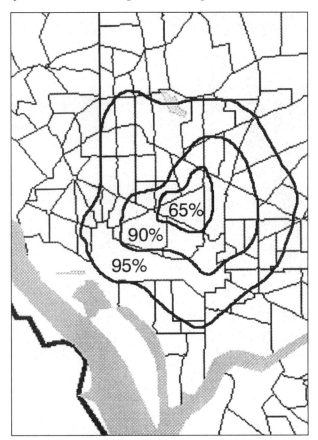

Figure 8.2   CGT choropleth probability map

For the CGT model to be valid, the score it assigns to the point containing the offender's residence should be higher than the scores for most of the other points on the hunting area map. How well this requirement is met can be examined with a distribution curve that indicates the number of points with various scores. The "success" of the CGT model in a given case can then be measured by determining the ratio of the total number of points with equal or higher scores to the total number of points in the hunting area. In other words, in what percentage of the total area would the offender's residence be found by a process that started in the locations with the highest scores and then worked down? The smaller that percentage (referred to as the "hit percentage"), the more successful the model.

While the geographic pattern for a crime series may yield several forms of information (coordinates, crime location type, area characteristics, nearest neighbor distances, point pattern, clustering, temporal ordering, etc.), the randomness inherent

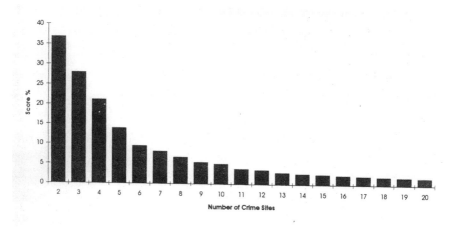

Figure 8.3   CGT Model Learning Curve

in most human behavior limits the conclusions that can be derived from a small number of crime sites. The use of more locations reduces the impact of chance. The performance of the CGT model is thus related to the number of points available for analysis – the more crime locations, the more information and, therefore, the more precision. Validity of the CGT model is hence a function of the number of crime locations.

Monte Carlo testing (a heuristic method that uses repeated simulations), accomplished through a computer program that creates random crime site coordinates based on a buffered distance decay function, was conducted to estimate the theoretical maximum efficiency of the model. The testing produced the "learning curve" shown in Figure 8.3, which displays the relationship between the number of crime sites available for analysis and the hit percentage produced by the CGT model. This process established that at least six crime locations are necessary to produce hit percentages under 10%.

The reliability of the CGT model is high, as the calculations are mathematically straightforward and the procedure has been computerized. The determination of exactly which crime locations in a given case are relevant to the analysis, however, is a subjective process dependent upon the knowledge, experience and interpretation of the profiler. The qualitative dimensions of geographic profiling are also subject to personal biases.

No matter how valid or reliable a particular investigative technique, it will have little practical value if it cannot be effectively used by police detectives in the real world of crime investigation. The utility of the CGT model is best demonstrated by the various geographically based investigative strategies that such a process makes possible. Some examples of these are described in the following section.

Investigative Strategies

Once a geographic profile has been constructed, a variety of criminal investigative strategies can be employed in a more effective and efficient manner. While the specific approaches are best determined by the police investigators familiar with the case in question, some examples of tactics used or suggested in the past are presented below. The development of further spatially based applications and innovative investigative techniques is an interactive process which involves the police officers responsible for the case in question.

Suspect Prioritization

If a lengthy list of suspects has been developed, the geographic profile in conjunction with the criminal offender profile can help prioritize individuals for follow-up investigative work. The problem in many serial violent crime investigations is one of too many suspects rather than too few. Profiling can help prioritize lists of sometimes hundreds if not thousands of suspects, leads and tips.

Patrol Saturation

Areas that have been determined to most probably be associated with the offender can be used as a basis for directed or saturation police patrolling efforts. This strategy is particularly effective if the offender appears to be operating during certain time periods. Prioritized areas can also be employed for neighborhood canvassing efforts, area searches, information sign posting, and community cooperation and media campaigns. Police departments have used this approach to target areas for leaflet distribution, employing prioritized letter carrier walks for strategic household mail delivery. For example, LeBeau (1992) mentions the case of a serial rapist in San Diego who was arrested through canvassing efforts in an area determined from the locations of his crimes.

Police Information Systems

Additional investigative leads may be obtained from the information contained in various computerized police dispatch and record systems (e.g., computer-aided dispatch systems, records management systems, the Royal Canadian Mounted Police Information Retrieval System, and the like). Offender profile details and case specifics can help focus the search at this point.

For example, the police may be investigating a series of sexual assaults that have been psychologically profiled as the crimes of an anger retaliatory rapist. Such an offender is "getting even with women for real or imagined wrongs ... the attack is an emotional outburst that is predicated on anger" (Hazelwood 1987:178–179). His rapes are often initiated by conflicts with a significant woman in his life, and he will frequently select victims who symbolize the source of that conflict. One possible investigative strategy, then, is a search of police dispatch data for domestic disturbance calls near the dates of the rapes to see which ones originated from the area where the geographic profile suggests that the offender most likely resides.

Those police agencies that maintain computerized records detailing the descriptions, addresses and modus operandi of local offenders can also use profiling information, including probable area of residence, as the basis for developing search criteria. Many departments have such files for specific types of criminals, such as parolees or sex offenders.

Outside Agency Databases

Data banks, which are often geographically based, as well as information from parole and probation offices, mental health outpatient clinics, social services offices and similar agencies located in the most probable areas can also prove to be of value. For example, LeBeau (1992) discusses the case of a serial rapist who emerged as a suspect after the police checked parolee records for sex offenders.

Zip/Postal Code Prioritization

The geographic profile can also prioritize zip or postal codes in a city. If suspect offender description or vehicle information exists, prioritized zip or postal codes (representing the most probable 1 or 2% of a city's area) can be used to conduct effective off-line computer searches of registered vehicle or driver's licence files contained in provincial or state motor vehicle department records. These parameters act as a form of linear program to produce a surprisingly small set of records containing fields with all the appropriate data responses. Such a strategy can therefore produce significant results by focusing on limited areas that are of a manageable size for most serious criminal police investigations.

The following is one example of the use of this approach. The postal codes for a city neighborhood within which a violent sexual offender was attacking children were prioritized by using the criminal geographic targeting model. Planning and zoning maps were used to eliminate industrial, commercial and other non-residential areas. Socioeconomic and demographic census data were also consulted to reevaluate the priority of those neighborhoods that were inconsistent with the socioeconomic level of the offender, as suggested by a previously prepared psychological profile.

The remaining postal codes, ranked by priority of probability, were then used to conduct an off-line computer search of the provincial motor vehicle department records that contain postal codes within the addresses connected to the vehicle registered owner and driver's licence files. Suspect vehicle information and an offender description had been developed by the detectives working on the case, and this was combined with the geographic data to effectively focus the off-line search. The conjunction of such parameters can narrow down hundreds of thousands of records to a few dozen vehicles or drivers – sufficient discrimination to allow a focused follow-up by police investigators.

Task Force Computer Systems

Task force operations that have been formed to investigate a specific series of major crimes usually collect and collate their information in some form of computerized system. Often these operations suffer from information overload and can benefit from the prioritization of data and the application of correlation analysis. Geographic profiling can assist in these tasks through the prioritization of street addresses, postal or zip codes, and telephone number areas. The details of the specific computer database software used by the task force, including information fields, search time, number of records, and correlational abilities, determine the most appropriate form that the geographic profile should take to maximize its usefulness to the police investigation.

Conclusion

Geographic profiling infers spatial characteristics of the offender from target patterns. This method uses qualitative and quantitative approaches that attempt to make sense of the pattern from both subjective and objective perspectives. Criminal geographic targeting is a specific statistical method that enhances the efforts of geographic profiling by delineating the most probable areas to which the offender might be associated.

Since geographic profiling is based on an analysis of crimesite locations, a linkage analysis is a necessary prerequisite to determine which crimes are part of the same series and should be included in the development of the profile. It must also be noted that not all types of offenders or categories of crime can be geographically profiled. In appropriate cases, however, such a spatial analysis can produce very practical results from the police perspective. There are a variety of ways which geographic information about the offender can assist the investigation, including the prioritization of suspects by address or area, the direction of patrol saturation efforts and the establishment of computerized database search parameters.

Geographic profiling therefore appears to have significant investigative value in certain types of criminal cases. It is also an example of the application of criminological theory to a criminal justice problem. Through a process of "inverting" criminological and geographic research that has focused on relating crime places to offender residences, the locations of a series of crimes can be used to suggest where an offender might reside. Environmental criminology, because of its rich context and diverse roots, has been particular fruitful in the development of practical applications and holds the promise of many future ideas for crime prevention and policing.

References

Brantingham, P.J. and P.L. Brantingham (eds) (1981). *Environmental Criminology.* Beverly Hills, CA: Sage. (1984). Patterns in Crime. New York: Macmillan.

Clarke, R.V. (ed.) (1992). *Situational Crime Prevention: Successful Case Studies.* Albany, NY: Harrow and Heston.

—— and M. Felson (eds) (1993). *Routine Activity and Rational Choice.* New Brunswick, NJ: Transaction Books.

Cornish, D.B. and R.V. Clarke (eds) (1986). *The Reasoning Criminal: Rational Choice Perspectives on Offending.* New York, NY: Springer-Verlag.

Doney, R.H. (1990). The aftermath of the Yorkshire Ripper: The response of the United Kingdom Police Service. In: S.A. Egger (ed.), *Serial Murder: An Elusive Phenomenon.* New York, NY: Praeger.

Eden, R.S. (1985). *Dog Training for Law Enforcement.* Calgary, CAN: Detselig.

Felson, M. (1986). Linking criminal choices, routine activities, informal control, and criminal outcomes. In: D. B. Cornish and R. V. Clarke (eds), *The Reasoning Criminal: Rational Choice Perspectives on Offending.* New York, NY: Springer-Verlag.

—— (1987). Routine activities and crime prevention in the developing metropolis. *Criminology* 25: 911–931.

Gates, D.F. and D.K. Shah (1992). *Chief.* New York, NY: Bantam Books.

Harries, K. (1990). *Geographic Factors in Policing.* Washington, DC: Police Executive Research Forum.

Hazelwood, R.R. (1987). Analyzing the rape and profiling the offender. In: R. R. Hazelwood and A. W. Burgess (eds), *Practical Aspects of Rape Investigation: A Multidisciplinary Approach.* New York, NY: Elsevier.

Holt, C. (1993). Personal communication to the author from a former member of the Los Angeles, CA Police Department.

Jeffery, C.R. (1977). *Crime Prevention Through Environmental Design.* 2d ed. Beverly Hills, CA: Sage.

Kind, S.S. (1987a). Navigational ideas and the Yorkshire Ripper investigation. *Journal of Navigation* 40: 385–393.

Klockars, C.B. (ed.) (1983). *Thinking About Police: Contemporary Readings.* New York, NY: McGraw-Hill .

LeBeau, J.L. (1992). Four case studies illustrating the spatial-temporal analysis of serial rapists. *Police Studies* 15: 124–145.

Montgomery, J.E. (1992). Organizational Survival: Continuity or Crisis? Paper presented at the Police Studies Series, Simon Fraser University, Vancouver, BC, February.

Newton, Jr., M.B. and D.C. Newton (1985). Geoforensic Identification of Localized Serial Crime: Unsolved Female Homicides, Fort Worth, Texas, 1983–85. Paper presented at the meeting of the Southwest Division, Association of American Geographers, Denton, TX.

—— and E.A. Swoope (1987). Geoforensic Analysis of Localized Serial Murder: The Hillside Stranglers Located. Unpublished manuscript.

Rengert, G.F. (1990). Drug Purchasing as a Routine Activity of Drug Dependent Property Criminals and the Spatial Concentration of Crime. Paper presented at the annual meeting of the American Society of Criminology, Baltimore, MD.

—— (1991). The Spatial Clustering of Residential Burglaries About Anchor Points of Routine Activities. Paper presented at the meeting of the American Society of Criminology, San Francisco, CA.

Rhodes, W.M. and C. Conly (1981). Crime and mobility: An empirical study. In: P.J. Brantingham and P.L. Brantingham (eds), *Environmental Criminology*. Beverly Hills, CA: Sage.

Rossmo, D.K. (1987). Fugitive Migration Patterns. Master's thesis, Simon Fraser University, Burnaby, BC, Canada.

—— (1993). Target patterns of serial murderers: A methodological model. *American Journal of Criminal Justice* 17: 1–21.

—— (1995). Targeting victims: Serial killers and the urban environment. In: T. O'Reilly-Fleming (ed.), *Serial and Mass Murder: Theory, Research and Policy*. Toronto, CAN: Canadian Scholars' Press.

Vold, G.B. and T.J. Bernard (1986). *Theoretical Criminology*. New York, NY: Oxford University Press.

Wood, D. (1981). In defense of indefensible space. In: P. J. Brantingham and P. L. Brantingham (eds), *Environmental Criminology*. Beverly Hills, CA: Sage.

Chapter 9

The 'Road to Nowhere': The Evidence for Travelling Criminals

Paul Wiles and Andrew Costello

A group of offenders aged 16 to 43 years from Sheffield were interviewed. Half of the sample of offenders had been convicted of burglary offences, with the remaining half being convicted of TWOC, but as Table 9.1 shows, many had committed other offences too. Indeed, Over 50 per cent of 'burglars' had committed a TWOC and over 50 per cent of 'TWOCers' had committed a burglary. 'Burglars were much more likely to have shoplifted or committed drug offences and 'TWOCers' were much more likely to have committed theft from a vehicle.

Overall the offending profile of the interviewees is consistent with other research findings that most offenders are generalists and opportunists rather than specialists. All admitted to carrying out more than one type of offence and one offender admitted nine different types of crime.

Table 9.1   Self reported offending of Sheffield interviewees

Offence	All as burglars (%)	(n)	Interviewed as TWOCers (%)	(n)	Interviewed (%)	(n)
Burglary	82	(49)			56	(14)
TWOC	77	(46)	60	(21)		
Shoplifting	47	(28)	57	(20)	32	(8)
Theft from Vehicle	35	(21)	26	(9)	48	(12)
Robbery	23	(14)	17	(6)	32	(8)
Violence	45	(27)	40	(14)	52	(13)
Other theft	58	(35)	69	(24)	44	(11)
Ram Raid	7	(4)	6	(2)	8	(2)
Sexual Offences	3	(2)	3	(1)	4	(1)
Damage/Arson	20	(12)	17	(6)	24	(6)
Drugs (excluding cannabis)	70	(42)	80	(28)	56	(14)

Note
1. Percentages add up to over 100 because of multiple answers.

The Structure of the Interviews

The interviews all followed the same basic format with the interviewee being asked a series of set questions and then being invited to participate in an open-ended discussion about their pattern of offending and general lifestyle.

The structured interviews asked about pre-prison residence and whether it would be returned to. The offenders were then shown a map of the city and asked about their knowledge of 23 pre-identified neighbourhoods.[1] This was to ascertain whether the area was known to the offender, and if so, why; and whether the area was avoided, and if so, why this was the case. The offenders were then asked how they normally travelled around the city. The next questions were about areas outside Sheffield that they visited and why. They were then asked about their work/educational experience.

Only at this point were questions about offending introduced. The interviewees were asked detailed questions about their index offence,[2] and further data was sought about up to three other offences.

Background Details

With regard to pre-prison accommodation, 60 per cent lived with their parents or other relatives, 20 per cent in their own home or with a girlfriend and another 12 per cent lived in a local authority home. The average length of time at the pre-prison address was 5.5 years, with the shortest under one month and the longest 23 years. However, there was a basic divide between length of residence, with 43 per cent of the interviewees living at their most recent address for less than 12 months and 45 per cent for over 3 years. Of the offenders living with their parents or other relatives, primarily the younger ones, the average length of time at their current address was 9.5 years. Sixty percent said they would be returning to their pre-prison address on release. Half of the interviewees spent an average of seven nights a week at their home address and only 10 per cent spent less than two nights a week at home; there was no difference between burglars and TWOCers, and no difference between those living with their parents and the rest. Of those who said they would not be returning to their pre-prison address, almost three-quarters had not regarded it as a permanent address anyway.

Two-thirds of the interviewees had been unemployed at the time they committed their offence, with only 16 per cent working full- or part-time. Furthermore, three-quarters of the interviewees had no formal qualifications so were not in a

---

1 The city was divided up into areas based upon our knowledge of the city and interviewees were shown these on a map. The interviewees appeared not to have any difficulty recognising the areas we had identified or using the map. Only one potential interviewee refused to participate in the research.

2 The offence that led to their selection for interview.

strong position to enter the job market upon release. This lack of involvement in the labour market meant there was little point in analysing movement patterns in relation to place of work, even though some previous research has suggested that workplace is an important 'anchor point' around which offenders structure their movements (Brantingham and Brantingham 1994).

The problem of poor educational attainment was compounded by the fact that during the course of the interviews it became apparent that well over half of the offenders were hard drug users (overwhelmingly heroin). This would appear to support Bennett's (1998) recent findings of the high incidence of drug use amongst those arrested. It is important to note that the use of hard drugs was extremely skewed: only 40 per cent of the TWOCers admitted to a hard drug problem whereas this figure rose to 69 per cent for the burglars. As will be seen, perhaps drug use is the main way of differentiating between the burglars and TWOCers. It certainly had an impact upon the reason for offending and the location of the offence.

Offenders' Knowledge of the City

Almost half (45%) of the interviewees (excluding those offenders living in a local authority home) had lived in two or less of the 23 neighbourhoods pre-identified for the interviews. Moreover, 68 per cent had lived in six or less neighbourhoods; all were areas dominated by unpopular social housing.

When the interviewees were asked which of the areas they knew, the following findings emerged:

* on average each offender claimed to know 14 of the 23 areas; with the burglars claiming knowledge of just under 13 areas and the TWOCers claiming to know just over 15 areas. The areas known by the two groups were largely the same'.[3]
* the only area known by all the offenders was the city centre.
* another seven areas were known by over 66 per cent of interviewees, of these six are high offender/offence, unpopular social housing areas, and the other is a shopping and entertainment area in north Sheffield.
* six of the areas were known by less than 50 per cent of the respondents. On the whole these are working class/lower middle class suburbs on the edge of the city without high offender rates.

Why some areas are known and others not can at least be partially explained by where the interviewees had lived. Of the least known areas none had been lived in

---

3   The correlation between burglars' knowledge of areas and the TWOCers was +0.7879 which is significant at the 0.1 per cent level.

by more than 13 per cent of the interviewees. However, the six well-known high offender/offence rate areas had been lived in by between 32 per cent and 48 per cent of the interviewees. On average each offender has lived in 4.4 neighbourhoods and the sample produced 264 lived in/area matches. Of these 139 (53%) were formed by the six highest offender rate neighbourhoods in the city. Each offender also said that they had friends in these areas at rates between 82 per cent and 96 per cent. Unsurprisingly these areas were also ones where the offenders had the strongest family links. These interview findings tended to confirm police recorded data on offender residence: the 10 per cent of census enumeration districts with the highest number of recorded offenders contained over 35 per cent of offender addresses.

On average each interviewee avoided 1.5 areas. The reasons for avoiding areas varied considerably. Of the three most avoided areas one is a high offender rate inner-city area, which is considered to be the centre of the city's drug trade, another is a high crime council estate and the third is a lower middle class/working class area on the north-western edge of the city (one of the least known parts of the city according to the interviewees). The main reasons given for avoiding an area were fear of a particular individual and being too well known by the local police. What did not emerge was any real sense that offenders were avoiding middle class areas because they believed they would not fit in or would stand out, even though the interviews probed for this reason on the basis that previous research has suggested that offenders will avoid such areas because they will feel 'ontologically insecure' (see, for example, Carter and Hill 1979). A much more prosaic reason for avoiding middle class areas emerged – the offenders simply did not know them to any extent.

Table 9.2   Modes of travel normally used to get around Sheffield

Mode of travel	All		Burglars		TWOCers	
	(%)	*(n)*	*(%)*	*(n)*	*(%)*	*(n)*
Own Vehicle	60	(36)	49	(17)	76	(19)
Mate's Vehicle	85	(51)	77	(27)	96	(24)
Bus/Tram	83	(50)	86	(30)	80	(20)
Taxi	75	(45)	77	(27)	72	(18)
Walk	53	(32)	77	(27)	20	(5)
Bike	47	(28)	29	(10)	72	(18)
Stolen Car	72	(43)	51	(18)	100	(25)

Note
1. Percentages add up to over 100 because of multiple answers.

Travel Around the City

Most of those interviewed (72%) said they had access to a car or motorbike; but the TWOCers had more access (92%) than the burglars (57%). This translated into the findings in Table 9.2 with regard to 'normal' modes of travel used to get round the city.

Whilst the TWOCers had the opportunity to be more legitimately mobile than the burglars did, they nevertheless were more likely to steal a car in order to be mobile. Furthermore, the TWOCers were significantly less likely to walk as a means of travel.

Travel to Areas Outside Sheffield

Each of the interviewees were given the opportunity to identify up to four places they visited outside the city on a regular basis. Just over a third (38%) replied that they had no regular visits outside the city. There was no particular age bias to this reply. The remaining 37 interviewees mentioned 68 places as set out in Table 9.3 and they are not dissimilar to the places that police recorded crime data shows Sheffielders offended in (see Table 3.5). Furthermore, 74 per cent of places are in the immediate vicinity of Sheffield and, if Skegness is included, 80 per cent of places have very close links with Sheffield.

The interview responses showed that offending was the single most important reason for visits outside the city, but this was outweighed collectively by other reasons. The places visited primarily in order to offend were very similar to those regularly visited for other reasons (see Table 9.3) and again are close to and closely connected with Sheffield.

Table 9.3 Places regularly visited by Sheffield offenders and places travelled to primarily to offend

Place	*Visiting regularly*		*Visiting to offend*	
	(%)	*(n)*	*(%)*	*(n)*
Rotherham	31	(21)	33	(11)
Chesterfield/ North East Derbyshire	22	(15)	24	(8)
Doncaster	15	(10)	12	(4)
Barnsley	6	(4)	9	(3)
Skegness	7	(5)	12	(4)
Leeds	6	(4)	–	
Other	13	(9)	9	(3)
Total		68		33

Table 9.4   Reasons for going to places outside Sheffield

Reason for visit	(%)	(n)
Relative/friends	39	(28)
Shopping	3	(2)
To offend	46	(33)
Work	4	(3)
Holidays	8	(6)
Total	72	

Table 9.5   Correlations with offence locations

Independent variables	Correlations
Areas lived in at some time	0.6220**
Areas known well	+0.3916*
Areas currently lived in	+0.7963***

Notes
1. ***significant at the 0.1 per cent level; **significant at the 1 per cent level; significant at the 5 per cent level.
2. All the above correlations based upon Pearson Correlation Coefficient 1-tailed test.

Offender Travel-to-crime

The interview data provided the opportunity to analyse, in detail, the travel patterns of 90 burglaries and 72 TWOCs (7 burglaries and 3 TWOCs were lost because the offender could remember little of the offence, usually because of drugs). The spread of offending was wider than the spread of offender residence and only one of the 23 neighbourhoods (Meadowhall) did not have a burglary or TWOC. In other words, the concentration of offence locations is wider than the concentration of offender residences. Analysis of these offences in relation to the offenders' most recent address, areas previously lived in and areas known well (see Table 9.5), revealed that offences were most concentrated in the area of current residence, followed by areas previously lived in and finally areas known well.

As can be seen all are statistically significant, the most important being area of current residence which shows a very strong correlation. This confirms the earlier findings about the generally short distances travelled to offend. It also reinforces the importance of the earlier finding that offenders tended to live in, and move around, a relatively small number of residential areas of the city which had high, resident offender-driven offence rates.

Interviewees Travel-to-crime

The interview data was also directly compared with the Sheffield recorded crime data. For each offence the offenders were asked where they had slept the night before the offence and why they were in the area of offence commission. Table 9.6 shows the average offender travel distances to offend, for burglary and TWOC, based on (a) police data using place of offence and recorded home address of the offender; (b) the interview data using place of offence and home address of the offender; and (c)

Table 9.6   Offender travel: police data and interview data

	Burglary (miles)			TWOC (miles)		
	Recorded crime	Interview data		Recorded crime	Interview data	
	Police data	Apparent	Real	Police data	Apparent	Real
	travel	travel	travel	travel	travel	travel
	(a)	(b)	(c)	(a)	(b)	(c)
All offences	5.2	5.2	1.6	7.1	2.9	2.5
Within City offences	1.8	2.0	1.6	2.4	2.5	2.1
Out of City offences	31.4	38.5	1.0	30.8	6.5	6.5

Table 9.7   Reason for being in area of offence commission

Reason	All offences (%)	Burglary (%)	TWOC (%)
To offend	33	30	38
Near home	33	36	29
Chance	10	9	11
Visiting friends etc.	13	13	12
Leisure/shopping	7	7	7
Can't remember	4	5	2

interview data using place of offence and the address where the offender slept the night before the offence was committed.

Generally the short distances travelled to offend shown by police recorded crime statistics are an overestimate. For example, one of the interviewees committed two burglaries in Skegness, 90 miles from his home address in Sheffield. However, he was on holiday in Skegness and simply came across opportunities that were too tempting. The main point to note is the analysis based on police data is, if anything, likely to overestimate the distances travelled by offenders to offend.

Table 9.8   Reason for deciding to offend (index offences)

Reason	All offences (%)[4]	Burglary (%)	TWOC (%)
Easy Target/Good Opportunity	45	31	64
Needed Money	73	100	36
Bored	18	0	44
Drunk/Drugged Up	45	40	52
Influence of Mates	17	11	24
Fun	32	0	76
Other	17	11	24
Don't Know	0	0	0

Note
1. Percentages add up to over 100 because of multiple answers.

Table 9.9   Solo and joint offending

Number of Offenders	All offences (%)	(n)	Burglary (%)	(n)	TWOC (%)	(n)
Solo	37	(61)	51	(46)	20	(15)
1 other	40	(66)	36	(32)	46	(34)
2–3 others	21	(33)	12	(11)	30	(22)
4 or more	3	(4)	1	(1)	4	(3)

There is some evidence that TWOCers are more likely to travel with the intention of offending than burglars (see Table 9.7) but the differences are not very great. Whilst offending is a significant reason for being in an area, overall it is less important than other non-criminal lifestyle reasons.

There seems to be a greater search for an opportunity in the case of TWOC than burglary and this might be explained by the reason given for deciding to commit an offence, as shown in Table 9.8. The difference between reasons for being in an area (taking 'to offend' versus the rest) is significant at the 5 per cent level.

The main reported motivation for burglary is the need for money which was primarily for drugs. Car theft, on the other hand, is much more driven by the search for fun, with money a secondary issue even though most of the interviewees admitted they made money from car theft. The 'social' nature of TWOC can be illustrated by the joint nature of much TWOCing as opposed to burglary (see Table 9.9). Whilst over half of burglaries were carried out alone this drops to a fifth for TWOC and seems to confirm the different reasons for offending.

Table 9.10   Target selection: TWOC (index offence)

Reason for selection	No.	(%)
Nearby and available	13	(52)
Easy to steal	22	(88)
Type of car I usually take	6	(24)
Good car (i.e. stylish, fast)	8	(32)
Looking for that type (make money)	5	(20)
Chance	12	(48)
Other	2	(8)

Note
1. Percentages add up to over 100 because of multiple answers.

One important aspect of drug-related offending that came across anecdotally in the interviews is that the burglars believe that they get caught as a result of being reckless because the need for drugs has become pressing. They offended very close to home and in an unplanned way and argued that this was why they were caught. However, this may be post-hoc rationalisation as almost as many burglars who travelled (n=9) as those who did not (n=11) were drug addicts.[4] Of the TWOCers, six non-travellers and four travellers were addicts.

The financial imperatives for TWOCers seemed to be way down the list when compared with how easy the car was to steal, its availability and chance (Table 9.10). These answers might add weight to the findings of the Home Offices recent Car Crime Index which found that various older cars were the most likely to be stolen. Older cars generally have less sophisticated security systems than more modern cars, but they also are more likely to be owned by people living in the same residential areas as offenders are, thus contributing availability and chance.

Table 9.11 shows that the dominant reason for burglary target selection seems to be chance, either literally or in the sense that the offender just happened to be passing, whilst the proportion deliberately targeted was small.[5] One point that is worth making is the fact that repeat targeting appears uncommon and yet much recent research has suggested that offenders returning to the same target is a cause of repeat victimisation.[6] There was no evidence of significant repeat burglary targeting among those admitted by the interviewees.

---

4   Four of the five professionals were also drug users.
5   The offenders themselves treated these categories as mutually exclusive.
6   Although this suggestion has been made and been supported by some empirical evidence the evidential base is still presently slim (see Pease 1998 for a review of this literature).

Table 9.11   Target selection: burglary (index offence)

Reason for selection	(%)	(n)
Chance	63	(22)
Passing and looked easy (poor security)	31	(11)
Passing and looked easy (unoccupied)	26	(9)
Passing and looked easy (isolated/quiet)	26	(9)
Had noticed previously	20	(7)
Tipped off	17	(6)
Passing and looked wealthy	14	(5)
Revenge	6	(2)
Other	6	(2)
Burgled before	3	(1)

Note
1. Percentages add up to over 100 because of multiple answers.

Table 9.12   Travel patterns of 'travellers' and 'non-travellers'

	Index Offence: Apparent Travel	Index Offence: Real Travel	Other Burglary TWOC: Apparent Travel	Other Burglary TWOC: Real Travel
Travelling Burglars	3.6 miles	2.7 miles	12.8 miles	1.3 miles
Non Travelling Burglars	1.8 miles	0.4 miles	3.5 miles	0.6 miles
Travelling TWOCers	5.1 miles	3.8 miles	3.1 miles	2.5 miles
Non-Travelling TWOCers	0.2 miles	0.2 miles	1.9 miles	1.7 miles

Table 9.13   Travel of 'professional' offenders

	Apparent Travel	Real Travel
Burglars	1.5 miles	1.4 miles
TWOCers	4.0 miles	3.4 miles

The Identification of Travellers Versus Non-travellers

The research design was constructed so those offenders who appeared to travel and those who did not, holding age constant, could be compared (see Chapter 2). Travellers were defined as those offenders who for the index offence had travelled at least 2 miles. The travel patterns of the interviewees are shown in Table 9.12.

The differences between travellers and non-travellers becomes much less apparent when offences other than the index offence for which they were selected are examined. This confirms the interview data in which there did not appear to be any discernible difference between the travellers and non-travellers. There was no difference between the two groups in terms of issues such as type of offences admitted to, mode of travel round the city, or knowledge of the city's areas. In other words, the data does not support the idea that some offenders are regular travellers and others not.

The group of professional offenders who were identified by South Yorkshire police produced the travel distances shown in Table 9.13.

Given the relatively small sample of professionals it is difficult to say whether there are any differences from the main body of interviewees, although the interviews did not suggest any significant differences in terms of travel, target selection or reasons for offending.[7]

Perhaps the main finding, with regard to travel, from the offender interviews is the broad confirmation it appears to give to the police and DNA data which suggests that patterns of travel can be broadly established by using police data. In fact as has been noted above, police data, if anything, overestimates travel.

References

Bennett, T. (1998). *Drugs and Crime: The Results of Research on Drug Testing and Interviewing of Arrestees;* Home Office Research Study 183. London: Home Office.

Brantingham, P. and Brantingham, P. (1994). Burglar mobility and crime prevention. In R. Clarke and T. Hope (eds), *Coping with Burglary*. Boston; MA: Kluwer Nijhoff.

Carter, R.L. and Hill, K.Q. (1975). *The Criminal's Image of the City*. New York: Pergamon.

---

7   The reason for the lack of difference may be that the professionals identified for us were drawn from the police list of the most prolific 25 burglars and 25 TWOCers in the city. There are, of course, other notions of 'professional' which the police could have applied.

Chapter 10

Distance Decay Reexamined

George F. Rengert, Alex R. Piquero, Peter R. Jones

Similar to other social scientists, criminologists are interested in discovering fundamental and generalizable concepts that are basic to social relationships. One of the distinguishing features of social relationships is the ability of humans to interact over space. Geographers and regional scientists use the term *spatial interaction* to denote these flows over a study area (Haynes and Fotheringham 1984; Taylor 1975). Criminologists have adopted this concept to study the spatial movement of criminals in their search for a crime site (Brantingham and Brantingham 1984) and their transportation of illegal commodities (Rengert 1996). These criminal activities over space are considered special forms of a common social behavior – spatial interaction.

In the study of criminal behavior over space, criminologists seek to discover fundamental characteristics that underlie this behavior. If these fundamental characteristics can be identified, one can make generalizations that can explain or predict future criminal spatial behavior. The purpose of much of the spatial research in criminology has been to identify these fundamental spatial characteristics that allow one to formulate theories to explain criminal behavior and the resulting crime patterns.

Data collected on the spatial characteristics of crime and criminals may take the form of either individual movements or aggregate flows over space. The former contain a great deal of variance between subjects and seem to typify uniqueness. Such data can be mapped simply as a collection of lines joining the origin of the interaction to its destination (Costanzo et al. 1986; Lentz 1986).

Aggregated data are usually mapped using choropleth maps to denote varying densities of flow from a single origin or to a single destination. More commonly in criminology, such data are presented in tabular form (Rengert 1989b) and seem to represent generality rather than uniqueness. In either case, the goal of spatial analysis in criminology is to seek the general patterns and regularities that exist but are not always evident from the cartographic or tabular portrayal of the data.

The debate between uniqueness and generality has been an important one in environmental criminology (Rengert 1989a). If one adopts a strictly uniqueness standpoint, whereby all criminal decisions are different from one another, general concepts and the development of spatial theory are not possible in criminology. On the other hand, if one rejects the uniqueness doctrine, one can

LIVERPOOL JOHN MOORES UNIVERSITY
LEARNING SERVICES

develop general models and theories of criminal spatial behavior and the geography of crime.

It is when the spatial behavior of many criminals is aggregated that common tendencies begin to arise. These common tendencies are present in the seemingly unique individual cases although they are obscured by the disaggregated level of the data. This is not to deny the "individuality" of criminals; each of them does indeed make separate decisions. However, each decision is made within a framework of constraints. For many criminals, a major aspect of these constraints is represented simply by distance. In other words, no matter how much one may wish to emphasize "free will" of the individual, in practice, criminals are not free to commit crime anywhere they wish. Their ethnic characteristics may make them stand out in a strange neighborhood, their economic status will determine their access to different modes of transportation, and their past experiences (e.g., school, armed services, and so on) determine the area they have knowledge of. Criminologists can begin to understand the working of these constraints by measuring the *distance-decay* effect exhibited in criminal spatial interaction. This relationship between interaction and distance is one of the most fundamental relationships in theoretical environmental criminology.

Most of the research completed with regard to the distance traveled from offenders' places of residence to crime sites indicates that, similar to the pattern exhibited by other forms of human movement (Jackle et al. 1976), this distance is rather short such that the number of crimes decreases almost exponentially as the distance to the crime sites increases (e.g., Brantingham and Brantingham 1984: 344–346; Capone and Nichols 1975, 1976; Phillips 1980; Rhodes and Conly 1981; Rossmo 1995; White 1932).[1] This finding has been termed the distance-decay function, or the empirical generalization that most offenders select their targets close to their own homes and the farther the distance from their homes, the fewer the crimes committed (Phillips 1980; Van Koppen and De Keijser 1997: 505).

Space itself is something to be passed over and thus calls for an expenditure of time and energy (Hawley 1950: 237). Since crime is an activity that almost always has a spatial component, the frictional effect of distance has direct implications for many criminological theories. Given the effort required to utilize space, rational choice theory (Cornish and Clarke 1986) holds that all other things being equal (e.g., amount of gain, risk of apprehension), there is no reason to believe that a criminal would choose a more distant opportunity for crime over a nearer one. In the eyes of rational choice theorists, criminals would attempt to expend as little time and energy

---

1   This does not preclude the fact that for some crimes, the distance traveled may be farther than for other crime types (Baldwin and Bottoms 1976; Gabor and Gottheil 1984; Rengert 1989a; Rhodes and Conly 1981). However, the point is that for these types of crimes, the decrease in the number of crimes committed still decreases as the distance increases; it just happens to decrease at a slower rate than for other crimes. Further, in the case of confrontive crimes, in which an objective is to avoid recognition, the origin of the criminal search may be beyond a buffer zone surrounding the home rather than directly from the home.

as possible to accomplish their criminal activity. This claim is similar to one found in Gottfredson and Hirschi's (1990:92) general theory of crime. Arguing that "one of the defining features of crime is that it is simple and easy," Gottfredson and Hirschi imply that since offenders are interested only in the short term, they are likely to minimize the time and energy involved in criminal activities by selecting crimes that can be executed at relatively short distances from their homes as opposed to long distances.

The concept of distance decay also has direct implications for the criminological theory of differential association. Given the residential segregation that exists in major cities by both income and ethnicity (Massey and Denton 1993; Wilson 1987 1996), differential association theory (Sutherland 1947) would predict that criminals learn from others in their own communities .with whom they are in close contact. Pettiway (1982) has demonstrated that criminals also tend to commit their crimes within these segregated areas rather than travel farther to victimize other ethnic groups. Further, this relationship may provide an explanation of why black-on-black and white-on-white crime tends to be the rule rather than the exception for many personal crimes. Relatedly, most subcultural theories that postulate that criminal attitudes and techniques are transmitted by interpersonal contact also imply the frictional effect of distance since the probability of association between people declines with (increasing) distance from their home (Angel and Hyman 1972).

The criminological theory that may have the most relevance for distance decay is routine activities theory (Cohen and Felson 1979). 'Ibis theory states that a crime is not likely to take place unless a motivated offender comes in contact with a suitable target in the absence of a capable guardian. As such, it implies that the routine activities of criminals are as important as those of the victim in determining the location of a crime. Consider, for example, that the only two means by which criminals can identify a suitable target other than through a secondary source is to search along and around routine routes of spatial activity or to explore space that is not near one of their routine activity paths. Rengert and Wasilchick (1985) have demonstrated that spatial exploration is rare in criminal activity. Given that criminal activity seems to occur on or around routine paths through space that are centered on the home, from routine activity concepts one would expect criminal activity to center on the home and to decrease with distance from this node.

The above theories are used only as examples of the role of the friction of distance in determining the spatial arrangement of crime about the home of the offender. As can be seen, the frictional effect of distance is central to a complete understanding of many criminological theories, and especially to the spatial arrangement of crime that is likely to result from each.

Van Koppen and De Keijser (1997)

In a recent article in *Criminology*, Van Koppen and De Keijser (1997) examined the issue of distance decay and argued that criminological applications of the theory may be problematic. Specifically, they suggest that inferring individual distance decay from aggregate-level data may be inappropriate. Their critique is grounded in the pioneering work of Robinson (1950), who almost 50 years ago, demonstrated some of the problems involved with using aggregate-level data to draw inferences about individual behavior. Robinson (1950:357) argued that ecological correlations are almost certainly not equal to their corresponding individual correlations what has come to be called the *ecological fallacy*.

The thesis driving the simulation research by Van Koppen and De Keijser is that the aggregated distance-decay function conceals individual variations in ranges of operation, and therefore, most (if not all) of the research that has employed this function may be based on artifact:

> If individual criminals who commit a 'particular' type of crime have a *range of operation* within which they select their targets, a distance decay function will emerge at the aggregate level. This will also happen if targets are dispersed randomly within the range without *individual* distance decay. These individual patterns generate a distance decay function at the aggregate level as long as individual criminals differ in their ranges of operation (p. 507).

Their argument may be summed up as follows: Irrespective of differences in offense intensity, relatively small ranges of operation for criminals included in the data will aggregate to form a peak at the lower side of the distance scale although none of the behaviors of individual offenders might be characterized by distance decay (p. 508). To support their assertions, Van Koppen and De Keijser present a series of randomly generated data that confirm their predictions. Before we proceed, a brief review of their results is warranted.

In their first example, Van Koppen and De Keijser present a very simplified illustration of distance decay for three offenders, each of whom commits 20 crimes. After presenting evidence that the crimes of each individual offender are evenly distributed within their own range of operation (no distance decay), the aggregated function is calculated and demonstrates distance decay (pp. 508–509). In their next example, they created a model of 1,000 hypothetical offenders who committed 20 offenses each. Their range of operation varied from 200 meters to 200 kilometers. The distance of each offense from the offender's residence was found by multiplying the range by a factor. The conclude by arguing that even though none of the simulated offenders exhibited a pattern of distance decay within his own range, the aggregate curve for the 20,000 crimes was indicative of the classic distance decay function.

In their third example, Van Koppen and De Keijser did not fix the number of offenses for their simulated offenders; rather, each offender was randomly assigned a number of offenses, which ranged from 1 to 100. Once again, a distance-decay function emerged at the aggregate level[2]? In their final model, Van Koppen and

---

2 When they set the range for all offenders to 200 kilometers in this model, they found no distance decay at the aggregate level.

De Keijser allowed each of their simulated offenders to have a random number of offenses, a random range of operation, and a moderate distance increase. The results for this model showed that while each individual offender was given a slight distance increase, the distance-decay function was again evident at the aggregate level.

They conclude by suggesting that the common assumption that the distance-decay function in the aggregate data reflects distance decay in the offenses of individuals is unjustified (p. 511). To them, the distance-decay function may be due to differences in the ranges of operation of different offenders, and future research should focus attention on ranges of operation instead of distance to crime targets when studying the spatial distribution of crime (e.g., Canter and Larkin 1993).

The Current Focus

We do not dissent from Van Koppen and De Keijser's assertion that researchers cannot and should not make inferences about individual behavior with data collected at the aggregate level. However, their analysis raises four important issues. The first concerns Van Koppen and De Keijser's interpretation of the ecological fallacy. The second deals with their assumption of linearity in offenders' movements. The third issue concerns their interpretation of geographic work on profiling. The final issue relates to the assumption made by Van Koppen and De Keijser in their simulations that offenders randomly choose targets within a delimited range of operation. We discuss each of these in turn.

The Ecological Fallacy

The main issue here concerns the question: When is there an ecological fallacy? Van Koppen and De Keijser appear to suggest that any individual-level inference drawn from aggregate data is inappropriate irrespective of the initial unit of analysis. We take this to imply that their main concern is whether the aggregate distance-decay function represents a summary level pattern that simply does not exist (at the individual level).

In our understanding of this concept, the ecological fallacy involves the confusion of units of analysis, that is, inferring the nature of individual level processes from the aggregate-level data. Thus, the ecological fallacy would not be present if one started with individual-level data, aggregated all the individual data points to a higher level, and then made inferences about individual behavior from the aggregated data. This process is similar to the one used in risk prediction, wherein one gathers data at the individual level, develops aggregate classification models, and then provides individual-level predictions. In this scheme, the ecological fallacy would not be present since the analyses derive from individual-level data and inferences at this level of analysis are appropriate. This is especially true if distance decay exists at the individual level. In this scheme, an aggregate distance-decay function is simply a summary of individual patterns (characterized by individual-level distance decay).

Van Koppen and De Keijser (1997:511) summarize their argument by stating: "The common assumption that the distance-decay function evident in aggregate data reflects distance decay in the activities of individuals is unjustified." We disagree. This "common assumption" concerning distance decay has been supported by individual-level data. A review of research focused on criminal behavior in space at the individual level reveals several studies that identify a distance decay (Alston 1994; Rengert 1996; Rossmo 1993; Warren et al. 1995). These studies also demonstrate that it is not uncommon for the criminal to begin the search for a crime opportunity at a distance from home in order to avoid recognition. Rossmo (1993) refers to this avoidance of recognition behavior as a *buffered distance decay* function. This behavior seems to be especially applicable to confrontive crimes. In fact, Van Koppen and De Keijser's (1997) illustrations in which the criminal always begins the crime search at the home is an unrealistic case. Our best understanding of the relationship between distance and probability of crime indicates that the function exhibits distance decay, but for confrontive crimes, only after a certain point in space. For distances up to that point (the buffer zone), the probability of crime increases with the distance from the home. In this buffered distance decay function, the turning point is equal to the radius of the buffer zone (Rossmo, personal communication, October 1997). These findings have been discovered with research focused on the individual level of analysis and not derived from aggregate statistics.

In order to assess this issue, we next present an analysis of "real," or nonsimulated, offenders. The data reported on in this section come from an ethnographic study of residential burglars in Philadelphia (Pa.) and Wilmington (Del.) that was designed to examine a variety of issues surrounding the decision-making process associated with residential burglary (Rengert and Wasilchick 1989). The offenders were active at the time the data were gathered and were identified by a snowball sampling from original contacts provided by probation officers in Philadelphia and Wilmington (Rengert and Wasilchick 1985). Here, we report the journey to crime (in miles) for 14 burglars, 8 burglaries per burglar, for a total of 112 burglaries.

In Table 10.1, we present the number of burglaries committed by each burglar per mile. For example, burglar 1 committed 5 burglaries between 0 and 1 mile from his home, 2 burglaries between 1.01 and 2 miles from home, and so on. We present the ranges of operation on an individual basis for all 14 burglars to highlight two points. First, our nonsimulated offenders do not always start the search for crime from their residence. In fact, burglars 2, 4, 6, and 14 committed their burglaries at least one mile away from their homes. This stands in contrast to Van Koppen and De Keijser's assumption that all offenders start the search for crime sites from their residence. Second, while the majority of the 14 burglars exhibit clear distance decay at the. individual level, others do not. This is due to the unique nature of the criminals and the small number of offenses for which we have data. If we had

Table 10.1 **Number of Burglaries per Range of Operation for Individual Burglars**

Distance Band (Miles)	Number of Burglaries Committed by Each Individual Burglar Within Respective Range													
	B1	B2	B3	B4	B5	B6	B7	B8	B9	B10	B11	B12	B13	B14
0–1.0	5.00	.00	3.00	.00	5.00	.00	2.00	1.00	8.00	7.00	8.00	7.00	5.00	.00
1.01–2.0	2.00	.00	1.00	2.00	3.00	3.00	5.00	.00	.00	1.00	.00	1.00	.00	7.00
2.01–3.0	1.00	2.00	1.00	3.00	.00	.00	1.00	5.00	.00	.00	.00	.00	3.00	1.00
3.01–4.0	.00	3.00	2.00	2.00	.00	.00	.00	2.00	.00	.00	.00	.00	.00	.00
4.01–5.0	.00	2.00	.00	1.00	.00	4.00	.00	.00	.00	.00	.00	.00	.00	.00
5.01–6.0	.00	1.00	.00	.00	.00	1.00	.00	.00	.00	.00	.00	.00	.00	.00
6.01–7.0	.00	.00	1.00	.00	.00	.00	.00	.00	.00	.00	.00	.00	.00	.00

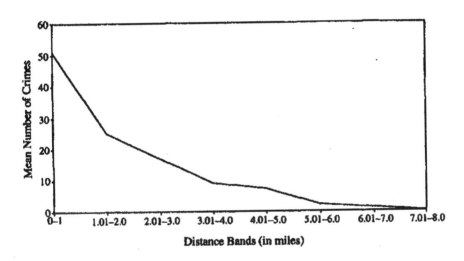

Figure 10.1 **Aggregated distance–decay function**

data on a hundred or more crimes for each individual, each would probably exhibit a distance decay. However, given the present data – in which not all criminals begin their criminal activity at the home, have varying ranges of operation, or have their crime sites clustered rather than randomly scattered across their ranges of operation – it is interesting to note that a classic distance decay appears at the aggregate level (See Figure 10.2). Since the aggregate distance-decay function is a

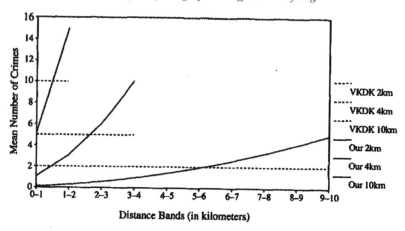

Figure 10.2   Von Koppen–De Keijser and our calculations

summary depiction of a series of individual-level data points, like other measures of central tendency, it may not always represent each and every individual.[3] In other words, while the aggregate-level analysis clearly indicated distance decay, this pattern may not be characteristic of every single burglar (e.g., burglar 6). Yet, the aggregate distance-decay function appears to mimic the majority of the burglars who individually exhibit distance decay in their offending.

These data support previous empirical research that illustrates that criminals exhibit a clear tendency to commit crimes closer to home rather than farther away. In other words, distance decay at the aggregate level is not a statistical artifact, but rather exemplifies the true tendency of criminals to minimize the distance to their crime sites.

Modeling the Absence of Distance Decay

Van Koppen and De Keijser claim to model the absence of distance decay at the individual level by assuming a uniform distribution of offenses (or in the final case, a slight increase in offenses) at varying linear distances from the offender's home. But this is only half the story. If there truly were no distance decay at the individual level, criminals would "slide" frictionlessly to varying distances from the home before they began their criminal search process. In other words, not only would the range

---

3   As the Editor pointed out, this situation is analogous to computing a measure of central tendency when the distribution of a variable, say sex, is completely bimodal (0,1). Although it in fact is the expected value, it does not come close to characterizing anyone in the sample. A mean value of .345 for the above example does not characterize anyone's value on the sex variable.

vary, but also the origin of the search must vary if one truly is to model no distance decay (i.e., not all offenders start at point zero as they are portrayed in the Van Koppen and De Keijser models).

A second physical property of a frictionless space used in Van Koppen and De Keijser's formulation is a uniform random distribution of opportunities for offenses over space. Thus, when they model a constant number of offenses with increasing distances from the home, they imply that they have modeled a lack of distance decay at the individual level. They have not considered that with a uniform distribution of opportunities over space, the number of opportunities at a given distance increases with increasing distance from the home at a ratio of πr^2 (see Turner 1969). In other words, if one drew circles around the home at 1000-foot intervals, as opposed to the linear distances found in the Van Koppen and De Keijser model, the circles would increase in size and area covered. As Turner (1969:14) notes, "going out one unit of distance from a point includes all the area swept out by a radius of one unit length; but going out two units from the same point sweeps out much more than twice as much area."

Therefore, if one thought of each unique crime opportunity as a pill in an urn with each representing a place in space, with a model of no distance decay, the probability of randomly drawing a pill representing a greater distance from the home increases at a ratio of πr^2. It is not a constant number with increasing distance. Without knowing it, Van Koppen and De Keijser actually modeled a distance decay at the individual level when they assumed a constant number of offenses at increasing distance from the home of the criminal.

If Van Koppen and De Keijser were truly to model an absence of distance decay, their distribution of offenses would match the distribution of opportunities for crime at varying distances from home. This would be the equivalent of the area contained in each distance band. For example, if a criminal committed 20 offenses in the first band of two kilometers surrounding the home, he must commit 60 offenses in the next band of two kilometers surrounding the first band, 120 in the next, and so on. Table 10.2 illustrates the difference between Van Koppen and De Keijser's distribution of offenses and the one required by a uniform random distribution of opportunities for crime and no distance decay affecting the offender's choice of a crime site.

Figure 10.2 illustrates the difference between Van Koppen and De Keijser's distribution of offenses over space and the one required if they were correctly to model an absence of distance decay. Notice that in the first instance, instead of 10 crimes in each of two distances of a kilometer each from the home (as in Van Koppen and De Keijser's model), we would require between 5 and 10 crimes in the first distance band and between 10 and 15 crimes in the next distance band away from home. Figure 10.2 illustrates that the same relationship holds for the range of 4 kilometers and 10 kilometers away from home. The point to draw from this analysis is that the number of offenses is not a constant value with increasing distance if there is no distance decay. A constant number of offenses would only occur in the unlikely event of the criminal always traveling in a straight line in the same direction.

Table 10.2   Expected crimes with and without distance decay

Distance Zone From Home (in Feet)	Van Koppen and De Keijser's Crimes	Distance Decay Crimes
200	20	20
400	20	60
600	20	120
800	20	200
1,000	20	300

Using the aforementioned nonsimulated burglars, we next present the number of burglaries that would be predicted on the basis of πr^2 and test whether the observed distribution of burglaries departs significantly from the expected values. Before proceeding, we describe in detail the procedures for undertaking this calculation.

First, we determine the number of burglaries within each distance band (in miles). This number is obtained by summing the number of burglaries within each distance band for each burglar. Thus, the total number of burglaries in the first distance band (0–1.0 miles) is arrived at by summing the total number of burglaries committed by each of the 14 burglars in that distance band (i.e., 5+3+5+2+1+8+7+8+7+5 = 51). Thus, we observe 51 burglaries in the first distance band. This procedure is completed for all seven distance bands. It is important to note that no burglaries were committed after the seventh distance band (6.01–7 miles).

Next, we calculate the total area by which seven miles is covered. This is obtained by multiplying πr^2, where r is equal to 7 because the farthest distance traveled in our data is seven miles. This result is equal to 153.938 square miles. Then, we calculate the total area within each zone. We obtain this area by multiplying πr^2, where $r = 1$ for the first distance band, $r = 2$ for the second distance band, and so on up through distance band seven, at which point $r = 7$. With this information in hand, we then calculate the marginal area within each distance band. This area is arrived at by subtracting the total area of the previous distance band from the total area of the current distance band. For example, when obtaining the marginal area of distance band two, we take the total area of distance band two minus the total area of distance band one.[4] The total area of distance band two is equal to πr^2, where $r = 2$ miles, or 12.566371 square miles. The total area of distance band one is equal to πr^2, where $r = 1$ mile, or 3.1415927 square miles. Thus, the marginal area of distance band two is equal to 12.566371 − 3.1415927, or 9.424778 square miles. We then proceed to calculate the marginal area for each of the seven distance bands.

---

4   By definition, the marginal area of distance band one is simply πr^2 because that distance band does not subsume any distance band before it.

Then, to obtain the expected number of burglaries within each distance band, we calculate the following equation:

$$\frac{(112 * M_i)}{153.938}$$

where 112 is the total number of burglaries, 153.938 square miles is equal to the total area covered by the seven distance bands, and M_i is equal to the marginal distance band. This is performed seven times, once for each distance band. So, to arrive at the expected number of burglaries for the first distance band, we take the total number of burglaries (112) and multiply it by the marginal area for the first band (3.1415927) and then divide that product by the total area (153.938). This gives us 2.2857149 expected crimes for the first distance band. To obtain the expected number of crimes for the second distance band, we take the total number of burglaries (112) and multiply it by the marginal area for the second band (9.424778) and then divide that product by the total area (153.938). This gives us 6.38571446 expected crimes in the second distance band. This procedure is then completed for all seven distance bands.

In Table 10.3, we present the observed crimes and the expected crimes from the πr^2 argument. Two things should be apparent from Table 10.3. First, both the observed and expected number of crimes sum to 112. Second, the expected number of crimes increases with increasing distance. This is to be expected because as the distance increases, larger and larger areas are included (Turner 1969: 14), and as a result, more offenses are to be expected.

The null hypothesis behind the πr^2 argument is that distance does not matter or, conversely, that crimes do not vary because of distance decay. What this argument says is that with a uniform distribution of crimes (as modeled in Van Koppen and

Table 10.3   Observed and Expected Burglaries for Nonsimulated Data

Distance Band (Miles)	Observed Burglaries	Expected Burglaries
0–1.0	51	2.2857149
1.01–2.0	25	6.8571446
2.01–3.0	17	11.4285740
3.01–4.0	9	16.0000040
4.01–5.0	7	20.5714340
5.01–6.0	2	25.1428640
6.01–7.0	1	29.7142900
	112	112.0000255

Note: $\chi^2 = 1,150.0077$, d.f. = 6.

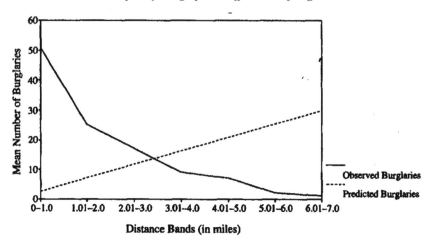

Figure 10.3   Observed vs. predicted burglaries

De Keijser), crimes are expected to vary with area. A test of whether the observed and expected distribution are equal to one another rejects the null hypothesis ($\chi^2 = 1,150.0077$, d.f. = 6).[5] By rejecting the null hypothesis, this result suggests that distance does matter and that burglaries in our sample are not committed at a uniform distribution. Thus, burglaries do vary because of distance decay. We also present a graphical comparison between observed and expected burglaries for the nonsimulated burglars in Figure 10.3.

Geographic Profiling

Van Koppen and De Keijser also do not accurately represent Rossmo's (1995) concept of *geographic profiling*. They mistakenly confuse the concept of *buffered distance decay* with that of *distance decay*. For example, a criminal may commit more crimes at a greater distance from home than closer and one can still predict the probable location of the home of the criminal. There is a directional component to geographic profiling determined by the spatial distribution of offenses that is absent in distance decay functions. Geographic profiling contains the implicit assumption of the frictional effect of distance but not linear distance decay. The two concepts are not equivalent. To understand the difference, one must understand the distinction between the concepts of *spatial behavior* and *behavior in space* (Rengert 1989a). Those who investigate the first concept attempt to identify overriding laws that govern human behavior, such as distance decay or the gravity model. Other researchers

---

5   The degrees of freedom are equal to the number of cells –1. Since there are 7 distance bands, d.f. = 7 – 1, or 6.

recognize that individuals do not operate on an isotropic plane, and thus, they search for social, environmental, and physiological constraints that confound the isotropic plane at the individual level (Hagerstrand,1967). These researchers study behavior in space, space that is not uniform in all directions and at all distances. Therefore, it is not uncommon to find individual criminals who commit more crimes farther from home than closer.

Rengert (1996), for example, modeled the point pattern of offenses of residential burglars. He identified four patterns: (1) bull's eye centered on the home; (2) bimodal centered on the home and a second anchor point; (3) teardrop, that is, the offenses occurred between the home and a second anchor point; and (4) bull's eye centered on an anchor point other than the home. In only one of these patterns would one expect to find linear distance decay from the home at the individual level (bull's eye centered on the home). Yet, when the data are aggregated, one finds distance decay because more criminals choose crime sites closer to home than other criminals who choose crime sites farther away. In fact, Van Koppen and De Keijser (1997) modeled a distance-decay function at the individual level since they identified all criminals committing crimes near their homes and none who began the search process at a greater distance from home.

The Assumption of Random Target Selection

Our final critique concerns the assumption made by Van Koppen and De Keijser throughout their simulations that offenders randomly choose targets within a delimited range of operation. In other words, they adopt the assumption that "suitable targets are randomly distributed in space" (1997: 509). We are at a loss as to why they would impose such an assumption when a reading of the literature surrounding offender mobility and related ecological studies consistently shows that "target selection is far from random" (Gabor and Gottheil 1984: 271), especially for burglary (Wright and Decker 1994). Crime has never occurred randomly in time, space, or across demographic groups (Brantingham and Brantingham 1995: 129); rather, crime occurs in spatial patterns in certain locations (e.g., Sherman et al. 1989). Research shows that offenders are quite selective as to their targets (e.g., Rossmo 1995; Shover 1996; Wright and Decker 1994, 1997). For example, offenders tend to be sensitive to the presence of bystanders or guardians, surveillance levels, street lighting, perceived risk of capture, perceived gain associated with the offense, and so on (for excellent reviews see Gabor and Gottheil 1984; Newman 1973; Repetto 1974).

More specifically, a number of qualitative investigations into the decision-making process of offenders shows that they are sensitive to site selection factors. For example, in their study of burglars, Wright and Decker (1994: 77) found that most burglary targets did not appear to be "chosen randomly or on the spur of the moment." Further interviews revealed that certain offenders collected information such as the timing of police patrols, daily activities of neighbors, the presence of security precautions, and occupancy (Wright and Decker 1994: 79–96). Similar conclusions have been reached by other scholars. Shover (1996:161) for example, notes that burglars are more likely to burglarize multiunit dwellings without access to security, corner houses, structures surrounded by view-obstructing foliage, and unoccupied homes or suburban homes without burglar alarms.

Conclusion

At the outset, we pointed out how a variety of social science researchers, including criminologists, have been interested in studying criminal behavior over space and one of its outcomes-distance decay. Throughout this discussion, we also pointed to examples of how the spatial study of criminal behavior is related to a variety of criminological theories. Then we moved into a review of recent research by Van Koppen and De Keijser that reexamined the idea of distance decay. We raised four concerns with the analytical strategy presented by Van Koppen and De Keijser: their interpretation and characterization of the ecological fallacy, their modeling of distance decay in a linear fashion, their misunderstanding of geographic profiling, and their assumption of random target selection. We then showed how their theoretical and empirical analyses were limited through the used of both simulated and nonsimulated data.

Looking back on this work and other recent forays into the spatial study of criminal behavior, the integration of geographic concepts within criminology is a recent advance and has, for the most part, been welcomed by criminologists. At the same time, researchers must remain aware of the assumptions and complexities involved in the modeling of offending behavior at both the aggregate and individual levels. Science moves forward by researchers continually pushing the envelope. However, sometimes researchers need to take a step back in order to move forward. In the present case, we suggest that it may be time to step back and reconsider the meaning of distance decay. In this regard, distance decay conclusions are dependent on identifying generalizations from aggregate data. Now that we have reestablished that distance decay exists in criminal behavior, the next step is to identify how distance-decay parameters vary between groups of offenders (i.e., ethnicity, gender, region) and what that says about their offending behavior. In the end, a much fuller understanding of criminal spatial behavior should emerge.

References

Alston, Jonathan D. (1994). The serial rapist's spatial pattern of target selection. Unpublished Master's Thesis, Simon Fraser University, Burnaby, Canada.

Angel, S. and G. Hyman (1972). Urban spatial interaction. *Environment and Planning* 4, 99–118.

Baldwin, John and Anthony E. Bottoms (1976). *The Urban Criminal: A Study in Sheffield*. London: Tavistock.

Brantingham, Patricia L. and Paul J. Brantingham (1995). Location quotients and crime hot spots in the city. In Carolyn Rebecca Block, Margaret Dabdoub, and Suzanne Fregly (eds), *Crime Analysis Through Computer Mapping*. Washington, D.C.: Police Executive Research Forum.

Brantingham, Paul J. and Patricia L. Brantingham (1984). *Environmental Criminology*. Prospect Heights, Ill.: Waveland Press.

Canter, David and Paul Larkin (1993). The environmental range of serial rapists. *Journal of Environmental Psychology* 13, 663–69.

Capone, Donald L. and Woodrow W. Nichols, Jr. (1975). Crime and distance: An analysis of offender behavior in space. *Proceedings of the Association of American Geographers*, 45–49.

—— (1976) Urban structure and criminal mobility. *American Behavioral Scientist* 20, 199–213.

Castanzo, C. Michael, William Halperin, and Nathan Gale (1986). Criminal mobility and the directional component in the journey to crime. In Robert Figlio, Simon Hakim, and George Rengert (eds), *Metropolitan Crime Patterns*. Monsey, N.Y.: Criminal Justice Press.

Cohen, Lawrence and Marcus Felson (1979). Social change and crime rate trends: A routine activity approach. *American Sociological Review* 44, 588–608.

Cornish, Derek and Ronald Clarke (1986). *The Reasoning Criminal: Rational Choice Perspectives on Offending*. New York: Springer-Verlag.

Gabor, Thomas and Ellen Gotiheil. (1984). Offender characteristics and spatial mobility: An empirical study and some policy implications. *Canadian Journal of Criminology* 26, 267–281.

Gottfredson, Michael and Travis Hirschi (1990). *A General Theory of Crime*. Stanford, Calif.: Stanford University Press.

Hagerstrand, Thorsten (1967). *Innovation Diffusion as a Spatial Process*, trans. Alan Pred. Chicago: University of Chicago Press.

Hawley, Amos (1950). *Human Ecology*. New York: Ronald Press.

Haynes, Kingsley and A. Stewart Fotheringham (1984). *Gravity and Spatial Interaction Models*. Beverly Hills, Calif.: Sage.

Jackle, John A., Stanley Brunn, and Curtis C. Roseman (1976). *Human Spatial Behavior: A Social Geography*. Prospect Heights, Ill.: Waveland Press.

Lentz, Ralph (1986). Geographic and temporal changes among robberies in Milwaukee. In Robert Figlio, Simon Hakim, and George Rengert (eds), *Metropolitan Crime Patterns*. Mousey, N.Y.: Criminal Justice Press.

Massey, Douglas and Nancy A. Denton (1993). *American Apartheid: Segregation and the Making of the Underclass*. Cambridge, Mass.: Harvard University Press.

Newman, Oscar (1973). *Defensible Space*. New York: Collier.

Pettiway, Leon (1982). The mobility of robbery and burglary offenders: Ghetto and non-ghetto spaces. *Urban Affairs Quarterly* 18(2), 255–270.

Phillips, Phillip D. (1980). Characteristics and typology of the journey to crime. In Daniel E. Georges-Abeyie and Keith D. Harries (eds), *Crime: A Spatial Perspective*. New York: Columbia University Press.

Rengert, George (1989a). Behavioral geography and criminal behavior. In David Evans and David Herbert (eds), *The Geography of Crime*. New York: Routledge.

—— (1989b). Spatial justice and criminal victimizations. *Justice Quarterly* 6(4), 543–564.

—— (1996). *The Geography of Illegal Drugs*. Boulder, Colo.: Westview Press.

Rengert, George and John Wasilchick

—— (1985). *Suburban Burglary: A Time and a Place for Everything*. Springfield, Ill.: Charles Thomas.

—— (1989). *Space, Time, and Crime: Ethnographic Insights into Residential Burglary*. Final Report submitted to the National Institute of Justice, Washington, D.C.

Repetto, Thomas (1974). *Residential Crime*. Cambridge, Mass.: Ballinger.

Rhodes, William M. and Catherine Conly (1981). Crime and mobility: An empirical study. In Paul J. Brantingham and Patricia L. Brantingham (eds), *Environmental Criminology*. Beverly Hills, Calif.: Sage.

Robinson, W. S. (1950). Ecological correlations and the behavior of individuals. *American Sociological Review* 15, 351–57.

Rossmo, D. Kim (1993). *Multivariate Spatial Profiles as a Tool in Crime Investigation*. Chicago: Workshop on Crime Analysis Through Computer Mapping.

—— (1995). Overview: Multivariate spatial profiles as a tool in crime investigation. In Carolyn Rebecca Block, Margaret Dabdoub, and Suzanne Fregly (eds), *Crime Analysis Through Computer Mapping*. Washington, D.C.: Police Executive Research Forum.

Sherman, Lawrence, Patrick Gartin, and Michael Buerger (1989). Hot spots of predatory crime: Routine activities and the criminology of place. *Criminology* 27, 27–55.

Shover, Neal (1996). *Great Pretenders: Pursuits and Careers of Persistent Thieves*. Boulder, Colo.: Westview. Sutherland, Edwin

—— (1947). *Principles of Criminology*. Philadelphia: Lippincott.

Taylor, Peter (1975). *Distance Decay in Spatial Interactions*. London: Institute of British Geographers.

Turner, Simon (1969). Delinquency and distance. In Thorsten Sellin and Marvin E. Wolfgang (eds), *Delinquency: Selected Studies*. New York: Wiley.

Van Koppen, Peter J. and Jan W. De Keijser (1997). Desisting distance decay: On the aggregation of individual crime trips. *Criminology* 35(3), 505–515.

Warren, Janet, Roland Reboussin, and Roy Hazelwood (1995). *The Geographic and Temporal Sequencing of Serial Rape*. Final Report Submitted to U.S. Department of Justice, National Institute of Justice, Office of Justice Programs, Washington, D.C.

White, R. Clyde (1932). The relation of felonies to environmental factors in Indianapolis. *Social Forces* 498–509.

Wilson, William Julius (1987). The Truly Disadvantaged. Chicago: University of Chicago Press.

—— (1996). *When Work Disappears*. New York: Albert A. Knopf

Wright, Richard and Scott Decker (1994). *Burglars on the Job: Streetlife and Residential Breakins*. Boston: Northeastern University Press.

—— (1997). *Armed Robbers in Action: Stickups and Street Culture*. Boston: Northeastern University Press.

PART 3
Key Concepts in Geographical Offender Profiling

Chapter 11

Geographical Profiling of Criminals*

David Canter

The President: Ladies and gentlemen, this evening we are honoured to have Professor David Canter with us, who has come from Liverpool. He is the Professor of Psychology at the University of Liverpool, and has been for almost the last 10 years, not quite 10 years. He has a long and varied CV. He is a Fellow of the British Psychological Society and the American Psychological Association and a member of the Forensic Science Society. He has a PhD from Liverpool and is a Chartered Forensic Psychologist and is one of the first psychologists to be elected as an Academician to the Academy of Social Sciences. He is interested in a number of things, but he provided expert evidence in the case of prisoners, for example, in the Risley Remand Centre charged with riot, that their actions were an understandable response to the environment and the regime. I am not quite sure what he is talking to us about tonight. His recreations are listed as *clarinet and musical composition*. We are honoured to have Professor David Canter to speak to us this evening. (Applause.)

    Professor Canter: What I quite unashamedly decided to do this evening was to talk through the theme of my new book *Mapping Murder*, which is available in all good book shops. (Laughter) When I was asked to give this talk about a year ago it was really quite fortunate that it coincided with the recent publication of the book, so I thought I would talk through the issues that are dealt with in the book, which grow out of the work I have done as a psychologist working with the police and then, moving on beyond that work, to carry out research work that is of relevance to police investigation.

    I realise this is a very august gathering, though a rather difficult one for a psychologist to speak to, with doctors, who will tend to regard psychology as a footnote to their discipline, and lawyers, who will regard psychology as probably what they do anyway, and neither of them will be particularly familiar with the concept and techniques of the science of Psychology. So the presentation I have here is the one I gave to some sixth form students just a while ago, and hopefully that will cover ground that will be of interest to you. I came into crime rather late

*The Medico-Legal Society
A meeting of the Society was held at the Royal Society of Medicine, 1 Wimpole Street, London W1, on Thursday, 13 November 2003. The President, Miss Eleanor F Platt QC, was in the Chair.

in life, having been really an applied psychologist working in a variety of different areas of the application of psychology, including into the study of how the physical environment has relevance to people. I started off in a school of architecture as a psychologist lecturing to architects, and that was how I got caught up in looking at the design of the Risley Remand Centre and at the riot that happened there, just in case you were curious about that connection. It is quite an involved story as to how I got caught up in crime and you really have to read my first popular book *Criminal Shadows* to get the full story there, because what I thought I would talk about today is the development since that early work, really in the mid 80s, when I first became involved with police work, and since that time I have been involved in a number of police investigations trying to contribute in various ways to those investigations, but, as I say, really moving beyond that out into research matters.

It is worth starting with how this unfolded historically. In the mid 80s there were a series of murders around London and a series of rapes that the police linked together to a common offender and, by some curious roundabout route, the police asked me to give some comments on that. I will talk a little bit about that investigation, but it was really as a result of that that I then was given access to data that the police hold and was able to start doing some proper research on it, because the police are quite remarkable in that they won't give you access to any information unless they think it is going to be of some use to them, and as a scientist it is terribly difficult to be of any use unless you have some information to work with, and so there was a bit of a *pulling yourself up by your bootstraps*. I had to help as best I could in that early investigation working from first principles without being able to test the veracity of those principles in the particular context of violent crime.

The police became very enamoured at the result, as shown by the sort of Press cuttings in Figure 11.1. These were a product of the police selling the idea that psychologists were now contributing to police investigations and that here they were

Figure 11.1   Success Brought Police Support and Access to Data

at the cutting edge of the use of new scientific procedures. This recognition of the potential helped to open doors that allowed us to start doing proper research. This early case really opened up a particular way of thinking about criminal activity that then turned out to be very productive.

Figure 11.2 is a map of London. Each of the points is a location where crimes had been committed, mainly rape, over a four-year period. This is typically what the police would have, a record of where the crimes had occurred, for operational purposes to give them some basis for starting to decide where they were going to deploy officers and how they were going to carry out their investigations.

I was asked if I could help. I still remember very clearly the day when I went to where a number of senior police officers were meeting at Hendon, the training college for the police, and being asked "Can you help us catch this man before he kills again?". The full details of how my response to this unfolded are given in my book *Criminal Shadows*. But, in essence, I started by exploring how the crimes unfolded over time as indicated in Figure 11.3.

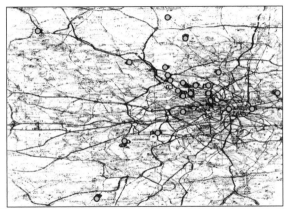

**Figure 11.2   The series of rapes and murders carried out across London 1982–
1986**

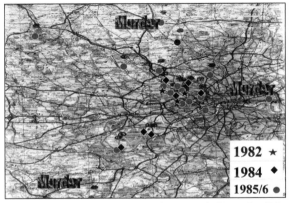

Figure 11.3   The series of rapes and murders carried out by John Duffy

As an environmental psychologist, interested in how people make sense of their surroundings, it seemed to me that there was likely to be some sort of process involved there, and this is what we found: in 1982 a series of rapes had happened in one limited area, in 1984 there had been a few more in a broader area, in 1985/86 there had been some more spreading out even wider as can be seen in Figure 11.3. There was no indication of anything happening in '83 that could be tied into these cases. Then there were three murders that happened really further away. It seemed just painfully obvious that there was some development in this process, with the murders occurring round the edge and, as can be seen, the movement out from the area of the earliest crimes. When we looked at the details of the behaviour there also seemed to be a psychological development.

The early crimes seem to have been committed by two individuals, tended to be at the weekend, one of the individuals even seemed to be a bit remorseful and on occasion apologised to the victims that they had raped. The later crimes tended to be during the week, tended to be by an individual alone, were much more determined, much more planned. This indicated the possibility of a developing commitment to a criminal life, and related criminal activity. That psychological development seemed to be reflected in the growing geography of the crimes. Therefore it seemed very likely that what we should be thinking of is the early stages of the crimes being in a sense more amateur, almost sort of 'recreational', if you can describe rape in that way, and less committed, less determined, less part of a convinced career than in the later part. If that were the case then if we ran the crimes backwards we would actually be able to end up with the idea of the area circumscribed by the initial three 1982 crimes being where the individuals started from. Within that area, I thought, perhaps they were less likely to be thinking through what they were doing, acting as part of their day-to-day activities. I thus suggested to the police that they were looking for individuals who might be based in the Kilburn area of North West London in 1982.

I also made some other comments, like the fact that this individual, particularly who had raped and murdered young women, probably had a history of being violent against women and was quite a nasty character and would be known to be so. This turned out to be important in the sense that one of their suspects was in the police records and being looked at only, as far as they were concerned, because he had violently attacked his estranged wife at knifepoint and raped her. It was this that had brought him onto the list of suspects but at that stage some police officers considered this to be 'just' a domestic; they thought it was a tussle between a married couple and they couldn't see this individual going off to commit a series of rapes and murders. Consequently, the comment that the individual they would be looking for would actually have some history of that type of dealing with women was something I helped to emphasise.

There were a variety of other issues I mentioned to the police but the most significant one was the suggestion that the individual lived in a limited, identifiable area of London. It turned out that of all the possible suspects they were considering – and there were really only half a dozen that they had very serious consideration of

– only one of them lived in the proposed area. So, they were then able to put their surveillance resources on to that individual, John Duffy, and that gave them the information of where he was moving around, how he was watching and following women. He was seen in the areas where crimes had been committed. When they arrested him they found some very strong forensic evidence that led to a conviction. Duffy had indeed lived at the centre of the area marked out by the three rapes committed in 1982 at the time of those rapes.

What is interesting is that there are two photographs available of Duffy from around the time of these offences. As you can see in Figure 11.4, in terms of witness statements and descriptions of an offender, you would have really quite different descriptions potentially from different victims. So that there is a sense in which the geographical or spatial information is more indicative and more reliable in this particular case than maybe the sightings and the descriptions by witnesses, which is the normal source of what the police deal with. So it is quite an important and interesting example of the way in which trying to get to grips with the geography of the crimes is giving us some indication of what the characteristics of the individuals are. This has become an important theme, in exploring indicators of criminal behaviour, trying to make more sense of these geographical processes. My new book *Mapping Murder* explores those ideas in a number of different ways.

Now one of the things about this type of research is that it is potentially very frustrating. You generate some hypotheses, have some ideas about the criminal and what their characteristics are and you have to wait for the police to catch somebody to see whether you may be correct, and then they have to go through the legal process, and even then some people may get it wrong along the way, before you have got any real indication as to whether your own explorations may be appropriate.

It was therefore very exciting to learn that fourteen years after his conviction Duffy was willing to talk about the crimes and indeed to indicate who had been

Figure 11.4   John Duffy – the Railway Killer

committing the earlier rapes with him. He claimed that David Mulcahy had been involved in the murders as well as the rapes. This came to court a couple of years ago. That then gave us the opportunity, in Duffy's account, to see whether or not we had been correct in making these inferences from the geographical and spatial pattern about the individual's behaviour. What Duffy actually said in court could have been taken from the speculation in my book *Criminal Shadows*, but I don't think he had read it (there is always a bit of a risk that offenders play back to you what they think you want to hear). He said "To begin with It was in areas we knew well. We would plan it quite meticulously. We would have balaclavas and knives. We used to call it hunting. We did it as a bit of a joke, a bit of a game. It added to the excitement". And then he went on to say "You get into the pattern of offending – it is very difficult to stop". So he is describing the developing process that we had inferred from the geographical pattern.

What is also interesting is that these crimes were referred to as the crimes of "the railway rapist", because it was noticed that a number of the crimes occurred near railways stations and it was assumed that the offenders were travelling by train and that they had a very detailed knowledge of the railway system. In court Duffy described a situation whereby they had worked out that young women on their own tended to come out of railway stations at certain times of the evening and that therefore going to railway stations would give them that opportunity for finding these victims. But they were actually driving around to do this; they weren't travelling by train at all. This just shows how important it is from our point of view, from a psychological point of view, to try and get a more detailed understanding of what these processes are that underlie the actions and patterns of behaviour and how they are shaped by the experience of the individual. We cannot only consider the geometry of what is going on.

The publishers of my book *Mapping Murder* assigned the sub-title *The Secrets of Geographical Profile*. I am not sure that was such a good idea. It implies that there is some sort of clever geometry or mathematics, to me anyway, seeing that on the cover. So in an early chapter I made clear that the secret of geographical profiling is to go behind the dots on the map and to try and understand the psychological processes involved. This follows a general view I have that where people go to do all sorts of things does tell us something about their lives and their relationships to others. For criminals where they choose to commit their crimes does tell us something about the personal narratives that they are developing.

What I am describing grew out of the process that is known as 'profiling', and so in a general introduction to these ideas I am very concerned to get across that what we are talking about are the very early days of a rather complex discipline, in which there are certainly not very many hard and fast rules. The media tends to create the image of the 'profiler' as some sort of super hero, some sort of sleuth figure that has great insight that goes beyond the everyday and that every crime the hero tackles is a success.

So I think it is quite useful to mention one example of a case in Alaska, where the murders of five females were linked together to the actions of one unknown serial killer. The FBI, who claimed to have developed the whole procedure of profiling, came up with the opinion that the individual was single, around 40 years old and not in the armed services. The actual individual, a chap called Bunday, was married with two children, 34 years old and an Air Force instructor. (Laughter) What is important about this is that it slowed down the investigations, because originally this guy was excluded from the computer searches due to this profile being available.

A very similar thing happened in the Washington sniper case, where people, for totally bizarre reasons with absolutely no scientific basis, were quoted in the press as saying that the individuals involved in the sniping were likely to be Caucasian, were not black, were not from ethnic minorities and that it was likely to be one offender on his own. It turned out to be two people, one black and one from an ethnic minority group. They had been stopped a number of times but had not been looked at very closely because they didn't fit this 'profile' that was offered up.

Really what I am trying to get to is that there is a whole ethos, a whole literature, a whole quasi-fictional account of profiling that suggests that there is a lot of expertise, there is a lot of knowledge out there that can be drawn on very readily. The police, in desperation, in many countries, will draw upon whoever is prepared to offer up an opinion without really evaluating the basis of that opinion is. Since the Duffy case I have become increasingly aware of how much general chatter is around, without any real foundation, and the need to develop a proper scientific discipline that can be the basis of contributing to police investigations.

One way of developing the science is to explore the internal representations that offenders have of their surroundings; trying to see how where they go and where they choose to operate is influenced by their knowledge and their understanding of their locality. One way of doing this is to explore what psychologists have called their mental maps. It is not a terribly good term mental maps, it is misleading in a number of ways, but essentially what you do – and I will show you somebody doing this in a minute – what you do is you ask an offender to draw a sketch map of where they commit their crimes and to indicate on it where the crimes occurred and where they were living at the time.

Figure 11.5 is such a mental map drawn by a burglar. The crosses are where he committed his burglaries – as you see, he is a busy chap – where he lived is marked a 'home' towards the middle of the right side of the area. You can see a number of interesting things begin to emerge about his mental representation in this sketch map. For instance, there are very clear boundaries; although there is a canal clearly indicated to the right running down the map, there is nothing indicated on the other side of this canal from his home. The canal acts as a sort of mental barrier that he doesn't go beyond. He is quite happy to commit crimes near the police station, but going past and coming back is problematic for him. (Laughter) Another outer limit is the DHSS, where he gets his Giro, and clearly he steps out of his familiar area to the bottom once he gets to the roundabout, which seems to act as another boundary

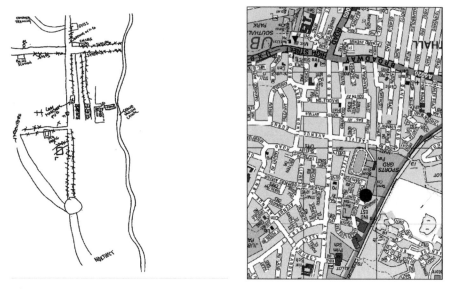

Figure 11.5   Comparison of actual and "mental" map

point. Besides the clear boundaries is the very interesting issue of the way in which the whole areas is shaped by where he had his base, where his home was.

In Figure 11.5 is also the actual map of that area. The comparison of the 'mental map' with the actual map shows a lot of processes that we find in all mental maps, as I discussed in my book many years ago *The Psychology of Place*. For instance, we tend to simplify our ideas of crossroads as simple right angles when in fact they are usually much more complicated than that. The gap to the right above his home makes sense because it is a sports ground and there aren't any houses there. For him it does not have any presence. Further the comparison of the two maps shows how his understanding is very much structured by the dominant road that operates through the middle of the area. So, he has shaped his crimes around what he knows and around that development of the understanding that gives him of what the opportunities for crime are. That understanding is very strongly influenced by where he has his base; where his home is.

Perhaps we can look at the video, and you will see, as we call him, *Bob the Burglar*, not his real name, going through this process.

(The video was then played)

It is a very interesting interview, not least for hearing the term *swag* used without any sense of irony. (Laughter.)

Of the many matters that the interview illustrates, for our purposes here there are just two points I would draw attention to within that interview. One is that this is an individual who claims he had a very disorganised lifestyle; he was on drugs and moving around. Yet the logic of where he went was still very powerful; he was still very rational. This is one of the points that comes through our research over and over again. What the person is doing may be bizarre in all sorts of ways and the reasons for them doing their crimes, whether it is rape or murder, or burglary or arson, these reasons may be actually very difficult to fathom and may be very complex, but the processes that they are going through still have a very strong logic to them. They are still trying to avoid detection and they are still trying to achieve their criminal objective as effectively as they can. Consequently there is likely to be a pattern to these activities that we can make sense of, if we can understand that logic.

The second point I would draw your attention to is, as I have already mentioned earlier, the significance of the home, the fact that the individual is moving out from where they have that base in order to carry out the activities in locations that are open to them and where they know those crimes are possible. This gives us the basis for starting to develop more involved models of location choice that can be very interesting and indeed very directly helpful to police investigation.

The idea is a very simple one. Just to get the model started, we assume the individual has some sort of base. In fact, if you are a vagrant and moving around it is actually quite difficult to continue a criminal career without either being picked up or really without making yourself vulnerable to detection in a variety of ways. So we find that many of the offenders we are dealing with do have some sort of base. If they have that base, and if the opportunities for crime are evenly distributed around that base, then they are going to move to a location for the first time that is likely to be a distance away from their base that is comfortable, is convenient for them. This location, as Bob mentioned will not be too close to their base with the risk that they may draw attention to themselves when people are looking for who committed the crime, or where they may be recognised. However, they will also not want their crime location to be so far away that they are moving into some sort of alien territory and they don't know where they are or they may have difficulty getting back. Having been to a location for a crime, that area is now potentially one in which they are vulnerable. But the same processes in terms of distance are likely to operate in other directions, so they'll move on in other directions to carry out their crimes. Now that new area is one where they may be recognised and where they may be more at risk, so they will then move on in other directions. These simple ideas lead to the build-up of a pattern of crimes, of individuals moving out from a base as illustrated in Figure 11.6. We have given a name to this pattern of 'marauder'. It is quite intriguing what potential this pattern has.

Figure 11.7 is a map that were sent to me by a colleague from New Zealand. It shows the locations where a man was seen prowling. Where is that individual likely to be based; where are they likely to be living? From my previous argument I would suggest that one possibility is that the offender is living within the areas circumscribed by the crimes, possibly quite central to that area. The easiest way of being precise about the area and location is to take the two crimes furthest from each other and to draw a circle with those two crimes as the ends of the diameter. The hypothesis is that the offender is based near the centre of that diameter, at the centre

'MARAUDERS'

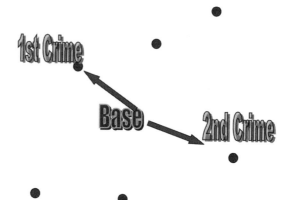

Figure 11.6   Modelling offence location choice

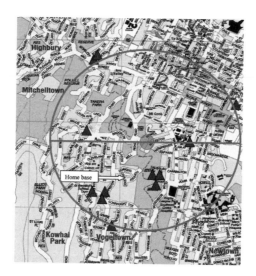

Figure 11.7   A marauding prowler – the Circle Hypothesis as a predictor of home location

of the circle. This circle is drawn on the sightings in New Zealand in Figure 11.7. The offender's home is also indicated and as can be seen it is remarkably close to that central point. This is just one example of many crime series we have explored. As we have shown in published papers, although this result certainly does not occur in all cases it is remarkable how often it does. In burglaries we find it applies in around half of crime series, but for more violent crimes like serial rape and serial murder it seems to be apply to as many as three-quarters of crime series.

This simple idea gives us the starting point for developing more mathematical models about offenders' crime location selections, admittedly based on a number of assumptions, as I have outlined, but at least giving us a starting framework that we can test out in a variety of contexts.

Having become aware of the surprising prevalence of these geo-behavioural patterns I began to look into a broader literature on the study of people's movement around an area. I was delighted to discover that there is quite a long history, going back to the 1850s, of looking at patterns of human behaviour and seeing how the geography of those actions reveals some interesting and useable structures.

I am sure in this august setting you are all familiar with the work of John Snow, the father of modern epidemiology? But, for those of you who can't remember his seminal work, there was a cholera outbreak in the Soho area of London, and in those days there was still a debate, I am told, about whether cholera was airborne or waterborne. Snow's argument was that it was likely to be waterborne and therefore the pumps from the wells that were used to get water were likely to be the main source of the cholera. To test this idea he did something very elegant and precise. He marked on a map where the cholera cases had occurred and also marking on the map where the various wells were. This showed very clearly that the majority of the cases occur around only one particular well. The story is told that he went to the well and took the handle off the pump over the well so that it could not be used and the cholera epidemic then subsided.

This shows a process parallel to that I have been describing for criminals, whereby people, minimising their effort, will go to the nearest pump. The cumulative effect of this is to mark out the pump that is the source of the disease. There are some rather nice analogies between a criminal moving out and spreading his particular sort of criminal contagion, by similar analogous processes, to the way cholera operates, and on the basis of this we have been able to start developing a research tool that helps us to study patterns of crimes and to draw out interesting results that are also of value for police investigations.

The idea behind our research tool, which I have called Dragnet after the old movie series, can be seen in Figure 11.8. Here we have a series of crimes, five crimes in this particular instance. What we are trying to do is to see each crime as a source of some process that relates to where the offender is living. Therefore around each crime there is what might be considered a kind of force field. Indeed the mathematics of gravitational fields are very applicable here. As you get further away from any crime then the chances of the offender living there are reduced. By overlapping

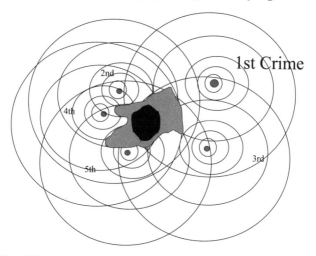

Figure 11.8   Offence map – developing the search tool

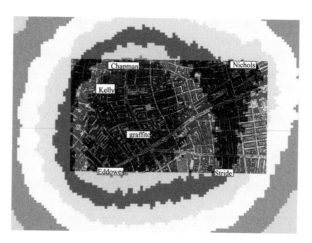

Figure 11.9   Dragnet analysis of five murder locations and graffito

the fields you get a distribution of probabilities. This gives a more detailed way of calculating where the offender may be based.

To illustrate the application of a Dragnet analysis the five crimes in Figure 11.8 are located in relation to each other as are the crimes of Jack the Ripper in the Whitechapel of 1888. Figure 11.9 gives the names of the victims at each location for the five victims that most people agree are likely to have been murdered by the same man. I have superimposed on that map the Dragnet analysis showing the highest probability areas for the base of Jack the Ripper. This points to an area, not too far from Liverpool Street Railway Station, to the West of Whitechapel. Well, it is an intriguing analysis. It shows you how you can use these ideas with existing material.

Of course, we don't know who Jack the Ripper is, but a quite fascinating document emerged that I rather like, because it is apparently written by a Liverpool cotton merchant. The document, often referred to as *The Diary of Jack the Ripper*, purports, in effect, to be the confession of the Whitechapel murderer, written by James Maybrick, who bought and sold cotton in Liverpool. (I rather like the idea that the first serial criminal in modern history is a Scouser, especially as Liverpool has now been designated the European Capital of culture for 2008!).

There would need to be a whole, rather involved lecture around James Maybrick, and the diary that has been published. But in summary, what happened was that about ten years ago a document emerged that professed to be the diary written by James Maybrick. It described his activities as Jack the Ripper recounting the various crimes that he committed and what he got out of them and why he was doing it. This 'diary' raises many fascinating issues and I can happily answer questions about it later. But for the moment there is an interesting challenge to what I have been suggesting to you in the whole existence of that diary.

James Maybrick was a Liverpool cotton merchant who lived 200 miles away from Whitechapel. Yet my analysis of the five Whitechapel crimes suggests that this individual was likely to have a base in Whitechapel. What is intriguing about the diary – it is a curious document, it is more or less a rather rambling journal that mixes attempts at doggerel with comments on how cold his hands are with details of the murders, but what is intriguing about it is that it says briefly in it "I took some rooms in Middlesex Street". It is the only reference in the diary to any specific location in the Whitechapel area, and, would you believe it, Middlesex Street is exactly in that area of Whitechapel that I mentioned, as shown in Figure 11.9 . So it is intriguing that the diary quote fits our Dragnet analysis

It is one example of a case that will go on forever. One example no more makes a science than a swallow does a Summer, but it provides a taste of what may be possible and is an interesting illustration and raises some significant questions, but really the important thing is to begin to develop the approach further testing it on many other examples, which is what we have been doing, giving rise to many publications in various journals.

However, let me show you one more example of the application of this approach to illustrate further its potential. This is an interesting illustration is in relation to a series of bombs that were left around London in banks and supermarkets about six years ago as part of an extortion campaign. These 'bombs' were homemade devices in video cassette cases and he put on the cases "The Mardi Gra Experience", (annoying misspelling Gras which really confuses spell-checkers). This criminal became known as *The Mardi Gras Bomber*. These devices were left around London in the locations indicated in Figure 11.10, which has the Dragnet analysis superimposed. The locations were the devices were left are spread London. But it is clear that there is a cluster in the Western area of London and another in the Eastern area. In other

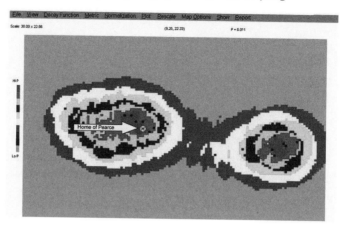

Figure 11.10   The Mardi Gra Bomber – Location of the Bomber's Home

words, the dragnet analysis, intriguingly, draws attention to two foci of activity. I wasn't involved in this investigation, but the police did use something very similar to this. What they were able to do was to hypothesise that the area to the West was the dominant one for this individual and, and to identify a core of that area where he was drawing his extorted funds from ATM machines. The police were therefore able to put surveillance on credit card machines in that area of the West of London. This paid off because they were able to spot him using a machine and thereby arrest him. So it was helpful in narrowing down the area of attention for the police. It turned out that the man, Edgar Pierce, lived very close to the location indicated in the Dragnet plot. The intriguing thing, of course, is the other focus of his activity in the East of London. Well, it transpired that his ex-wife lived in that area and he used to visit her on occasions and sometimes prepare his bombs there. So there were two bases that he was operating from as indicated in the geo-behavioural analysis.

We are beginning to develop out of this is an exploration of the variety of strategies that offenders use and how these can be modelled in various ways. Some of them we know don't move out from a base in the same way that the marauders do. They move out to an area where they know crimes are possible and then back again, and we have used the term *commuters* to describe these individuals. More recently in *Mapping Murder* I prefer to refer to them simply as 'travellers' because there are many strategies involved, not just that of travelling from home to a crime area and back again as implied in the 'commuting' analogy. The residential location of these travellers is much more difficult to pinpoint. You can't use the sort of Dragnet modelling that I have been talking about to identify the base of these individuals.

This therefore raises the question of what proportion of offenders operate in these different ways. I know it is getting a bit late to show you graphs and charts and I realise there are members of the legal profession here who, from my experience, break out into a cold sweat if you give them a percentage, unless it's a fee for them

Commuters

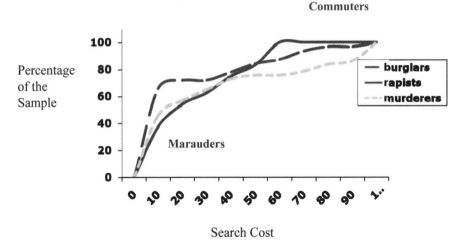

Search Cost

Figure 11.11 Cumulative search cost functions for a sample of serial burglars (n=32), rapists (n=24) and murderers produced using decay function with β value 1.0

– no, that's not fair, a cheap joke. But I just want to show you some science behind this, and there are actually some interesting analyses that emerge.

What we have in Figure 11.11 – which is derived from work carried out by one of my graduate students, Brent Snook – is the proportion of the Dragnet area that has to be searched before you find the individual. We have three samples here, serial burglars, rapists and killers. Interestingly enough, virtually all of these individuals seem to have a base within the overall Dragnet region, as shown by the fact that nearly 100% of the individuals in the sample are found within the whole Dragnet area. It took me a long time to figure out what was going on there, but it must mean that most serial criminals commit some crimes close to home. If the opportunity is there close to home they will commit the crime there. The graph therefore shows the proportion of the area that needs to be searched, in order to find the cumulative proportion of the sample who are resident in that area. Now, if this graph just crept up steadily I wouldn't be talking to you, because it would mean that there was nothing of note happening if criminals' residential locations were just spread out generally across the area available. But what you can see is an elbow in the graph, which means that quite a high proportion, 70% typically, of the offenders are within about 15 to 20% of the area defined by the analysis. Now I am always very struck by this. The same general shape is found for serial burglars, serial rapists and American serial murderers – you have to go to America to get enough serial murderers to actually do the analysis. You can see they all have broadly the same shape to them. To the bottom left of the graph are those individuals who are close to the highest probabilities for the Dragnet calculations, the 'marauders'. To the top right are those who are rather further from the added highest probabilities and therefore are more peripheral to the area surrounded by the crime locations. These are the 'commuters' and other travelling offenders.

Besides the practical value of such findings it strikes me that this does tell us something about criminals, that really in the end criminals are fundamentally lazy. They are seeking easy opportunities that are available to them within easy reach of the base from which they are operating, and although there are some who are travelling further and are much more spread out in terms of the area in which the operate, there is still quite a high proportion who are operating within their particular context.

The individuals who are travelling offenders operating over different sort of structures and routes from the marauders are the ones that we need to explore much further, and indeed one of the big research questions at the moment is whether there is anything we can tell from the pattern of the crimes which will allow us to know whether or not the offender is a commuter or a marauder. We are still exploring various possibilities of how we may be able to tell that, and part of that we are doing by exploring the strategies that different offenders use.

Figure 11.12, for instance, is a mental map drawn by a woman who used to do basically shoplifting to order, collected as part of Karen Shalev's studies. She would be given a list of things that her neighbours and associates wanted and then she would go off to a Marks and Spencer, or whatever else it was, to steal them. You can see it is a very, very different structure from what I showed you earlier. This is an individual for whom the route to where she could find the opportunities for crime is dominant. She is not really aware of any other possibilities other than where she can get to. She knows the security systems in different supermarkets and different department stores in the area. She knows where she may be recognised, and it is really getting to them and getting back which is the dominant issue, and so the route there becomes the dominant part of her way of thinking about it.

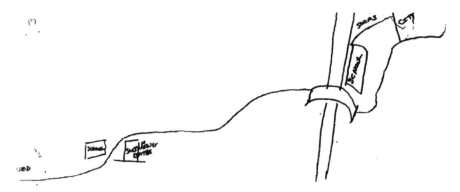

Figure 11.12 Shoplifter – targeted attack

Figure 11.13 is an individual where also his crimes are construed in terms of the journeys and the opportunities and the motorways that were available to him. He thinks of where he goes to commit crimes in terms of major motorway journeys. He has no 'mental map' in the sense of a knowledge of an area related to his crimes. He just has an idea of the dominant routes. Certainly his crimes will be shaped much more by route availability than where he is living.

Also there are individuals for whom the crimes do not have an objective in the same way. Figure 11.14 is a youngster whom I interviewed. This is what he drew when I asked him to draw where he committed his crimes. He used to steal cars and drive them away, and when asked to draw his mental map of the crimes, what he did was to draw himself in a car, with the skid marks, being chased by the police, very aware of the helicopter view with the car number on it. He just wrote on the sketch " many cars chasing all over most areas". It is really the excitement of the chase that is important to him, rather than the particular localities and routes that operate. Following on from this we are doing some research now looking much more closely at the emotions associated with different types of crime and what the actual emotional benefits are that criminals seem to be getting out of their crimes.

So you can see we have moved on quite a bit from the studies in the late 1980s, where the geography was the dominant process. We are now beginning to look at a variety of strategies that offenders use and trying to get much closer to the way in which these strategies really reflect an internal narrative and account that the offender has about what the nature of his life is, what the nature of their criminality is, and

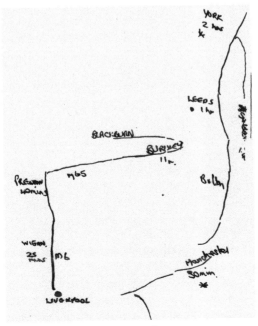

Figure 11.13 Raiding forays – prolific burglar

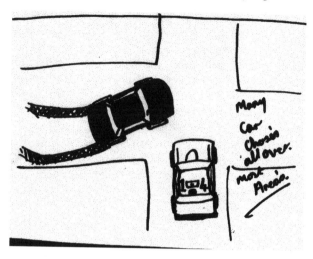

Figure 11.14 Spatial opportunity – joy rider

how that is shaped around the locations that they move to. We are considering the way in which the geographical journey reflects a psychological journey and reflects different modes of transacting with people in the criminal context. It is trying to read that process out of the map, as well as the patterns of behaviour that have been involved. That is opening up a whole new area of research, taking us a long, long way away from the early idea of profilers, who were really more concerned with trying to indicate some psychopathology that was producing the criminal activity, rather than trying to understand the logic that drives these crimes and makes it possible for offenders to get away with them for so long.

So I am happy to leave it there and to respond to questions. Thank you very much. (Applause)

Discussion

The President: Any questions. Who wants to put the first question? Could you give your name and your specialty.

Mr Straw: I am Robert Straw, a barrister. I was intrigued sort of watching, as this is developing, the areas you are looking at. With the sort of areas where it might be a homogenised, fairly standard sort of urban gridlocky town centre and somebody who is on foot, I can see how effectively it shows up your acquisitive burglar feeding a habit. I can see how this is "Well, yes, just draw the dot in the centre". Is there any way that you can take into account the topography of the area? Bearing in mind that if somebody is travelling by car, for instance, or a van or a truck, or is some sort of odd traditional sort of serial killing lorry driver, can you actually take that into account with the software you are doing, so effectively, because somebody goes there, one might say "Oh, that's totally off the graph. It might be somebody different. Perhaps he turned back there. That's a 10-minute journey and that thing was half a mile away from the 10-minute journey".

Professor Canter: That is precisely the development of our research activity. I think the misleading point would be to suggest that the software can do it all. For instance, one of the cases that I use in *Mapping Murder* that illustrates the issue very clearly is Robert Black, who travelled up and down the country abducting children and then leaving their bodies 80 to 100 miles away from where he had taken them. It turned out that there was nobody else who had ever travelled those sort of distances and disposed of the bodies so far away from where the child was first abducted. It is not hugely surprising that that individual had a job that took him round the country. You mentioned lorry drivers, but there is still the point that there is something that takes them round the country that the crimes follow, and it is very unusual to have individuals who actually shape their geography solely in relation to the opportunity for crime. Without flogging the book too much, there was a very interesting case in Belgium, *Detroux*, where very consciously and deliberately he would set out on a mission to abduct girls to sell on in various ways and was very deliberately going to the four corners of the country. He admitted as much. So what I am saying is that the scale of the operation and the way it is structured can tell us something about the individual, if we know how to read it. Also we know from studying, for instance, the difference between rural offenders and urban offenders that although the same sort of patterns occur, the scale of the patterns are different, and those graphs I showed with the elbows in them, what we are doing is looking at the proportion of the search area, we are not looking at the size of the area.

Mr Straw: Does that graph apply to an urban area/a rural area somewhere in the UK/somewhere in the US? Is that a common factor, that 60 to 70 per cent of people will only commit crime …

Professor Canter: There are not that many studies, but studies done in Australia have found that 60 to 70 per cent of rapists have a similar pattern and about 50 per cent of burglars, which is what we found in Britain. It would seem that there is always a proportion of offenders who operate close to home, and in fact when you start looking into the literature there are studies done in the Ps in Chicago that give the average distance that burglars are travelling from home as about a mile to a mile and a half. We have got data from Liverpool in the '0s that is very similar. So some of these processes are consistent, but I wouldn't want to give the impression that it is all very simple. There are lots of other things going on. You mentioned topography. Actually, when I submitted a paper exploring this I got my knuckles rapped and was told "In fact, it is land use you are talking about, not topography". That is clearly an important issue, and in fact this very afternoon I was discussing with somebody how we can get more of a grip on the different patterns of usage of areas and how that is going to influence where criminals travel, and clearly it does. That is certainly the direction the research is moving in.

Mr Samuels: Alec Samuels. One can understand that the criminal may not want to go too far from home and may want to be able to get back to his home, as it were. How far does he have any kind of intimate knowledge of the areas which he is going to in your kind of circular location? Does he know this area, or is it just simply proximity, rather than knowledge?

Professor Canter: Well, that is part of the issue that needs to be explored. There is also the issue and complicating factor, which is how recognisable he is. In other words, for instance, if you look at people knocking on doors and saying that they have come to read the meter and then stealing things, clearly they are very recognisable, because you can't do that with a balaclava on, so that they are going to be distributed rather differently from an individual who climbs into the back of the house, is never seen and climbs out again. So that does have an influence on that geometry, on those factors of activity. So there are those issues as well. The other thing that complicates matters is evolution over time. As I have hinted, that can be quite important, but it can operate in a number of different ways. Individuals may operate in a particular area and then move on to another area where they operate, so in both of those locations their base is important. But also one of the things that happens (and Duffy illustrates it remarkably well) is that as individuals begin to become more committed to certain sorts of crime their criminal activity takes over, and so they may start off burgling on the way to work or on the way to some sort of casual job or to a pub that they use, but once that becomes something that they feel they get some benefit from, they may then start wandering around an area and start looking out for opportunities. Certainly for serial rapists who attack strangers there is a lot of evidence that they will develop a knowledge of an area, in terms of what the opportunities are for committing that crime, so then they will very deliberately build up an understanding and quite clearly become much more sensitised to the opportunities. A somewhat frivolous example is if you are trying to post a letter you suddenly become aware of all the red objects in the area that may be post boxes. You become much more alert to where the post boxes are. Once you have posted the letter that then fades into the background, your attention is not drawn to that. Well, that is a very natural psychological process whereby our attention is focused in terms of our objectives, and quite clearly criminals become very alert to opportunities. There is quite a lot of research interviewing burglars about how they decide what house they are going to burgle, and they do become very alert to the cues that the house gives off about, for instance, whether it is occupied or not, or, as our man Bob said, areas where there is going to be something that they can steal, or they become alert to the fact that a place is run down and the individual living there may be old and vulnerable. So they become sensitive to those opportunities, and that may show their knowledge and familiarity, but it starts off from proximity. That is the start of it.

The President: Can I ask you, Professor – the examples you have given us have been about several crimes probably by the same individual – does any of your work assist in cases where there is only one crime?

Professor Canter: Well, the basic process is relevant to any crime, and the very interesting ...

The President: Well, you can't get the sort of round picture.

Professor Canter: But you are still saying that the individual is likely to be local, for example. The very interesting example is the murder of Jill Dando, whereby, because of her public image and the fact that so many people knew about her and the way the whole police process became caught up in a huge media interest, there was a tendency for the police to explore very widely all the possibilities. Quite early on in the investigation a name was offered to them of an individual who lived round the corner. Now using the principles that I am talking about – and I have discussed this directly with the senior investigating officer, whom I have a lot of admiration for and he had a tremendously tricky job, but he admits that this basic idea had never occurred to him in that early stage in the investigation. So when this name Barry George was offered to them early on in the investigation it just wasn't looked at seriously, and that meant, when after six months of the investigation they realised they were getting nowhere, they were so organised they could then restructure their investigation and say "Well, what have we left out? They then realised they had these individuals, including Barry George, who for a variety of reasons should have been a relevant suspect, and if they had added the extra ingredient that he was actually quite local, they could have looked at him more closely. It was then very late by the time they arrested him. They could have been interviewing him within the first couple of weeks. My point is, whether he was guilty or not, at that stage there may have been more evidence available to support the case one way or the other, but they didn't get him until very late in the day, because this basic idea that really goes back to the notion of crimes being committed by local residents. As I've mentioned there is information from the 1920s on the study of how criminals travel that fits this general idea. It is not true in all cases. I As I said, Black is an obvious case, Robert Black, who travelled up and down the country abducting children, in which the idea of locality was not the important one. In fact, in Robert Black's case his van was his home, and his van was the place in which he had all the tools for abducting his victims and binding and controlling these girls, and that is what was moving around. So I must say proximity is a significant issue whether you have a series of cases or just one case. It is just that the more information you have about the criminal the more you have got to work with.

The President: Thank you. I think we have got time for one more question, please.

Dr Josse: Edward Josse, medical practitioner. In 1985 it so happened I examined one of the rape victims of the Duffy duo, so to speak. She was a German au pair and she was very, very badly injured. In my experience of 40 odd years of examining rape victims by and large they have not been very badly physically injured. This girl was very badly injured, and when Duffy split on his partner there were two specimens at the time, I remember, and 15 years later I looked at my original notes, because I had to redo them for the court, and the guy was eventually tagged, so to speak, from DNA. DNA had virtually not started in 1985, but it was available in 1990 when it eventually came to Old Bailey Court No. 1, and of course their series of rapes were also, as you stated, associated with murders. I just dealt with that one case and I didn't know that any profiling was going on. What I wasn't entirely clear was did the serious nature of the injuries – because I think the other rape victims were also badly injured – did that help with the profiling and did that give the police a clue, or was it really the shopping of Duffy, after so many years in prison, deciding "I've had enough", and he gave the information to the police?

Professor Canter: Well, the behaviours are very varied across cases and of course there is always the problem, that still exists to some extent, as to which were the cases that were actually linked. I have skated over that, but that is a big issue, if there is no forensic information, as to which cases are linked. Also the point is certainly that in the mid-80s when the statements were being taken the amount of detail that was recorded was often very weak, and certainly in those early cases we were not given any of the forensic medical examiners' reports. So although we took some account of the varieties of violence, I wouldn't have said at that stage we would be very alert to the issue that you have raised. Since then we have been able to do a lot more studies on rape and we now have models of the varieties of behaviour that occur in rape, and therefore we can identify what are the rare behaviours and what are the common behaviours. We didn't know that at that stage. For example, when I first started nobody had any idea about how prevalent anal intercourse was in rape. The police would say "We have got a series of rapes. We are linking them together because there was anal activity in all of these rapes", and we said "Well, perhaps that is common. How do we know? Where is the database for that? It is quite interesting, isn't it, that pretty well in the last two months I have learned that Duffy actually had a history of sadistic violence against his wife. I was never given that information. So what you mention could actually have been more relevant and indeed, although there is also the prejudicial issue, could have been important in terms of certainly narrowing down the whole investigation. It really draws attention to what is really the fundamental problem, and that is really effective databases, really effective information. The information, the knowledge you have, is almost certainly not recorded in any systematic central way that researchers can get access to and people can work with, and that is what we are still up against in many cases. The police have information about crimes, they have information about offenders, but rarely are these two sets of information integrated, so drawing on trends is extremely difficult.

So, as always happens at these gatherings, I learn something more each time, and particularly about that case, because it is amazing how many people have some sort of indirect contact with that case. So that is very, very interesting what you say. Thank you.

The President: Do come and sit down, Professor. Thank you very much indeed for a fascinating evening. We have all learnt something, I think, this evening we didn't know before – just what you were saying just now – and we must go away, I think, and read your book, or books, and perhaps we ought to give you something a little extra to go and purchase one of your choice.

Professor Canter: Oh, thank you. I would also like to record my thanks to Bert Raffan for the remarkable skill he has shown in taking detailed notes of my presentation in order to facilitate this publication of my lecture.

The President: Thank you very much. (Applause)

Chapter 12

Identifying the Residential Location of Rapists

D.V. Canter and A. Gregory

Introduction

Previous studies have suggested that offenders often travel only small distances from home to commit crimes [1–5]. As long ago as 1942, Shaw and McKay [6] established that there was a limited area within which criminals offend, and that these areas were geographically close to the areas in which the offenders lived. However, to date, most research has concerned itself with case studies, such as the Yorkshire Ripper [5], or has considered the aggregates of offenders [2], neither of which are likely to be of any direct use as investigative aids. Very little research has concentrated upon criminal spatial ability at the individual level, and the possibility that it may be modelled precisely enough to contribute to investigations.

Besides the practical benefits of a model of the discrete behaviour of offenders, there would be considerable theoretical value. It would help to clarify the psychological determinants of criminal actions and thus contribute to our understanding of crime. A plausible starting point for such modelling is that the choice of an offender's crime location will relate in some way to the home or base from which he operates. Amir [7], in a large scale study, presented evidence that rapists tend to operate from an established base, rather than being drifters of no fixed abode. LeBeau [8], also presented data to support the idea of a rapist having a fixed home or base from which he operates, and furthermore suggested that the geographical patterns of series sexual assaulters are not random. It is therefore feasible that an offender will spend a considerable proportion of his time in or around this home/base, whilst involved in noncriminal activities such as shopping, visiting friends or going to the pub. These journeys around the offender's "home range" would familiarise the offender with his surrounding area, and might provide sources of information around which further crimes could be planned, as suggested by Rengert and Wasilchick in their study of the spatial behaviour of burglars [9].

Brantingham and Brantingham [10], suggested that the security offered by the familiarity of this home range, to the offender, would outweigh the risk of recognition in all but those regions in the direct vicinity of the home/base. This indicated, therefore, the existence of both a maximum and a minimum distance from a criminal's home/base to his choice of offence location. This earlier research and more recent studies [11] support the idea that an offender forms a "mental map" of his home range; a unique representation of the network of familiar objects and routes habitually used by any particular individual, complete with its own particular distortions. It is suggested that this mental map is likely to shape and constrain the criminal and non-criminal spatial activity of any offender.

The literature, then, indicates that there are two important regions which must be considered in order to develop a theory of individual spatial behaviour of sex offenders: firstly, the "Home range"; an area well known to the offender, since it is the region surrounding the home or base from which he operates; and secondly the "Criminal range", a finite region which encompasses all offence locations for any particular offender.

The research task was to carry out empirical tests of the models of relationship between offender's home and criminal ranges.

Sample

Although the general arguments above are applicable to any offences, the present study focused on sexual assaults. This type of crime is a particularly strong test of the essentially rational models that have been outlined. Sexual assault overtly has a profound emotionality to it, and it may be regarded by many as containing some impulsive aspects [7]. However, when a rapist does commit a series of assaults on women, with whom he has had no previous contact, it is likely that some pattern will exist in these offences of which the offender may or may not be aware, just as for burglary or drug abuse. Indeed, it is true that, in some cases, offences of rape can be regarded as an extension of less serious crimes such as burglary or theft. Sexual assault may therefore be seen as an extreme case that tests the fundamental assumptions that an individual criminal's crime venue has some distinct relationship to his place of residence.

To carry out the study, details of 45 sexual assaulters were made available by British police forces. The material used to generate the data matrix was derived from victim's statements, offence schedules, microfiche and criminal intelligence documents. It included criminals who had been convicted of crimes legally regarded as "rape", in which vaginal penetration had taken place, as well as other forms of sexual violence. All offenders had been convicted of two or more offences on women whom they had not known prior to the offence. A total of 251 offences had been committed by these 45 offenders. The mean rape series consisted of 5.6 offences (SD = 3.6) with a minimum U2, and a maximum of 14. The sample of offenders had a mean age of 26.6 years (SD = 8.7) ranging from 15 to 59 years; 21 offenders could be broadly classified by the police as "white" in ethnicity and the other 24 as "black". All the offenders operated within the Greater London area and/or the South East of England during the 1980s.

Study 1

Two models broadly representing the spatial characteristics of offenders were proposed for the association between the home range and the criminal range. The first was the "Commuter" model (Figure 12.1a) which proposed that the offender travelled from his home/base into a selected area from which he moved out when travelling to his offence venue. This may be determined by the general geometry of the city, as would be consistent with Shaw and McKay's proposal of the use of the city centre [6], or it may be an area determined by regular routes that the offender took, as Rengert and Wasilchick [9] suggested. It could also be an area in which potential victims were known to reside, e.g., an area of nurses' residences. However, whatever the particular determinants of the specific area of crime, it is central to the commuter hypothesis that although there will be a region or domain within which the crimes are committed, and this domain will be related to where the offender lives, there will be no clear relationship between size or location of the criminal domain and its distance from any given offender's home.

The commuter hypothesis then proposed that there would be little or no overlap between the offender's criminal and home ranges. This is not to suggest that the area in which the offender committed his crimes is unfamiliar, but that it is an appreciable distance from the area in which he habitually operated as a non-offender.

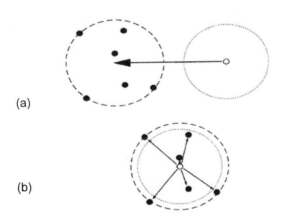

(a)

(b)

Figure 12.1 Hypothetical models of serial rapists' behaviour, adapted from Canter and Larkin (1993). (a) Commuter hypothesis; (b) marauder hypothesis. ----- criminal range; ..... home range; *offences; ● home/base.

The second model of a criminal's spatial activity was what may be called the "Marauder" model in which the offender was assumed to move out from his base to commit his crimes and then return, going out in different directions on different occasions. This hypothesis had most in common with the suggestions of Brantingham and Brantingham [10], who saw the home as a focus for each crime location. It implied a much closer relationship between the location of the crimes committed and the criminal's home, such that the further the distance between crimes, the further, on average, the offender must be travelling from home.

In other words, the marauder hypothesis proposed that there was a large overlap between the areas of the criminal and home ranges. and that the offender operated from a home/base located within the boundaries of his area for criminal activity.

One direct method of ascertaining which of the two models was better supported by this sample's data, was to look at the spatial distribution of each offender's crimes in relation to his home/base. If the home/base was found to be within this region of crimes, support would be given to the marauder model, whereas a home/base outside this region would suggest the commuter model as being appropriate.

In order to define the area of the offences, the two offences furthest from each other were identified and the distance between them was taken as the diameter of a circle that was drawn. Such a circle was likely, but not certain, to encompass all the offences. In the present sample, only 7 of 251 offences were not within the circle circumscribing the two furthest offences. This method is simpler than any technique utilising "centre of gravity" measurements, and owes more to psychological theories of the mental representation of an area [11]. However, with larger data sets and more crimes per offender, more geographically-oriented procedures might be effective, as LeBeau [8], for example, suggested.

By using offence coordinate information, a geographical representation of offences was produced for each offender, onto which the relevant home/bases were plotted.

Results

The residential location of the offenders was found to be within their offence circles in 39 of the 45 cases, (87%), and the mean area of the circular regions produced was found to be 177.11 square miles, (SD = 490.60). Of the other six offenders, two were found to involve the victims being picked up and driven away from the offender's home before being assaulted, and a further two involved targeting a specific street far away from the offender's home area. All six were typical of the commuter type offender.

From this evidence, the marauder hypothesis seemed to be more applicable to this particular set of sexual assaulters as a general model, whilst the commuter model seemed to have application only in more specific instances such as the targeting of prostitutes. For these reasons this more specific adaption of the marauder model, the "Circle Hypothesis", was used throughout the remainder of the study.

Study 2

It having been established that the geographical patterns of rapists' offences had a broad relationship to their home/base, other procedures were explored to see if the distances travelled could be modelled more precisely. The central hypothesis here was that, in general terms, offenders could be differentiated by means of the resources of time, travel costs and knowledge of an area, such that longer distances travelled from home to an offence location would relate to greater access to means of financing travel, greater availability of time and more extended knowledge of an area.

This heuristic formulation led to the hypothesis that older offenders would travel further than young offenders, and that offenders travelling at the weekend would travel further than those travelling during the week. It could be the case that due to disadvantages faced by ethnic minorities, white offenders would be able to travel further than offenders classified as black in this sample. It might also be suggested

Table 12.1   Data from the 45 offenders relating ethnicity, offence venue, offence timing and age at arrest, to the distance of the crime from their home/base

Resource facets	<0.5 mile	>0.5 mile	Total
Ethnicity			
Black	17	6	23
White	4	18	22
Total	21	24	45
Offence venue			
Inside/Mixed	14	6	20
Outside	7	18	25
Total	21	24	45
Offence timing*			
Weekend	3	3	6
Weekday	7	10	17
Mixed	12	8	20
Total	22	21	43
Age at arrest			
Under 25 y	13	11	24
Over 25 y	8	13	21
Total	21	24	45

*Data missing for 2 offenders.

that offenders attacking outdoors would travel further than those attacking indoors, since offenders who chose a location outside were likely to have to travel further in order to find a place they considered appropriate.

Results

The results of this study are shown in Table 12.1.

Ethnicity   White offenders were found to be more likely to have high home/base to offence distances than black offenders. For black offenders there was a 4:1 chance that the home/base was within half a mile of one of the offences (Chi-square = 1188, $p < 0.01$).

Offence venue   Outside attackers travelled approximately 2.7 times as far to offend as those who attacked inside or in mixed locations. There was also a 2.6 times greater chance that they would travel further than 0.5 miles to commit each offence, when compared to the same group (Chi-square = 6.28, $p < 0$-02).

Offence timing Offenders who attacked at the weekend were likely to travel further from their home/base to do so. Their average minimum distance from home was 2.5 times greater than that of "week-day" offenders. However, the ranges of values were so great that these differences were not significant.

Age at arrest Trends were found that gave some support to the hypothesis that older offenders, (>25 y), would travel further than younger offenders, though these trends were not strong enough to be statistically significant.

These results indicated that ethnicity and offence venue, individually, were able to discriminate offenders in terms of the minimum distance they travelled to offend, and that offence timing and age at arrest were sufficiently strong to be incorporated into a computer program with the. first two facets of offenders' backgrounds. This computer program was designed to overcome the interactions between variables which might be responsible for the weakening of the two latter trends.

Study 3

Phase I – test of a small expert system

Using the four parameters of age, ethnicity, offence timing and offence venue, a computer program was designed such that from limited offender background knowledge and known offence locations, a region could be plotted, within which, it was predicted, the offender was most likely to live or be based.

The program worked by matching a current offender, in terms of his "resource facets", to all other similar offenders within the database, for which distance information was known. By doing this, the maximum and minimum distances from home/base to first offence, found within the chosen sample group, could be plotted as the radii of two circles, both of whose centres were the location of the first offence of that particular offender. The area between these two circles was then the most likely region for the current offender's home/base to be located.

The choice of the first offence as the point of reference for the prediction of home/base was taken for a number of reasons. Firstly and most importantly, the primary aim of this research was to provide the police with a support aid which would hopefully be of use in live inquiries. Therefore it was obviously more useful if predictions of offenders' residential location could begin after the first offence rather than requiring a series of sexual assaults or rapes to occur before being of any value to police or forensic procedures. Secondly and more psychologically, it was plausible that the first offence represented the occasion where the offender was most influenced by his home/base and was most likely to use it as a reference point, around which the crime locations might be chosen. For example, in the early stages of a crime series, the offender is unlikely to be planning, in any great detail, the range or areas in which he will choose to offend, and is therefore more likely to be influenced by the areas familiar to him. Also, the choice of first offence venue is less likely to be distorted by his perception of increased vulnerability in places in which he has already committed crimes.

It was found that the mean area covered by this program prediction region was 8748 square miles (SD = 7756), and that this region, when centred around the location of the first offence of any offender, did indeed contain that offender's home/base; i.e., all 45 offenders within the sample had their home/base within the predicted region.

This sample of 45 offenders included the 6 offenders who were classified above as being of the "commuter" type. This was done so as to make the sample more representative of a variety of offenders, and to allow the system to make predictions based upon various spatial patterns, rather than just those which happen to fit the "marauder" model. This is important, since in a real crime situation it would be unknown at the outset as to whether the offender was a commuter or a marauder.

Phase II – further development of the system

The computer program was further developed to include the Circle Hypothesis information, so that the circle passing through the two furthest offences was plotted in addition to the minimum and maximum distance to home circles as used in phase 1. This additional information was found to reduce the prediction area considerably, from 17711, and 8748 square miles, yielded by circle theory and offender resource theory respectively, to 1139 square miles (SD =1683), for the overlap region, given by the combination of both.

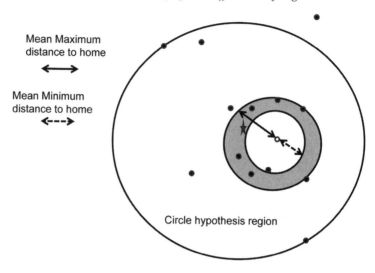

Figure 12.2 Example of a series of 14 offences by a white, 32-year-old, inside serial rapist. *Home/base: ○ first offence, ● subsequent offences

This area is a far more manageable size and likely to be of greater use as an aid to police investigations, and 83% of the offenders within the sample were found to have their home/base within this final prediction region.

Illustration

As the first steps in cross-validation, the software's utility was explored by applying it to data outside the original sample. One example of this (Figure 12.2), gives an example of the potential of the program as a visually lucid tool for establishing the likely area of offender residence. The figure is a representation of a sexual offence series committed by one man in Melbourne in 1986. The offender was a 31-year-old, "white", inside attacker. The "home" shown within the figure was the home/base from which the offender committed most of his rapes, and at which he was apprehended. The figure also shows the Circle Hypothesis region bounded by a circle passing through the two most distant offences, and maximum and minimum distances to base prediction circles. In this example the minimum distance circle has radius 0-0 miles. The darker shaded region represents the program's final prediction area for residence location.

This prediction was based on the combination of the Circle Hypothesis and determinant facet suppositions. As can be seen, the offender was resident within the prediction area, and 93% (13 out of 14) of his offences were committed within his predicted criminal range.

Discussion and conclusions

Work undertaken has demonstrated that the location of the base from which a sex offender operates can be predicted from information about the offender and the location of his offences.

Hypotheses have been proposed and pilot tested with considerable success. The models developed from these hypotheses have been used to generate a prototype decision support system, in the form of a computer program, to aid procedural enquiry within investigative situations. The faceted rule systems generated by statistical analysis have been linked within the program to generate a graphical representation of the predicted residence area of the sexual offender. It generates an illustration of the offence series and superimposes a hypothetical residential region based upon the models currently developed.

The models have been generated from information provided by various police forces in England. The material used to generate the data matrix was relatively small (45 offenders with 251 offences) but the relationships obtained so far have been very strong. The prototype decision support system itself has yielded between 82·5% and 100% accuracy for different derived models that have been used to predict offence location.

The prototype program's utility has been explored by applying it to ongoing investigations. To date, the program has been cross-validated on three English sexual assault series, one from Australia and one from Canada. The degree of success, on a global scale, highlights that there may be strong underlying processes involved in the selection of a sexual offence venue which may cross geographical and cultural boundaries.

It is therefore proposed that the clarity of the mathematical results obtained so far be expanded upon by the development of an intelligent expert system which is able to develop in parallel with new data. It is intended that such a system will have the facility either to let an investigator intervene in the decision process itself, or make a decision of the most likely area of residence of the offender, based upon best estimates generated from a larger, more reliable database.

Thus the prototype will be developed into a tool which can be used on a local level, based upon national data, to predict within known error boundaries the most likely residence location of a serial sexual offender. The program will be written in such a way that its underlying code can be applied to other serious offences. The faceted rule structures generated would apply to the offence type being processed and would constantly adapt to new information received by a large scale database.

Thus, as the system is used, it by necessity becomes more accurate and reduces valuable police time spent analyzing offenders' spatial offence patterns.

Acknowledgements

We are grateful to Paul Larkin for developing the computer software and to Ellen Tsang for the original data analysis.

References

1. White R.C. The Relation of Felonies to Environmental Factors in Indianapolis. *Social Forces* 1932; 10(4), 459–467.
2. Pyle G.F. et al. (1974). *The Spatial Dynamics of Crime*. Department of Geography Research Monograph No. 159. Chicago: The University of Chicago.
3. Repetto T.A. (1974). *Residential Crime*. Cambridge, MA: Ballinger.
4. Curtis L.A. (1974). *Criminal Violence*. Lexington, MA: Lexington Books.
5. Kind S.S. (1987). Navigational Ideas and the Yorkshire Ripper Investigation. *Journal of Navigation*, 40(3), 385–393.
6. Shaw C.R. and McKay H.D. (1942). *Juvenile Delinquency and Urban Areas*. Chicago: University of Chicago Press.
7. Amir M. (1971). *Patterns in Forcible Rape*. Chicago: University of Chicago Press.
8. LeBeau J.L. (1987). The journey to rape: Geographic distance and the rapist's method of approaching the victim. *Journal of Police Science and Administration* 15(2), 129–161.
9. Rengert G. and Wasilchick J. (1985). *Suburban Burglary: A Time and Place for Everything*. Springfield, Illinois: CC Thomas Publishing.
10. Brantingham P.J. and Brantingham P.L. (1981). Notes on the geometry of crime. In: *Environmental Criminology*. edited by Brantingham P.J. and Brantingham P.L. Beverly Hills: Sage, 27–54.
11. Canter, D. and Larkin, P. (1993). The environmental range of serial rapists. *Journal of Environmental Psychology*, 13, 63–69.

Chapter 13

Spatial Patterns of Serial Murder: An Analysis of Disposal Site Location Choice

Samantha Lundrigan and David Canter

Although the murders committed by serial killers may not be considered rational, there is growing evidence that the locations in which they commit their crimes may be guided by an implicit, if limited rationality.

The hypothesized logic of disposal site choice of serial killers led to predictions that (a) their criminal domains would be around their home base and relate to familiar travel distances, (b) they would have a size that was characteristic of each offender, (c) the distribution would be biased towards other non-criminal activities, and (d) the size of the domains would increase over time.

Examination of the geographical distribution of the sites at which 126 US and 29 UK serial killers disposed of their victims' bodies supported all four hypotheses. It was found that rational choice and routine activity models of criminal behavior could explain the spatial choices of serial murderers. It was concluded that the locations at which serial killers dispose of their victims' bodies reflect the inherent logic of the choices that underlie their predatory activities.

Introduction

In recent years, growing attention has been paid to the locations at which criminals commit their crimes (Brantingham and Brantingham 1981; Canter and Larkin 1993; Rengert and Wasilchick 1985). This has indicated that these locations are not arbitrary, but relate to the specific experiences of the offenders themselves and imply some form of logical selection on the part of the criminal, even if the basis of the selection is not always clear to the criminals themselves. Any locational choice involves a complex set of decision processes. Attempts to model these decisions have emphasized the logic of the choices made by the offender. For crimes in which there is a direct economic gain, such as robbery or burglary, such models based on

*We are grateful to Christopher Missen for providing the data. We are also grateful to Malcolm Huntley for the development of Mplot and subsequent analyses.

the weighting of the perceived costs and benefits have much to commend them. But for violent and emotional crimes, such as the murder of strangers, it may be assumed that such logical models may be inappropriate. However, this is to confuse an inherent logic of the location choice with an overt and conscious rational decision. A logical choice would be one that does not lead to detection and apprehension, even though the criminal activity and its motivation may be irrational. This study examines whether the body disposal patterns of serial murderers can be understood using logical models of location selection.

Serial murderers are stereotypically thought of as bizarre, genetically disordered individuals who randomly prey on victims (Revitch and Schlesinger 1981). Logical or rational behavior is not a term typically associated with such offenders. However, while their motivations and murder actions may be unique, there may be other aspects of their criminal behavior that do bear commonalties with other types of offender. In particular, it may be that, spatially, serial murderers share more in common with other types of offender than typically assumed. For while individual motivations for murder are often thought to be the result of a unique combination of biogenetic, sociological, and psychological factors, it can be suggested that the manner in which any individual interacts with the environment will be influenced by a number of spatial processes that are generic to both criminals and non-criminals alike. For instance, a serial murder whose motivation is a bizarre desire for sadistic sexual excitement is unlikely, in terms of motivation and murder actions, to share any similarities with other types of offender. However, the extreme nature of his motivation and murder actions will not necessarily be reflected in his spatial behavior. For although driven by a unique motive intrinsic to himself, he will nevertheless be subject to both the external influences of, and the internal conceptions of the larger environment. In the present study it is hypothesized that more generic spatial processes such as the psychological importance of the home (Canter and Larkin 1993), familiarity with one's surroundings (Brantingham and Brantingham 1981) and individual mental maps (Downs and Stea 1973) will influence the spatial decision making of serial murderers in a similar way to other types of offender.

Previous attempts to define serial killers in terms of their geographical mobility have classified offenders according to the distances they travel to offend. Hickey (1991) presents a threefold classification of serial killers that he calls (a) travelers crossing state boundaries, covering thousands of miles, (b) 'locals' who remain in their home state, and (c) 'place specific' killers who do not leave home to kill. Hickey's definition of these three groups lacks some precision in that no actual distance ranges are suggested to differentiate between the groups. More recently, Holmes and Holmes (1996) distinguished between geographically stable and geographically transient serial killers. Geographically stable killers live in the same area for some time, kill in the same or a nearby area, and dispose of bodies in the same or a nearby area. In contrast, the geographically transient killer travels continuously (probably to confuse police) and disposes of bodies in far-flung places. As with Hickey's classification, there is a lack of precision and no attempt to define the distances traveled or the size of area for each group. However, both typologies do draw attention to variations in the size of domain over which serial killers operate. They throw little light, though, on what determines the location of that domain or its scale.

Studies of crimes other than serial murder have provided hypotheses for the reasons why people offend in particular areas. In essence, they have proposed that the home base of criminals provides experience and familiarity with an area, and thus shapes where crimes are committed. As long ago as 1946, Erlanson found that 87% of rapists attacked within their own neighborhood. Amir (1971) supported the claim of an influence of home, location by showing that 68% of rapists in Philadelphia during 1958-60 offended within five city blocks of their homes. Brantingham and Brantingham (1981) developed the consideration of the familiarity a criminal has with an area beyond the home. They included job and recreational experiences, drawing attention to an action space, consisting of a network of paths and nodes with which an offender would be familiar.

In proposing an action space for criminals, Brantingham and Brantingham (1981) saw crime as a byproduct of other activities in which the criminal engages. Originally developed by Cohen and Felson (1979), this has become known as 'routine activity theory'. Routine activity theory sees crimes as opportunities taken within the awareness space of day-to-day life. The routine activity explanation for offender spatial behavior had traditionally been put forward to explain the target or victim selection stage of an offence. The approach focuses on the discovery of 'opportunities' in the form of victims and targets during non-criminal activities. However, it is proposed here that routine activity theory can equally be applied to the body disposal stage of a murder. The difference lies in the temporal stage of the offence. The likely offender has become an actual offender, the suitable target has been located and the crime has been committed. The search moves from that for a victim to that for a disposal location.

The rational choice explanation of spatial behavior involves the making of decisions and choices which exhibit a trade-off between increased opportunity and greater reward the further an offender travels from home, as well as the costs of time, effort, and risk (Cornish and Clarke 1986). The benefits of a criminal action are the net rewards of crime and include not only material gains, but also intangible benefits such as emotional satisfaction. The risks or costs of crime are those associated with formal punishment should the offender be apprehended. For example, a serial murderer may place a great distance between his home and the place where he disposes of a victim's body in order to distance himself from the offence, or to reach a particular location with which he associates some emotional satisfaction (the benefit). However, the risk of apprehension may increase the further he travels (the cost).

Bennett and Wright (1984) suggest that the concept of limited rationality best explains the spatial behavior of offenders. Here, it is not presumed that offenders weigh all the relevant factors every time an offence is contemplated, and other factors (moods, motives, perceptions of opportunity, alcohol, the influence of others, and their attitude toward risk) apparently unrelated to the immediate decision often take over. Bennett and Wright conclude that offenders are behaving rationally as they see it at the time, but what might be perceived as rational on one occasion might not be so perceived on another.

The proposal of limited rationality implies some random process in disposal site selection. This would mean that offenders would not be expected to move systematically through an area disposing of bodies. Instead a domain of operation would be hypothesized in which the central influences of familiarity were having an effect, but with the subjective factors introducing some degree of randomness into the selection of sites. In so far as routine activity was the dominant influence, the home would play a pivotal role. In so far as rational choice was dominant, the actual qualities of the disposal location would be primary.

The different emphases of these two models are reflected in the distinction that Canter and Larkin (1993) made between offenders whom they labeled 'commuters' and those they called 'marauders'. The rational choice would be to 'commute' into an area where the optimum benefits of disposal locations to the offender outweighed the risks. Routine activities would tend to lead to disposal locations occurring on routes from the residential location in the 'marauding' fashion. In other words, the distances traveled by an offender from home to dispose of a body are likely to be less clearly related to residential location for 'rational choice' offenders than for 'routine activity' offenders. There is thus an open question as to which model will be most appropriate for serial killers.

It is hypothesized that serial killers will choose locations for the disposal of their victims' bodies in accordance with aspects of the two models outlined. The different models do give emphasis to somewhat different aspects of the disposal sites and therefore do lead to different predictions but they all emphasize the possibility of a logical location choice. Therefore, if any of these models were supported, they would challenge the view that such killers are totally bizarre and further open up the feasibility of studying serial killers empirically in the same way as other criminals.

Hypothesis

(1) *The role of residential location.* Both models see the home as a significant determinant of offence locations. The difference lies in the centrality hypothesized for the home. Rational choice is more likely to lead to disposals occurring at some distance from the home in locations determined by the attractiveness of the location rather than nearness to home. Routine activity would tend towards the home location being biased at one end of an area within which the disposals occur.

(2) *Variations in domain size.* The actual size of the area over which serial offenders operate would be expected to vary if they are driven by rational choice. For such offenders, the home will not have as strong a modifying influence in their decision of where to dispose of their victims' bodies. Rather the resources available to the offender will influence the size of the area. Variations would be expected to occur between offenders in relation to both their targets and criminal objectives.

A number of studies of criminals have demonstrated analogous patterns of space use. Baldwin and Bottoms (1976), for example, found that the more valuable the property stolen the further the offender had traveled to steal it. In contrast, routine activity theory places greater importance on the role of the home and the notion of familiarity in influencing spatial mobility. Routine activities may be rather variable for different offenders, and this would lead to expectations of variations in the size of the area over which they would offend, but a relatively small range of distances for each offender because of the modifying influence of home. In terms of any given offender, then, routine activities would predict a reasonable, defined area of criminal activity.

(3) *Directional bias in geographic distribution.* The rational choice model leads to the hypothesis that the area in which the disposal sites are located will be distinct from the location of the home. By contrast, the routine activity model predicts a bias along pathways that link other activities specific to the offender and implies a more random distribution with the home at one edge.

(4) *Changes in domain size over time.* One further hypothesis that distinguishes between the two models relates to the change in the distances traveled from home over time. The rational choice would be to move on to avoid risk of detection or higher vulnerability due to increased vigilance. Routine activities would keep a person in an area unless the activities themselves took the criminal further afield. A slightly different perspective would be to argue that bodies might be disposed of under the influence of routine activities in the early stages of an offender's career, but as he becomes more committed to this form of crime, more rational considerations would push him further from his home base to dispose of the bodies.

Table 13.1 summarizes the predictions made by the two models for each hypothesis.

Table 13.1   Summary of routine activities and rational choice theory hypotheses

	Routine activities	*Rational choice*
Role of residential location	Home base within disposal area	Home base separate from disposal area
Size of criminal domain	Small range of sizes	Large range of sizes
Directional bias	Along pathways with home at edge	Away from home area in separate area
Change over time	Extension of familiar areas	Move to a different area

Sample and Procedure

Within the literature, there are many definitions of serial killers, usually differing in terms of the number of victims any given offender must kill in order to be termed a serial killer. The most common number is a minimum of three victims (Holmes and Holmes 1996). However, some researchers, such as Jenkins (1994), use four or more as the cut-off point. Our definition recognizes serial killers as those individuals who have killed two or more victims over a period of time with a cooling off period between each murder. The inclusion of a cooling off period ensures that mass murderers are excluded from the definition. The use of "two or more victims" as the defining number allows for those serial killers who, although being responsible for only two known murders, may still exhibit the traits of serial killers who are known to have killed more than twice.

Data Collection

The data used in the present research were obtained by consulting published accounts of serial killers who had been convicted since 1960. The location at which they had been residing at the time of their offence was then determined from at least two independent sources. If these sources did not corroborate each other, the offender was dropped from the sample. Attempts were then made to contact police officers or local journalists who had worked closely on the cases in question in order to further test the reliability of the residential location information. At this stage, corroboration was also sought from published information on the locations at which the bodies of the victims were found.

While there are a number of geographical locations associated with any one murder in a series (e.g. point of encounter, murder scene, holding location), the present study focuses on the locations and meaning of the body disposal sites that the offender selects. The locations at which the victims' bodies were left were used because it is the least contentious, most objective information available about the location of a murder. Interestingly, in an analysis of the Hillside Strangler case, Newton and Swoope (unpublished manuscript) discriminated between point of fatal encounter, site where the body was left, and victim residence. They found that the geographic center of the location where the body had been placed most accurately predicted the location of residence of murderer Angelo Buono.

It is important to recognize a number of potential problems associated with such data sources. The information available to the authorities itself may have unreliability in it and they may not have recorded the information correctly. Distortions can also arise due to reporting strategies and concern to protect the victims' families. Unreliability is also introduced due to confusion over which location the offender really was residing in at the time that any particular victim's body was disposed of. Attempts to counteract all these problems were made during the data collecting process that took a number of years to complete. However, although the full reliability of the data can never be precisely gauged, cross checks on its internal consistency have been encouraging. Furthermore, the errors introduced by unreliability are most likely to add noise to the data and thereby reduce the possibility for finding support for the models tested. Any support for the models may therefore be considered, in part, as support for the reliability of the source data. But as in other areas of research, the acid test is through examination of other data sets by other researchers.

Locational information concerning 126 American and 29 British serial killers was collected in the manner described. Collectively, the U.S. killers were known to be responsible for 898 victims, and those in the U.K. for 207. They had been convicted of killing between 2 (1) and 24 (1) people each. Once the relevant geographical information had been collated, the offenders' home bases and the sites at which they left the bodies of their victims were recorded onto local street maps. Where more than one base was known, the one that was used during any particular series of killings was recorded. Thus the base recorded was always linked directly to the offences known to have been committed from that base. The addresses of the body disposal sites and offender's residence were located through street maps and local gazetteers. These were input into a specially developed mapping system, "Mplot", which recorded the locations as relative coordinates in a two-dimensional Euclidean space. The software calculates a variety of distances from the co-ordinates as well as statistical derivations of these distances.

Statistics for Distance Data

The data used in the present study was not normally distributed. Therefore, as the mean is a parametric statistic, it was found not to be the most appropriate measure of central tendency. Furthermore, because of a small number of offenders who traveled vast distances, the average was inflated and not representative of the sample as a whole. Therefore, where distributions of the entire sample are being described, the median is used to measure the central tendency of the data. Similarly, the standard deviation is a parametric measure and therefore not very useful in describing the data in the present research. Instead, the inter-quartile range is used to describe the range of the sample.

Results and Discussion

The Home as a Determinant of the Criminal Domain

Evidence for the home acting as a base that forms a focus for criminal activity was sought by Canter and Larkin (1993). They used the simple device of drawing a circle with a diameter either end of which were the offenses furthest from each other. This was a way of defining the area in which the offenses took place with the hypothesis being that if the home did have an important role it would be found within the defined area. They found that 86% of a sample of 45 serial, stranger rapists living in the area of London lived within the "circle."

Taking the sample of 126 U.S. serial killers, the same "Circle Hypothesis" was supported by finding that 89% of the offenders lived within a circle defined by the disposal sites that were furthest from each other. For the British sample of serial killers, 86% fit the hypothesis. This indicates that similar proportions of serial killers are operating as "commuters" both in the U.K. and the U.S. as were the London serial rapists. The great majority were acting in accordance with routine activity theory, in which a strong relationship between the location of the home and crime sites is proposed.

A further gauge of the relevance of the home in disposal site location choice is to calculate the distances traveled from home to dispose of victims' bodies. The median distance is 15 km (mean of 40 km) for the 126 U.S. serial killers and 9 km (mean of 18 km) for the 29 U.K. offenders. The difference in medians is likely to be a reflection both of topography and the ease of travel in the two countries, but both appear to be within conventional local travel distances. Figure 13.1 shows that while nine of the American serial killers did travel further than 140 km from home, 50% traveled a mean distance of less than 15 km to leave the bodies of their victims. Furthermore, over 25% traveled an average of less than 5 km. These figures suggest that the criminal domain in which the home is based typically covers a relatively small area. This is possibly within about half an hour's cross-city drive. However, these figures are much larger than those given for other types of offense.

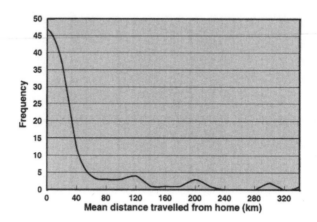

N = 126
Median = 15 km
Inter - quartile range
25% = 5
50% = 15
75% = 40

Figure 13.1   Frequency distribution of mean distance travelled from home for 126 US serial murderers

This suggests that serial killers may be at the extreme of some kind of criminal continuum. For example, Rhodes and Conly (1981) found that the mean distances rapists, burglars and robbers traveled in Washington, DC, were 1.84 km, 2.60 km and 3.38 km respectively.

The size of the average minimum and maximum distances traveled from home to leave the bodies of victims also indicates that these offenders operate within identifiable domains that related to familiar traveling distances. For the U.S. sample, the median minimum distance is 4 km (mean of 9 km) and the median maximum distance is 33 km (mean of 89 km). For the U.K. sample, the comparable figures are 2 km (6 km) and 15 km (36 km).

Overall, these averages do cover quite large ranges but nonetheless put the scale of these disposal domains into perspective. Vast distance traveled from home, running into hundreds of kilometers, do occur but these are very much the exception, and offenders traveling these large distances may be expected to have some identifiably distinct demands on them, such as jobs that require them to travel long distances.

Variations in Domain Size

Both models predict that offenders will operate over a range of distances from their home that is characteristic of them. They do not predict anything like a random exploration, in which there would be a complete overlap between offenders, all of them offending at a great range of distances. The hypotheses above have dealt with the average distance an offender might travel from home. Range hypotheses are concerned with the variations around that average that will be typical of an offender. Routine activities would predict a range small in area. Rational choice would produce great variations in individual ranges, with the probability that no overall pattern could be found without knowledge of the details of the offender's location selection process.

One test of this hypothesis is the relationship between minimum and maximum distances traveled from home. If serial killers are reasonably consistent in their criminal range, there should be a substantial correlation between the minimum and maximum distance they travel from home. There is no arithmetic reason why the two should be correlated. An offender traveling very short minimum distances need not be traveling very short maximum distances, unless the same processes are influencing both distances. Figure 13.2 illustrates the strong correlation of 0.81 (p < .0001) between minimum and maximum distances traveled by the U.S. serial murderers. This supports the view that, for these serial killers, an increase in the maximum distance traveled from home was accompanied by a parallel increase in the minimum. Although the sample is much smaller for the U.K. serial killers, the correlation of 0.5 is still significant at p < .01.

A consequence of this process that has practical value is the possibility of establishing whether identifiable sub-groups exist that have clear distinctions in the sizes of area over which they operate. For the purposes of the present examination,

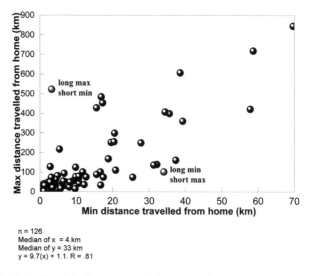

n = 126
Median of x = 4 km
Median of y = 33 km
y = 9.7(x) + 1.1. R = .81

Figure 13.2   Relationship between minimum and maximum distance travelled to disposal sites for 126 US serial murderers

the mean interpoint distance (MID), a measure of the average area over which an offender traveled, was used. The MID was calculated for each offender by adding the distances between every disposal site (as defined by measuring the 'as the crow flies' distance between two points) and dividing by the number of distances measured. By examining the distribution of MID among the offenders, it was evident that the offenders are operating along a continuum with more restricted spatial mobility at one end and less restricted at the other. Interestingly, the majority of the U.S. offenders (58%) are operating with MIDs of less than 25 km, with 19% within 5 km, indicating again that the criminal ranges involve d are relatively small (Figure 13.3). This indicates, once more, that most serial killers act as if on the basis of their routine activities rather than against a strong rational choice model. The findings also challenge Hickey's threefold classification of spatial mobility and imply that serial murderers cannot be easily allocated to groups based solely on their spatial behavior.

Directional Bias in Criminal Domains

The domocentric nature of the domain, as supported by the home being within the 'crime circle' in the great majority of cases, does not require that the home is at the center of this domain. The different models predict different forms of eccentricity of the location of the home, from the extreme of rational choice to the moderate eccentricity of routine activities.

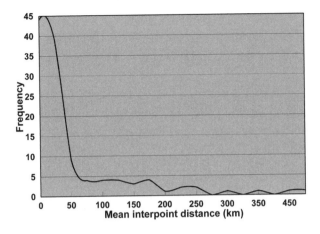

n = 126
Median = 20 km
Inter-quartile range
25% = 7
50% = 20

Figure 13.3 Frequency distribution of mean interpoint distance for 126 US serial murderers

One possibility for exploring the bias in the location of the home away from the center of the domain is by considering the regression equation created by the relationship between the distances traveled from home with the distances traveled between sites. In other words, if the home is within a region that can be defined by the location of the disposal sites, then the distances *(h)* that offenders' travel from home should have a strong monotonic linear relationship to the distance *(c)* between the sites. The function *(f)* in the relationship $h=f(c)$ will be a consequence of the eccentricity of the home within the disposal domain. This will be true of the relationship of the distances between any pair of sites and the distance from home for either of those sites, provided that all sites are not equidistant from the home. As *f* approaches 0.5, the home typically approaches the center of the domain. As *f* approaches 1.0, the home is more eccentrically located towards the periphery of the domain. A value greater than 1.0 would not be expected in the present samples because that would imply that the home is external to the criminal domain as defined by the two sites furthest from each other.

Figure 13.4 shows the scatter plot for the relationship between the maximum distance between disposal sites and the maximum distance traveled to a site. As anticipated there is a very high correlation, $r=.99$ ($p < .0001$). Of more interest is the evidence given by the regression equation $h=0.79c+3.7$ that the home tends to be towards the edge of the domain. The high value here *(0.79)* though, is in part a product of those few offenders who do not operate within a domain that includes their home. The U.K. sample (for which $r=.98$, $p < .0001$) provides an equation where $h=0.80c+0.56$.

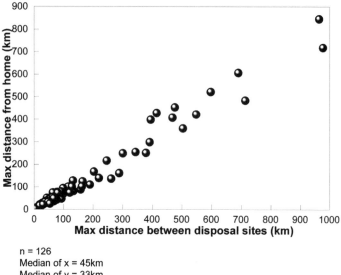

n = 126
Median of x = 45km
Median of y = 33km

Figure 13.4 **Relationship between maximum distance from home and maximum**
distance between disposal sites for 126 US serial murderers

A rather better estimate of the typical eccentricity of the home location can be obtained from considering the minimum distances traveled to disposal sites and between sites. Although errors of measurement will be relatively large for small distances and thus produce a lower correlation, the equation is less sensitive to those offenders who move out of a domocentric domain to dispose of their victims' bodies. Figure 13.5 shows the relationship between the minimum distance between sites and the minimum distance traveled by the sample. The correlation for this plot is r=.81 ($p < .0001$). The regression equation for minimum distances for the U.S. sample is h=0.54c+3.23.

The constant in this equation of approximately two miles (3.23 km) is of some note because it indicates the distance that these U.S. offenders typically put between their home and their nearest disposal location. This lends support to rational choice influencing the distance a person will keep from home rather than the location they choose in which to offend, a process called a safety zone (Turner 1969) or buffer zone (Brantingham and Brantingham 1981). It may be that there are areas immediately around the home base that the offender would avoid disposing of bodies in. For the U.K., sample h=0.72c+0.66. The 'safety' zone would appear to be even smaller here, around half a mile.

A further test of this eccentricity is to consider the angle between disposal sites. If, as proposed, an offender's activities are biased towards a particular orientation in his domain, then the angle subtended from his home between his sites would be hypothesized to be acute rather than oblique. In other words, rather than radiating out from his base in all directions, the majority of his sites would be expected to be in

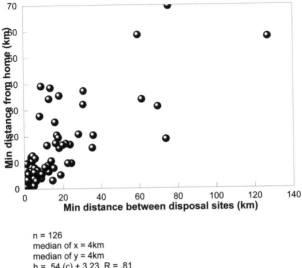

n = 126
median of x = 4km
median of y = 4km
h = .54 (c) + 3.23. R = .81

Figure 13.5 Relationship between minimum distance from home and minimum distance between disposal sites (km) for 126 US serial murderers.

a dominant direction. To test this hypothesis, Mplot was used to calculate the angle from home between each disposal site and every other site for each offender and then calculate the mean angle for each offender. The distribution of these mean angles is shown in Figure 13.6. As can be seen, whilst there is variation in these means, the modal value of 60° lends strong support to the hypothesis of a bias in orientation.

Change Over Time

The two theories that have been put forward to explain spatial behavior both predict the possibility of a change over time. The difference between them lies in the nature of this change and why it may occur. The rational choice perspective would predict a change in order to avoid risk of detection because of greater vulnerability due to increased police vigilance. Routine activities would keep a person in an area unless the activities themselves took the criminal further afield. Such a change would be indicative of individual offender development, a choice rather than a necessity.

In order to establish whether there was change over time in the spatial behavior of serial murderers, the mean distances traveled to each successive site in each series was examined. Figure 13.7 illustrates the mean distances traveled to each site up to and including the tenth offense. A change in the size of criminal domain over time would be reflected in a gradual increase or decrease in the mean distances traveled. As can be seen, there is a general increase in the distances traveled up to and including the sixth site. It appears that the offender may then backtrack to within the previously established range.

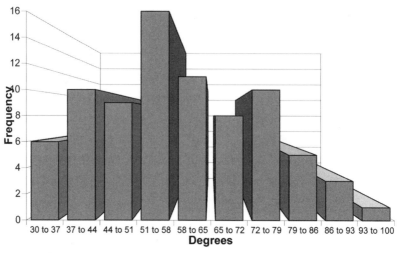

n = 79
Note: The degrees of the acute angles represent the smallest
width between each disposal site

Figure 13.6   Frequency distribution of mean acute angles as seen from the home base for 79 local US serial murderers

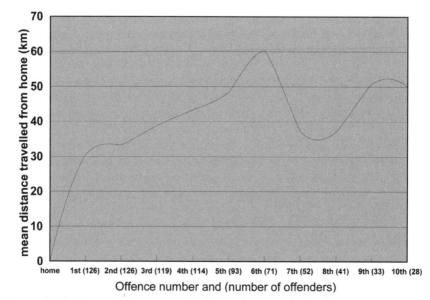

Offence number and (number of offenders)

Figure 13.7   Mean distance travelled from home to body disposal site for each of the first ten offences in series for 126 US serial murderers

In order to determine whether the overall changes illustrated in Figure 13.7 were significant, a non-parametric version of the repeated measures ANOVA was used. Anon-parametric test was used because all the results show the distribution of distances traveled do not have a normal distribution or even a symmetric distribution. Analysis using Friedman's ANOVA gave a significant result (χ^2 =14.95, p < .01). In order to determine which of the changes in distance traveled were significant, Wilcoxon matched pairs signed ranks tests were carried out between each site and each other site. The sites between which significant differences in the distance traveled were found are shown in Table 13.2.

Table 13.2 shows that there is no significant development until the fifth site is selected. This suggests that the offender will exploit the areas closest to him before moving to locations further afield. Interestingly, although the offender appears to "retreat" into an already established area after the sixth offense, there is still a significant difference between the first and last (included) disposal location. This gives support to a general increase in scale across a series despite the relative decrease in distance after the sixth site.

Table 13.2   Disposal site numbers where a significant change over time was found

Site numbers	Significance
1st and 5th	$z = -2.25 \; p = .05$
1st and 6th	$z = -3.03 \; p = .01$
1st and 10th	$z = -2.31 \; p = .02$
2nd and 6th	$z = -2.71 \; p = .01$
2nd and 8th	$z = -2.33 \; p = .02$
5th and 8th	$z = -2.39 \; p = .02$
5th and 9th	$z = -2.48 \; p = .02$

Summary and Conclusions

This study has explored the disposal site location choices of serial murderers from a routine activities and rational choice perspective. It was found that the majority of the murderers operated within an area that bore a strong relationship to their home. However, it is worth emphasizing, that it appears that there are a small proportion of offenders that do not live within such a "disposal domain." It has been suggested that these are offenders who are more likely to be selecting their disposal sites in an attempt to minimize the risk and maximize the benefits to themselves. In contrast, the majority of serial killers appear to be leaving the bodies of their victims in an area that provides ready opportunities for them, possibly familiar to them because of the routine activities in which they are engaged. The relatively small size of the area over which serial killers move from home to leave the bodies of their victims also accords well with routine activity models of behavior.

In the present study, it has been possible to show that serial killers, like other criminals, do operate within distinct domains and that these domains are likely to be indicative of the experiences and conceptualizations of the offender. They are not haphazard and do show an inherent logic. In practical terms, Rossmo (1995) has highlighted an important implication of the empirical modeling of offender spatial behavior. He has illustrated the ways in which the crime locations of an individual serial killer can be used to create a probability surface, where the higher the probability of any point, the more likely it is to contain the offender's home. Rossmo has shown how such models can be used by law enforcement agencies to narrow their area of search for offenders. In other words, it is possible that, once robust models are established of how serial killers' locational choices relate to their residential location, they can be built into computer models of use to police investigations.

References

Amir M. (1971). *Patterns in Forcible Rape.* Chicago: University of Chicago Press.

Baldwin J, Bottoms A.E. (1976). *The Urban Criminal.* London: Tavistock.

Bennett T., Wright R. (1984). *Burglars on Burglary: Prevention and the Offender.* Aldershot, Hants: Gower.

Brantingham, P.J., Brantingham, P.L. (1981). *Environmental Criminology.* Beverly Hills: Sage.

Canter D., Larkin, P. (1993). The environmental range of serial rapists. *Journal of Environmental Psychology,* 13, 63–69.

Cohen, L.E., Felson, M. (1979). Social change and crime rate trends: A routine activities approach. *American Sociological Review* 44, 588–608.

Cornish, D.B., Clarke, R.V. (1986). *The Reasoning Criminal: Rational Choice Perspectives on Offending.* New York: Springer.

Downs, R.M., Stea. D. (1973). *Image and Environment.* Chicago: Aldine Publishing.

Erlanson, O. (1946). The scene of a sex offence as related to the residence of the offender. *American Journal of Police Science* 31, 39–342.

Hickey, E.W. (1991). *Serial Murderers and Their Victims.* Pacific Grove, CA: Brooks-Cole. Holmes RM, Holmes S. 1996. *Murder in America.* Beverly Hills: Sage.

Jenkins, P. (1994). Serial murder in the United States 1900-1940: A historical perspective. *Journal of Criminal Justice,* 17, 377–392.

Rengert, G.F., Wasilchick, J. (1985). *Suburban Burglary: A Time and a Place for Everything.* Springfield, IL: Thomas.

Revitch, E., Schlesinger, L.B. (1981). *Psychopathology of Homicide.* Springfield, IL: Thomas.

Rhodes, W.M., Conly, C. (1981). Crime and mobility: An empirical study. In *Environmental Criminology,* Brantingham, P.J., and P.L. Brantingham (eds), Beverly Hills: Sage, 167–188.

Rossmo D.K. (1995). Place, space and police investigations: Hunting serial violent criminals. In *Crime and Place*, Eck J.E., Weisburd D. (eds), Monsey, NY: Criminal Justice; 217-235.

Turner S. (1969). Delinquency and distance. In *Delinquency: Selected Studies*, Wolfgang M.E., Sellin T. (eds), New York: Wiley.

Chapter 14

Criminal's Mental Maps

David Canter and Samantha Hodge*

Background

Many people have noted that criminals tend to offend in a limited area and that area tends to be close to where they live. Indeed the basis of penal reform in the 19th century was precisely to remove people from their areas of criminal activity that was regarded as supporting their crime-oriented life-styles. The first fully documented account of the geographical localisation of criminals is usually regarded as the work of what is known as the Chicago School of sociologists (Shaw 1942). Subsequently, with the development of empirical criminology especially in the 1970s and 1980s, a variety of studies drew attention to the limits on criminal mobility (e.g. Capone and Nichols 1976, Pettiway 1982).

These studies of criminal localisation paralleled broader developments in what became known as *Environmental Psychology*. This examination of how people make sense of and relate to their surroundings led to the development of the concept of 'mental maps', those internal representations of the world that we all use to find our way around and make decisions about what we will do where. The importance of the 'mental map' can be traced at least to the writings of Trowbridge (1913), who called them 'Imaginary Maps', but it got new impetus from the writings of various psychologists, notably Bartlett (1932) and an urban planner, Lynch (1960)

These psychological ideas provided one form of explanation for the limitations on the geographical mobility of criminals, as well as most other people, by suggesting that it was their limited mental maps that structured their activities. Awareness of the possibility of such limited psychological structures rather than the vagaries of local geography encouraged researchers to examine how locations of crimes could be modelled in general as schematic systems rather than as particular geographical instances e.g. Brantingham and Brantingham (1981), Constanzo et al. (1986). In other words there has been a growing body of research that attempts to develop general principles that will characterise the geographical patterns of individual offenders in many places rather than aggregate patterns of samples or populations of offenders in particular locations (e.g. Canter and Larkin 1993). These principles have been found to have practical significance in helping to solve crime (Canter 1994) as well as the broader theoretical issues to which they contribute.

*We are grateful to Jonathan Boehm for collecting some of the maps used here.

This all points to an explanation of the selection of the location for offence activities on the basis of some sort of personal mental representation of the locations in which the crimes are committed. This mental representation is often, a little inaccurately, referred to as a 'mental map'. A considerable amount of research over the last 30 years has demonstrated that such internal representations only approximate to the maps with which geographers are familiar. They are more akin to a summary of a person's knowledge and experience of a place, being distorted by many of the processes involved in committing experiences to memory and later retrieving them. However, precisely because of these psychological distortions in such 'maps', they help us to understand how people conceptualise their surroundings and the activities that take place there.

Criminological Cognitive Cartography

There has been very little examination of the mental representations criminals have of the locations in which they commit their crimes, so the suppositions that form the basis of many debates in environmental criminology have yet to be tested. For example routine activity theory would indicate that an offender's mental map of the locations in which he commits his crimes would be seamlessly linked to the areas in which he carries out other activities. By contrast, a perspective that emphasises crime emerging out of awareness of opportunities might be expected to give more salience to the routes and paths that people follow when carrying out their crimes. Alternatively, crimes that are a dominant part of an offender's life might be expected to dominate their conceptualisations of places and be the primary focus of the maps they draw.

There are also interesting questions about the sorts of details that offenders may recall or choose to symbolise in their representations of their geographical experiences. Do these indicate a studied examination of their surroundings or a haphazard, opportunistic approach to their selection of locations in which to offend? Of course the nature of the crime may be expected to relate to how the environment is conceptualised by the offender. Crimes that are closely tied to particular locations, such as burglaries, may be hypothesised to have stronger geographical structures than those that follow the possibilities for finding vulnerable victims, such as rape. Furthermore, some crimes may be location specific, such as targeting a specific warehouse, whilst others can take place wherever the opportunity presents itself. In all these cases the question arises as to whether the offender has some mental representation that reflects the selection of crime locations and in its turn possibly helps to enhance the geographical focus of his crimes.

Exploring Urban Images

The exploration of the essentially, subjective, internal, mental representations is notoriously difficult, but this has not stopped psychologists and other social and behavioural scientists in at least gaining approximations for the way people cognitively structure their transactions with the world. One procedure of especial interest that has been widely used actually owes its scientific origins to an urban planner, Kevin Lynch (1960). He used the device of asking people to draw sketch maps of their cities as a way of exploring their mental representations, or 'image' as he called them, of those cities. His early studies of Boston, Jersey City and Los Angeles have encouraged many other people to follow his lead, in the main because of the distorted and limited maps that people draw. These distortions and limitations are seen as indicators of the cognitive processes that shape people's transactions with their surroundings.

Of course, as was illustrated in some detail many years ago (Canter 1977) and has subsequently been elaborated with great precision (Kitchen 1994), there are a number of methodological difficulties in basing psychological models solely on 'sketch maps'. The skills of the producer may distort what they draw, the ability to understand the nature of the exercise may relate to cartographic training and the precise details of the instructions may have a very strong influence. However, there can be little doubt that important aspects of the respondents conceptual system are indicated by what they choose to draw and how they choose to draw it when asked to "draw a map from memory" of any particular area.

There does therefore appear to be considerable potential for understanding criminals' ways of thinking about their crimes and the locations in which they commit them by asking them to "please draw a map that indicates where you have committed crimes". What follows are some illustrations of the results of such explorations. They indicate the potentials for this line of research. At the present time these results are presented as indications of the possibilities for such a methodology in the hope that they will stimulate others to develop them further.

1. Icons of Experience

The instructions, to "draw a map", does assume some understanding of the mapping process.

In the British education system children are given such exercises throughout their school career. It may start at the age of seven or eight with being required to draw a map (or more accurately a plan) of their classroom, or to draw a map of their route to school. It is therefore reasonable to assume that British offenders have some idea of what is required from an early age. Indeed in the explorations we have carried out we have never found individuals who did not understand the instructions, even though they may have found it challenging to follow those instructions in relation to their own criminal activity. Therefore when a respondent chooses to interpret the instructions in an unexpected way it is worth considering the implications of that reaction.

In interesting illustration of this is Map 14.1. J who had a heroin habit from the age of 14 drew this. He had a long history of drug dealing, burglary and car

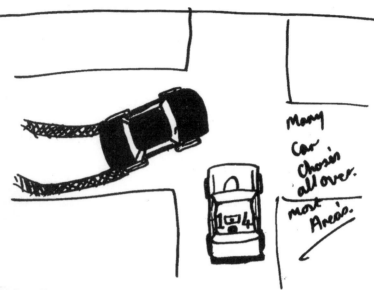

Map 14.1   **J's 'map' of his crimes, showing his excitement with being chased by the police**

theft etc. all over England. He would often spend 24 hours away from home on a burglary spree, travelling along country roads over great distances to commit crimes. Drawing a map of these activities would clearly be very demanding for any person. J therefore had to choose some aspect of his criminal activity to represent. He chose to draw a number of sketches of particular locations without any indication of the links between them, perhaps illustrating something of his haphazard approach to his criminal activities.

Map 14.1 one, though, is especially instructive. As can be seen he chose to draw a bird's eye view of a particularly dangerous moment in a car chase. He wrote on the 'map' "many car chases all over most Areas". The drawing has strongly emphasised skid marks and even the numbering on the top of a police car. The drawing captures the excitement that J obviously feels in the chase and serves to illustrate the importance of the component of adventure he finds in his criminal activities.

J's 'map' also indicates the metaphorical qualities of attempts to represent the locational qualities of thoughts and feelings. This is worth bearing in mind even when a map appears to be an attempt at some cartographic exactitude. It is really just one set of symbols that aims at reconstructing experience. The geographical cross-reference in the symbols will always refer to or mask many other psychological associations. Of course, care must be taken in treating the drawings offenders produce as a 'projective' technique, like a Rorschach inkblot. But as Lynch (1960) stressed, sketch maps and related drawings may often function as a fruitful focus for a more extended interview, exploring the emotions and conceptualisations associated with the image produced. J's drawing therefore serves to illustrate that even the most impoverished attempt at a sketch map may emphasise important aspects of the offender's relationship to his crimes and the targets he selects.

2. Routes to Crime

Map 14.2 is clearly just a set of routes as might be sketched out by a delivery employee seeking to make a note of the journeys that need to be made to various drop-off points. The names on the map are names of small towns and cities in the North of England. The numbers are those that designate the main inter-city highways (Motorways as they're called in the UK, hence M6, M65). The times are the journey times from the base in Liverpool. In some senses that is what this sketch is, although for F it was the routes she took to go shop-lifting, taking from stores rather than delivering to them.

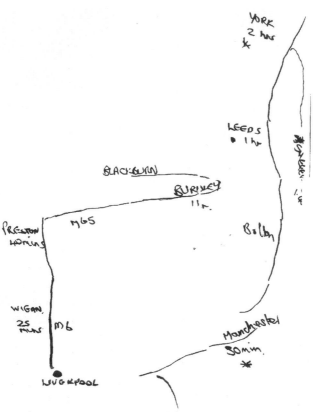

Map 14.2   **F's map of the routes she takes to steal from chain stores in small towns around Liverpool**

For her stealing from well-known department stores was a job that she did to collect goods that people had ordered from her. So she visited the well-known chain stores in the knowledge that they would have what she wanted, preferring those in the smaller towns because their security was more lax. A mother with seven grandchildren she rarely visited the places on her map except on 'business'. She just parked in the central car park near the stores where she did her thieving, leaving each load in the car while she moved on to the next shop, and then returned straight home.

For F then her mental image of crime scenes is a set of opportunities distributed throughout a network of available small towns. The reliability of goods on offer in chain stores across the country mean that the only thing she needs to know is whether any small town boasts a Woolworth's or Marks and Spencer. If it does then the town name implies a standard pattern of activity. She would even steal from the shops in a standard sequence that she had developed over her years of theft.

It is also noteworthy that F gives no details of Liverpool, where she is based, or the link roads from her home in Liverpool to the Motorways. She just sets out of there on the road to crime. Indeed, she reported that she would never steal in her local shopping centre, in part because she only goes there on her 'days off' from work, and also because she does not want to risk losing membership of her local golf club if she should be caught.

3. Designations of Locality

When crime is an integral part of the offender's day to day activities the sketch maps that are drawn can be taken as indicators of how they see their local world structured. This can be seen clearly in D's map 3, which is not untypical for young, prolific burglars. His home is in the middle of the map but the Grand Union Canal to the right very distinctly demarcates the area he chooses to draw. A more direct representation of the no-man's land into which a criminal will not venture to commit crimes could not be drawn.

In contrast the area around D's home is marked in some detail. The salient locations in it, his local pub, which interestingly forms the centre of the map, the DHSS office where he gets his welfare cheques, and the police station are all marked as well as the sets of tower blocks that create the area in which he has an apartment. But what is particularly noteworthy is his memory of the locations in which he has carried out a burglary, each carefully marked with a cross. The prolific crosses are clearly on the main routes he takes between this home and the DHSS office and out towards the main road junction that defines for him the edge of his domain.

D's map reveals a dense world of criminal opportunity. The crosses that mark his crime sites are not casually placed there. The thinner pattern of crosses around the 'old house', and on the way to the police station, show that he has carefully marked actual sites. The street in which he has burgled virtually every house or shop are also so marked that it can be seen the assiduousness with which he has broken into

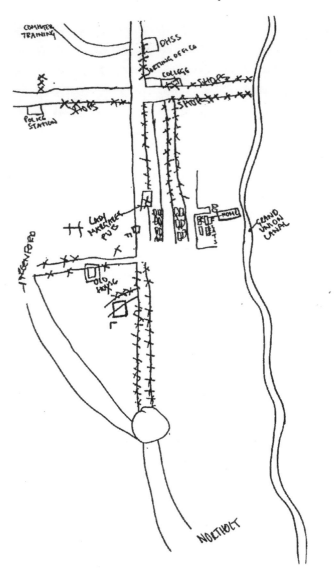

Map 14.3   **D's map indicating his burglaries and the apparent boundaries to his offending territory**

every place on both sides of the road. This map reveals a burglar for whom all the properties that he has easy access to are feasible targets for his criminal activities. But this is also a constrained world that he knows, bounded by the limits of his familiarity, the police station, the DHSS office, and the canal.

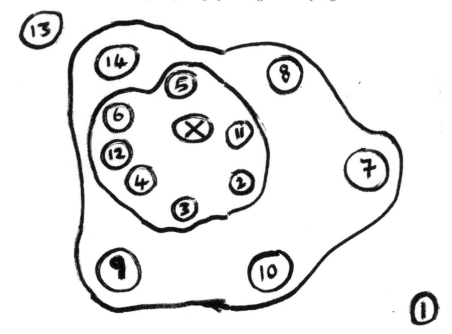

Map 14.4. **P's indication of the locations across a UK city where he had raped women he saw walking in the street**

Sometimes young burglars like D, produce maps with even more detail. Proud to mark on every building the particular form of security devices and burglar alarms it has. For these people the sketch map reveals the plan of work that shapes their deeds It can almost be regarded as an action plan that will be drawn on in the future as well as a record of what they have enjoyed doing in the past.

4. Indications of Involvement

When the crimes become an all embracing drive which takes over the offender's life then the sketch maps the offenders draw can be chilling in the sense they give of dominating the offender's life. Map 14.4 was drawn by a man in his mid-20s to indicate the locations in which he had raped 14 different women, all strangers to him, over a period of a few months.

P has taken the trouble to mark on the locations of his assaults their chronological order as well as indicating with an X the location of his home during the period he was attacking these strangers. It is remarkable, not to say unnerving, to see how closely this schematic pattern reflects the model put forward by Canter and Larkin (1993) on the basis of the crime locations of serial rapists in the South of England. The home is clearly at the conceptual centre of P's map. He is also aware of a process in which his first attack is some distance from his home, but then a wave of attacks happen in the closer area around his home, which he has bounded with a line. He then sees himself moving out from that location, after his sixth crime, to a further region before moving back again for the eleventh and twelfth and further on again for the thirteenth, before attacking closer to home for the fourteenth, where he was caught.

After his initial rape of a girl-friend he took to following women as they left railway stations on their way home, attacking them as they walked through areas where there was no-one to witness his assault. For P the whole of the city around where he lived became his stalking ground, moving from one locality to another in case he was recognised. The sequence shows clearly that he would never carry out more than a couple of assaults in adjacent localities before moving on to somewhere distinctly different. He was very aware of doing that and felt he had been caught because he moved back to an area where he had committed crimes earlier and where the police were therefore waiting for him.

The lack of any other detail in P's map than the rape sites and his home show how important these assaults became in defining his existence. He could move anywhere he liked and find possible victims. The only thing that brings significance to a location appears to be whether he carried out an attack there. Within this framework he seems to have a notion of boundaries that relate the offence to his home location. This gives the impression of his being aware that he had been moving into unknown territory, although interestingly he puts a lot of space between his first assault and any of the others.

Conclusions: The Values of Imaginary Maps

The four examples presented here were selected to illustrate the ways in which criminal activity can be more fully understood if the mental representations that criminals have of where they commit their crimes are explored. It has been shown that asking offenders to draw maps of where they commit their crimes does reveal some interesting insight into their approach to their offending. However, the sketch maps on their own without any other background information can be very misleading. They are best as a focus for an interview that explores the criminal's life style and offending career.

Nonetheless despite the difficulties inherent in exploring what is going on in the minds of criminals this brief examination of their mental representations does show that there is another side to the maps that can fill an atlas of crime. These maps are the products of the amalgamated activities of many individuals. Without knowing how those individuals see the geography of their crime the maps produced by cartographers can only be seen as a relatively superficial account of the effects of criminals' actions with only indirect hints of their causes.

By understanding the limited horizons of some criminals, the way others shape their lives around their criminal activities and the dominant roles that others assign to the routes and pathways to criminal opportunities, it is possible to begin to see the psychological processes that underpin an atlas of crime. Development of this work will help us to understand not just the way criminals' mental geography shape their activities but how such processes shape the transactions that we all have with our surroundings.

References

Bartlett, F.C. (1932). *Remembering*. Cambridge: Cambridge University Press.

Brantingham, P.J. and Brantingham, P.L. (1981). *Environmental Criminology*. Prospect Heights, IL: Waveland Press.

Canter, D. (1977). *The Psychology of Place*. London: Architectural Press.

Canter, D. (1994). *Criminal Shadows* London: HarperCollins.

Canter, D. and Larkin, P. (1993). The environmental range of serial rapists. *Journal of Environmental Psychology*, 13, 63–69.

Capone, D.L. and Nicholas, W. Jr. (1976). Urban structure and criminal mobility. *American Behavioral Scientist*, 20, 199–213.

Constanzo, D.B. Halperin, W.C., and Gale, N. (1986). Criminal mobility and the directional component in journeys to crime. In R.M. Figlio, S. Hakim and G.F. Rengert (eds), *Metropolitan Crime Patterns*. Monsey, NY: Willow Tree Press.

Kitchen, R.M. (1994). Cognitive maps: What are they and why study them? *Journal of Environmental Psychology*, 14, 1–19.

Lynch, K. (1960) *The Image of the City*. Cambridge, Mass: MIT Press.

Pettiway, L.E. (1982). Mobility of burglars and robbery offenders. *Urban Affairs Quarterly* 18, 2 Dec. 255–270.

Shaw, C. (1942). *Juvenile Delinquency and Urban Areas*. Chicago: University of Chicago Press.

Trowbridge, C.C. (1913). On fundamental methods of orientation and 'Imaginary Maps', *Science* 38(990), 888–897.

Chapter 15

Putting Crime in its Place: Psychological Process in Crime Site Selection

David Canter and Karen Shalev

Introduction

How and why offenders decide to offend where they do is given little consideration in most geographical modeling of crimes. Geometric calculations are applied to crime location data taking no account of the offender's cognitive processes. If the offender's behavior is considered it is usually only in terms of the simple logic of his optimizing his benefits whilst minimizing his efforts. This costbenefit logic tends also to be based on the equally naive assumption that criminals have an informed understanding of the distribution of opportunities for crime. Yet for well over 40 years it has been clear that nobody makes use of his or her physical environment like an efficiently programmed automaton. There are many biases and heuristics built into our cognitive representations of our surroundings that influence what we do where. There is growing evidence that criminals are probably even more prone to these distorted mental representations of what is criminally possible (Canter and Hodge 2000). Future improvement of crime mapping systems will therefore need to take account of this Psychology of Place (Canter 1977).

As a contribution to these considerations a variety of criminal cognitive strategies are illustrated from offence series and interviews with offenders. The proposed strategies deliberately draw on non-criminal models of person-environment transactions to facilitate utilization of the rich models available in other studies of people's use of place. They avoid the animal analogies, such as `predator' and the like, to emphasize the cognitive processing involved rather than the spurious, exotic rhetoric that implies only base, atavistic instincts are involved.

In different ways these models all weigh in the balance the risk of detection. A fundamental assumption is that offenders are aware of the possible risks in the crimes they commit and that their actions incorporate attempts to control those risks. This is not an especially demanding assumption for serial offenders in many jurisdictions because if they did not manage their risks with reasonable effectiveness they would soon be caught. However, if police effectiveness is of a low standard, for whatever reason, then the assumption of offender risk management may not be so appropriate. The present considerations are therefore based on the assumption of a reasonably effective policing process.

Most considerations of human spatial behavior are curiously static, taking cross-sections of patterns of activity at a particular point in time. This is severely limiting when considering the spatial activity of serial offenders. Every crime they commit changes the ecology of risk to which they expose themselves. This in turn will be expected to modify their choice of subsequent offence locations. That introduces a dynamic quality that needs to be at the heart of any modeling of offence locations.

We are grateful to Dr Samantha Lundrigan for her assistance.

Strategic Location Selection

One way of modeling offenders' changing patterns of offence location choice is to consider the strategies they use for selecting where they will offend next. This is a development of the consideration of offenders as rational decision makers (Cornish and Clarke 1986). It recognizes the limited rationality in their activities and also attempts to specify the actual decision processes they utilize. The sequence of decisions creates a generalized, and probably loose, strategy that generates the geographical pattern of offending.

At the simplest level one overarching strategy may be hypothesized. For example when an offender steals from stores within walking distance, making sure not to return to the same store twice in any month. Such a strategy would generate the classic 'marauder' model (Canter and Larkin 1993) with the added component of adjacent offences being further apart than other offences.

Many other strategies can be hypothesized, drawing on the range of geographical, transport, consumer, environmental psychology and other models that are available to characterize human spatial behavior. Mix models are also very feasible. For instance an offender may use one offence strategy in order to obtain the funds that will allow him to utilize another more resource demanding strategy. Or an offender may vary strategies depending on times of day and target opportunities. Changes in offence strategies across offence career would also be likely.

The present considerations merely explore these possibilities, illustrating a variety of strategies revealed in current studies of serial offenders.

Methodology

Four possible strategies will be considered. These are drawn from a broad literature on spatial decision making, stimulated by consideration of two very different forms of data. One is the actual geographical pattern of known crimes assigned to a given offender, together with the known residential address of the offender at the time of the crimes. This material is the stock in trade of crime mapping analysts and any associated 'geographical profilers'. So, although this material does have the advantage of drawing directly on what is available to investigators and those providing support to the police, interpreting such patterns does rely on many untested inferences about the offender's way of thinking. Also, such interpretations are almost certainly based upon the limited set of offence activities for which the offender has been caught.

A second research process is to interview criminals about their offence locations. Because such explorations require consideration of the geography of their crimes it is helpful to require criminal interviewees to draw sketch maps of where they have offended, discussing their reasons in relation the maps they draw. This research procedure owes much to the pioneering work of the urban planner Lynch (1960), but it has been rarely used in the context of criminal decision-making. However, its potential was identified recently (Canter and Hodge 2000). The following proposals are a continuation of that recent work.

It is often not possible to explore decision processes directly with offenders, especially for more serious crimes. Criminals may also not be clearly aware of the basis of their own actions. There is also the risk of them portraying what they think the researcher wants to hear. Therefore both approaches to exploring offenders' conceptualizations of their criminal activity complement each other.

For the present considerations comparisons are made of two different sets of material. One set consists mainly of is a set of series of rapes carried out in New York kindly made available by the NYPD. These series are particularly interesting because they throw light on the many different patterns of offence site selection of serial rapists in New York. Interestingly, none of these patterns approximates closely to that assumed in 'geographical profiling' of the 'East Side rapist' and may therefore throw some light on why that profiling has been so ineffective in helping the police investigation.

The second set of material is derived from interviews with prolific offenders in Liverpool. These individuals were the focus of intensive study whilst they were undergoing rehabilitation for drug abuse. They were very willing to describe and discuss their criminal activities and to draw maps of where they committed their crimes. They therefore provide especially detailed insight into their personal criminal geographies.

A final example is drawn from the investigation into a series of murders and rapes that took place in London in the mid-1980s. The investigation that led to the conviction of John Duffy for these crimes was the first systematic use of psychological profiling in a UK investigation and also the first case in which Dr David Canter provided a geographical profile that was of very direct utility to the police enquiry. However, John Duffy steadfastly denied any memory of the crimes so the details could not be explored with him. Recently he has admitted the crimes as part of a police investigation into his co-offender Mulcahy. In the past few weeks he has been giving detailed evidence in court about the rapes and murders he carried out with his co-offender. These details have served to elucidate what was known of the geography of his offences, thereby providing a combination of the geographical and psychological decision making processes.

Four Decision-Making Strategies

1. Satisficing

This is the strategy of specifying the effort to be expended in advance and then obtaining what ever is possible within that time and space constraint. It characterizes local 'small-time' offenders. These offenders are dependent on what they know to be vulnerable sources for their criminal objectives.

There are many interesting parallels to other aspects of non-criminal consumer behavior. For example, people wishing to find a house to buy under severe time constraints may not set about developing a complete knowledge of all possible houses within their budget, but instead will limit their search to an area they know to be feasible and buy a house that is acceptable even if not the best possible (Michelson 1977). In house buying it may be the local school or other amenity that acts as the focus. For the offender it is often likely to be his/her base. The important parallel is that the offender will have some limited knowledge of possibilities for his offences and act on that knowledge, only changing if circumstances require it. This decision process has much in common that which the Nobel prize winner Herbert Simon referred to as 'satisficing'. A neologism he created to capture the mix of 'satisfaction' and 'suffice', meaning just enough to be acceptable but not the best possible answer.

Figure 15.1 shows the map drawn by a drug supplier. This 39-year-old man supplied drugs as a means of making a living, and committed hundreds of thefts (from people's gardens, sheds, cars, shops) and several robberies of night-clubs. Due to his involvement with drug supply, he constantly moved between different towns in the same county. He lived in the area drawn on the map for three years, when he was a teenager and again briefly as an adult. He obtained his drugs from about 3 miles away then returned to the area near his home to sell them on. He admitted to prefer selling drugs to shoplifting or robbery, due to the "easy money" involved. He chose places to sell the drugs that were immediately accessible to him and in which he felt that he would not be at risk from police enquiries. The selling locations were therefore very much part of his desire to minimize the effort needed to sell the drugs whilst keeping the risk under control, rather than maximizing the financial gain he might have obtained by going into an area where the drugs may have attracted higher prices.

The drug sales were the easiest way for him to obtain money with minimum effort and manageable risk. When he engaged in robberies he moved to the specific locations where he thought he could get what he wanted effectively. That required a rather different strategy for location choice.

Figure 15.2 shows the locations of offences and home base for a prolific rapist in Manhattan. With his base quite near Central Park this rapist found a convenient area of the Park, to which he had ready access and in which there were vulnerable victims. Having established an area for his criminal activities, which provided what

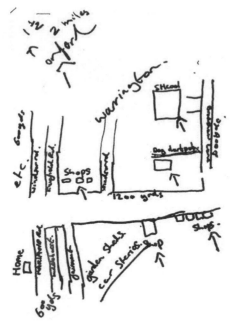

Figure 15.1   **The sketch map of a drug supplier showing (with arrows) the places where he sold drugs**

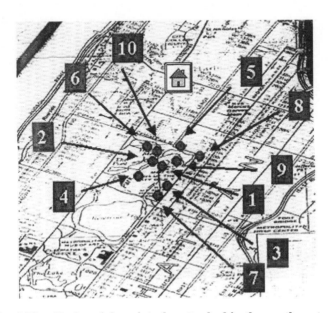

Figure 15.2   **A New York serial rapist who attacked in the north east corner of Central Park**

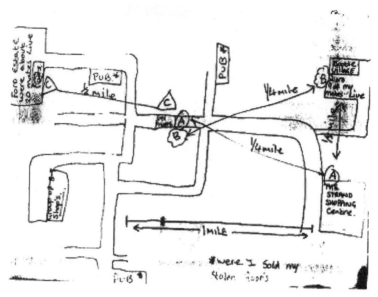

Figure 15.3 Sketch map of a shoplifter showing where he had associates and sold stolen goods

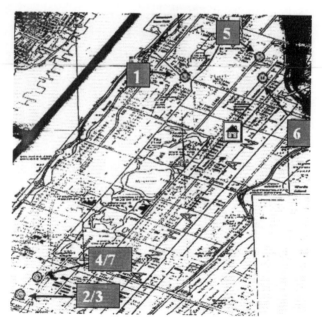

Figure 15.4 Distribution of a Manhattan rapist's offences around Central Park

he wanted, like the drug dealer, he kept going back to this area. The strategy required the minimum effort on his part for a sufficient return, making his activities not so different from a person who uses neighborhood shops for regular consumables.

2. Traveling Consumers

It has long been recognized that the distribution of market outlets may be effectively organized to "enable [a dispersed] population to have easiest possible access to markets" Bromley (1980) p.148. This means the trader can maximize the opportunities to make contact with potential consumers by the careful geographical distribution of the markets he attends. In this system the base of the market trader is central but s/he alternates around a polygon of points covering all compass directions. For offenders the distribution around the residence is aimed at finding new vulnerable victims rather than new markets, but analogous principles hold. These offenders are the typical 'Marauders' in the Canter and Larkin (1993) sense.

Figure 15.3 was drawn by a 32-year-old man who had a long history of shoplifting, and was involved in a few cases of assault, fraud and damage to property. In order to afford drugs he targeted the same are of shops every morning (points marked as A and C), and then walked to area B in order to buy the drugs. Returned home and used them. As can be seen from his sketch map he distributed his shop lifting around the area in which he was based, maximizing his access to opportunities whilst minimizing his journey distances. He also sold the goods that he stole in the pubs around the area where he lived a pattern remarkably similar to traders who visit a number of markets.

The distribution in this map has what we now recognize as the `classic marauder' pattern, modified by the presence of Central Park. The offender is distributing his offence locations in such a way that he diffuses his contact with potential victims and therefore minimizes the risk of moving back into areas where people may be more alert. He enhances this process by also using a strategy that we have noted in many studies; the tendency to avoid the area of the most recent crime, alternating around the points of the compass. This is a process that has been proposed directly for market traders by Bromley (1980). It is offenders whose activities most closely fit this general pattern who are most likely to be apprehended with the assistance of conventional geographical profiling procedures.

3. Collection Runs

For many offenders it is the selection of an offence route that is the dominant strategy. This may relate to their utilization of a particular target so that their conceptualization of their criminal activities is entirely in terms of their access to that target. It may also be a product of other locations besides their residential base that provide anchor points for their criminal journeys, this may be other relatives or

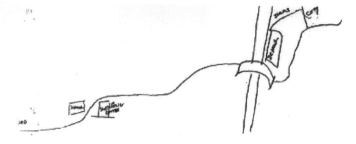

Figure 15.5 The sketch map of a shoplifter showing the dominance of the route in her thinking

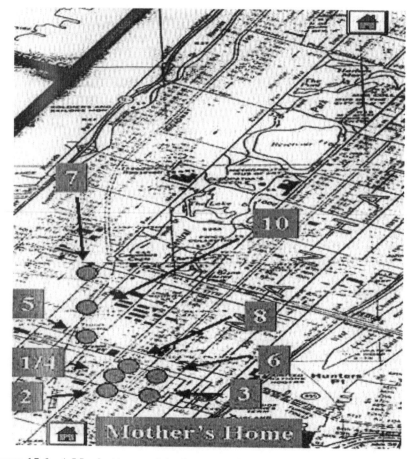

Figure 15.6 A Manhattan rapist whose attacks were on the route between his mother's home and his own

friends, criminal contacts such as drug supplies or receivers of stolen property. Public transport opportunities will be very relevant to some of these offenders, especially in metropolitan areas.

Joanne, who was a 30 year old woman began the interview by denying she was involved in crime, other than one drug possession she was charged with. However, whilst drawing the first map, shown in Figure 15.5, she disclosed that she shoplifted daily from a shopping center not far from her home. Joanne 'stole to order'. Stealing from the shopping center was a job that she did in order to collect goods that people had asked here to steal. Those were mainly food, bedding and clothes. The road she drew indicates the bus route that leads from her house to the shopping center. The route was considered "easy", because of the simple access to the shopping center and escape from it.

This prolific rapist, as can be seen in Figure 15.6, had a base North of Central Park whilst his mother's residence was South of the park. His crimes occurred between these two 'anchor points'. Their preponderance is nearer to the mother's home, possibly because he was less well known in that area, but all the offences lie along the dominant public transport route that connect the two important locations, that presumably acted as refuges for him.

4. Career Commitment

When criminal careers unfold over long time periods it may be expected that a mixture of strategies will be drawn upon. These will be expected to indicate increased sophistication in the utilization of route opportunities, risk reduction and target selection. It also is likely that what may have started as casual crime will evolve into much more serious and committed criminal activity. Rather than finding a sufficient opportunity for acceptable gain the offender will seek out higher gain opportunities in a more calculating way.

There are two aspects of this series of particular note for the present considerations. One is that the offences start from an area North of central London, an area known as Kilburn. The other is that they expand out from this area over time, with the murders at the edge of the sequence, occurring at the end of the series. It was this pattern that was used by Dr Canter as the basis for his advice to the police on the location of the offender's residence within the area demarcated by the initial three crimes (Canter 2000). This advice turned out to be very helpful indeed. The assumptions on which it was given, however, could not be fully tested because the man convicted of the rapes and murders, John Duffy, initially claimed traumatic amnesia. It is only now, a dozen years later, that he has admitted these offences as part of the legal process to convict his alleged co-offender at the time David Mulcahy. In the evidence he has been giving at the Old Bailey in the last few weeks the central thesis of outlined in *Criminal Shadows* (Canter 2000) has been remarkably vindicated.

This is the argument that the offences grew out of other less criminal activities of the offenders and that this behavioral evolution was directly reflected in the

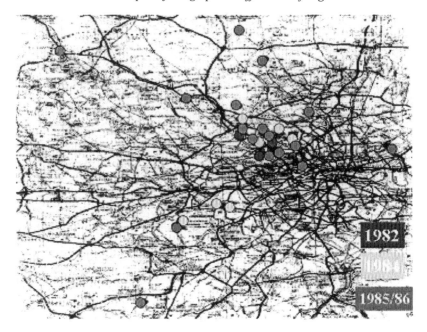

Figure 15.7   The series of rapes and murders carried out by John Duffy

geographical evolution shown in Figure 15.7. In court Duffy made it clear that when he and Mulcahy were both teenagers they had carried out unsuccessful burglaries during which they had planned to rape women. Duffy claimed that Mulcahy had identified the women for these assaults in the area where he was working as a builder. So the early exploratory thoughts and criminal activities were a casual part of other activities in which the offenders were engaged.

Duffy described in court the development from these teenage explorations, how he and Mulcahy went on from scaring people on Hampstead Heath, by driving stolen motorbikes at speed across the Heath and other forms of activity that he called "messing about" to attacking women.

The court report states that Duffy said in a soft, measured voice: "To begin with it was in areas we knew well. We would plan it quite meticulously. We would have balaclavas and knives. We used to call it hunting. We did it as a bit of a joke, a bit of a game. It added to the excitement."

These early stage eventually gave rise to a much more determined and violent set of offences in which three women were killed after being raped. As Duffy said "You get into the pattern of offending – it is very difficult to stop."

Discussion and Conclusions

Duffy illustrates how offenders will often use a combination of these strategies at different times and stages in their criminal careers. It is therefore important to avoid the suggestion that offenders exist as distinct types, each of which will have their own particular geographical pattern. Assigning offenders to groups such as 'predators', 'stalkers', 'poachers' or any other implicit animal sub-class is to loose sight of the dynamic qualities that create any observed pattern of offending. We need to consider the particular strategies that give rise to any pattern of offending. By understanding that strategy we will ultimately gain a better understanding of offence behavior that will have practical implications across a range of applications.

However, these initial considerations show that there is still a long way to go in modeling the spatial behavior of offenders. An important future task will be to model the combinations of the major components that these strategies consist of a) the time frame over which offences occurs, b) the targets of the offences, c) the routes to crime and d) the stages in the criminal career at which they occur.

References

Bromley, R.J, (1980). Trader mobility in systems of periodic and daily markets, in D.T. Herbert and R.J. Johnston (eds) *Geography and the Urban Environment* Chichester: John Wiley & Sons pp. 133–174.

Canter, D.V. (1977). *The Psychology of Place.* London: The Architectural Press.

Canter, D.V. (2000). *Criminal Shadows.* Texas: Authorlink Press.

Canter, D.V. and Hodge, S. (2000). Criminal's mental maps, in Turnbull, L.S., Hendrix, E.H. and Dent, B.D. (eds) *Atlas of Crime: Mapping the Criminal Landscape.* Arizona: Oryx Press. pp. 184–191.

Canter, D.V., and Larkin, P. (1993). The environmental range of serial rapists. *Journal of Environmental Psychology,* 13, 63–69.

Cornish, D.B. and Clarke, R.V. (eds) (1986). *The Reasoning Criminal: Rational Choice Perspectives on Offending.* New York: Springer-Verlag.

Lynch, K. (1960). *The Image of the City.* Cambridge, MA: M.I.T. Press.

Michelson, W. (1977). *Environmental Choice, Human Behavior, and Residential Satisfaction.* New York: Oxford University Press.

Bibliography of Geographical Profiling

Alston, J. D. (1994). *The Serial Rapist's Spatial Pattern of Target Selection.* Unpublished master's thesis, Simon Fraser University, Burnaby, BC.

Amir, M. (1971). *Patterns in Forcible Rape.* Chicago: University of Chicago Press.

Anselin, L., Cohen, J., Cook, D., Gorr, W. and Tita, G. (2000). Spatial analysis of crime. *Criminal Justice*, 4, 213–262.

Bair, S. (2005). *Movement-Based Forecasting of Serial Crime Events.* Paper presented at the 3rd National Crime Mapping Conference: Jill Dando Institute of Crime Science. Stream 3a: Where will the Offender Strike Next? 13th April 2005: London.

Baldwin, J. (1974). Social area analysis and studies of delinquency. *Social Science Research*, 3, 151–168.

Baldwin, J. and Bottoms, A.E. (1976). *The Urban Criminal. A Study in Sheffield.* London: Tavistock Publications.

Barker, M. (2000). The criminal range of small-town burglars. In D. Canter and L. Alison. (eds), *Profiling Property Crimes* (pp. 57–73). Aldershot, UK: Dartmouth.

Bennell, C. and Canter, D.V. (2002). Linking commercial burglaries by *modus operandi*: tests using regression and ROC analysis. *Science & Justice*, 42(3), 1–12.

Bennell, C. and Jones, N.J. (2005). Between a ROC and a hard place: A method for linking serial burglaries using an offender's *modus operandi*. *Journal of Investigative Psychology*, 2, 23–41.

Bennell, C., Snook, B., Taylor, P.J., Corey, S. and Keyton, J. (2007). It's no riddle, choose the middle: The effect of number of crimes and topographical detail on police officer predictions of serial burglars' home locations. *Criminal Justice and Behavior*, 34(1), 119–132.

Bennell, C., Taylor, P.J. and Snook, B. (2007). Clinical versus actuarial geographic profiling approaches: A review of the research. In press.

Bernasco, W. (2005). *The Use of Opportunity Structures in Geographic Offender Profiling: A Theoretical Analysis.* Paper presented at the 3rd National Crime Mapping Conference: Jill Dando Institute of Crime Science. Stream 3a: Where Will the Offender Strike Next? 13th April 2005: London.

Bernasco, W. (2006). Co-offending and the choice of target areas in burglary. *Journal of Investigative Psychology and Offender Profiling*, 3, 139–155.

Bernasco, W. (2007). The usefulness of measuring spatial opportunity structures for tracking down offenders: A theoretical analysis of geographic offenders profiling using simulation studies. *Psychology, Crime & Law, 13(2)*, 155–171.

Bernasco, W. and Luyxk, F. (2003). Effects of attractiveness, opportunity and accessibility to burglars on residential burglary rates of urban neighborhoods. *Criminology*, 41, 981–1001.

Beverton, R.J.H. and Holt, S.J. (1957). On the dynamics of exploited fish populations. *Fish.Invest.Lond.* Ser II, Vol. XIX.

Bernasco, W. and Nieuwbeerta, P. (2005). How do residential burglars select target areas? A new approach to the analysis of criminal location choice. *British Journal of Criminology*, 45, 296–315.

Block, R.L. and Block, C.R. (1995). Space, place and crime: Hot spot areas and hot places of liquor-related crime. In J.E. Eck and D. Weisburd (eds), *Crime and Place*. Monsey, NY: Criminal Justice Press.

Boggs, S. (1965). Urban crime patterns. *American Sociological Review*, 30(6), 899–908.

Bowers, K. and Hirschfield, A. (1999). Exploring links between crime and disadvantage in north west England: An analysis using geographical information systems. *International Journal of Geographical Information Science*, 13, 159–184.

Bowers, K.J. and Johnson, S.D. (2004). Who commits near repeats? A Test of the boost explanation. *Western Criminology Review*, 5(3), 12–24.

Bowers, K., Johnson, S.D. and Pease, K. (2004). Prospective hot-spotting: The future of crime mapping? *The British Journal of Criminology*, 44(5), 641–658.

Brantingham, P.L. and Brantingham, P.J. (1975). Spatial patterning of burglary. *Howard Journal of Penology and Crime Prevention*, 14, 11–24.

Brantingham, P.L. and Brantingham P.J. (1981). Notes on the geometry of crime. In P.J. Brantingham and P.L Brantingham (eds), *Environmental Criminology* (pp. 27–54). Beverly Hills: Sage Publications.

Brantingham, P.J. and Brantingham, P.L. (1984). *Patterns in Crime.* New York: Macmillan.

Brantingham, P. and Brantingham, P. (1994). Burglar mobility and crime prevention. In R. Clarke and T. Hope (eds), *Coping with Burglary.* Boston; MA: Kluwer Nijhoff.

Bromley, R.J. (1980). Trader mobility in systems of periodic and daily markets. In D.T. Herbert and R.J. Johnston (eds), *Geography and the Urban Environment* (pp. 133–174). New York: John Wiley & Sons Ltd.

Brown, M.A. (1982). Modelling the spatial distribution of suburban crime. *Economic Geography*, 58(3), 247–261.

Canter, D. (1977). *The Psychology of Place.* London: The Architectural Press.

Canter, D. (2004). Geographical profiling of criminals. *Medico-legal Journal*, 72, 53–66.

Canter, D. (2005). Confusing operational predicaments and cognitive explorations: Comments on Rossmo and Snook et al. *Applied Cognitive Psychology*, 19(5), 663–668.

Canter, D. and Alison, L.J. (2003). Converting evidence into data: The use of law enforcement archives as unobtrusive measurement. *The Qualitative Report*, June, 8(2).

Canter, D., Coffey, T., Huntley, M. and Missen, C. (2000). Predicting serial killers' home base using a decision support system. *Journal of Quantitative Criminology*, 16, 457–478.

Canter, D.V. and Gregory, A. (1994). Identifying the residential location of rapists. *Journal of the Forensic Science Society*, 34, 169–175.

Canter, D. and Hammond, L. (2006). A comparison of the efficacy of different decay functions in geographical profiling for a sample of US serial killers. *Journal of Investigative Psychology and Offender Profiling*, 3, 91–103.

Canter, D. and Hammond, L. (2007). Prioritizing burglars: Comparing the effectiveness of geographic profiling methods. In press.

Canter, D. and Hodge, S. (2000). Criminals' Mental Maps. In L.S. Turnbull, E.H. Hendrix and B.D. Dent (eds), *Atlas of Crime, Mapping the Criminal Landscape* (pp. 187–191). Phoenix, Arizona: Oryx Press.

Canter, D. and Larkin, P. (1993). The environmental range of serial rapists. *Journal of Environmental Psychology*, 13, 63–69.

Canter, D. and Shalev, K. (2000). *Putting Crime in its Place: Psychological Process in Crime Site Location*. Paper for Wheredunit? Investigating the Role of Place in Crime and Criminality. Crime Mapping Research Center of the NIJ, San Diego.

Canter, D. and Snook, B. (1999). *Modelling the Home Location of Serial Offenders*. Paper presented at the Third Annual International Crime Mapping Research Conference, Orlando, December.

Canter, D. and Youngs, D. (2003). Beyond offender profiling: The need for an investigative psychology. In R. Bull and D. Carson (eds), *Handbook of Psychology and Legal Contexts* (pp. 171–205). John Wiley and Sons Ltd.

Capone, D. and Nichols, W.W., Jr. (1976). Urban structure and criminal mobility. *American Behavioral Scientist*, 20, 199–213.

Carter, R.L. and Hill, K.Q. (1975). *The Criminal's Image of the City*. New York: Pergamon.

Catalano, P. (2000). *Applying Geographical Analysis to Serial Crime Investigations to Predict the Location of Future Targets and Determine Offender Residence*. Unpublished master's thesis, University of Western Australia, Australia.

Ceccato, V. (2005). Homicide in Sao Paulo, Brazil: Assessing spatial-temporal and weather variations. *Journal of Environmental Psychology*, 25(3), 307–321.

Chainey, S. (2005). *The Police Role in Community Cohesion: Using Geographic Information to Identify Vulnerable Localities*. Paper presented at the 3rd National Crime Mapping Conference: Jill Dando Institute of Crime Science. Stream 2a: Crime, Communities and Offenders. 12th April 2005: London.

Clarke, R. and Felson, M. (1993). *Routine Activity and Rational Choice*. New Brunswick: Transaction Publishers.

Cohen, J. and Tita, G. (1999). Diffusion in homicide: Exploring a general method for detecting spatial diffusion processes. *Journal of Quantitative Criminology*, 15(4), 451–493.

Cohen, L.E. and Cantor, D.C. (1981). Residential burglary in the United States: Lifestyle and demographic factors associated with the probability of victimization. *Journal of Research in Crime and Delinquency*, 18(1), 113–127.

Cohen, L.E. and Felson, M. (1979). Social change and crime rate trends: A routine activity approach. *American Sociological Review*, 44, 588–608.

Collins, P.I., Johnson, G.F., Choy, A., Davidson, K.T. and Mackay, R.E. (1998). Advances in violent crime analysis: The Canadian violent crime linkage analysis system. *Journal of Government Information*, 25, 277–284.

Conklin, J.E. and Bittner, E. (1973). Burglary in a suburb. *Criminology*, 11(2), 206–232.

Cook, D., Symanzik, J., Majure, J. and Cressie, N. (1996). Dynamic graphics in a GIS: Exploring and analysing multivariate and spatial data using linked software. *Computational Statistics*, 11, 467–480.

Cornish, D.B. and Clarke, R.V. (1986). *The Reasoning Criminal: Rational Choice Perspectives on Offending*. New York: Springer-Verlag.

Costello, A. and Wiles, P. (2001). GIS and the journey to crime: An analysis of patterns in South Yorkshire. In A. Hirschfield and K. Bowers (eds), *Mapping and Analysing Crime Data: Lessons from Research and Practice* (pp. 27–60). London: Taylor and Francis.

Craglia, M., Haining, R. and Wiles, P. (2000). A comparative evaluation of approaches to urban crime pattern analysis. *Urban Studies*, 37(4), 711–729.

Cromwell, P.F., Olson, J.N. and Avery, D.W. (1991). *Breaking and Entering. An Ethnographic Analysis of Burglary*. Newbury Park, NJ: Sage.

Curtis, L.A. (1974). *Criminal Violence*. Lexington, MA: Lexington Books.

Davidson, R.N. (1981). *Crime and Environment*. London: Croom Helm.

Davies, A. and Dale, A. (1995). Locating the stranger rapist. *London Home Office Police Department*, Special Interest Series Paper 3.

Douglas, J.E. and Munn, C. (1992). Violent crime scene analysis: *Modus operandi*, signature, and staging. *FBI Law Enforcement Bulletin*, 6, 1–10.

Downs, R.M. and Stea, D. (1973). Cognitive maps and spatial behaviour: Process and products. In R. Downs and D. Stea (eds), *Image and Environment* (pp. 8–26). Chicago: Aldine.

Downs, R.M. and Stea, D. (1977). *Maps in Minds*. London: Harper and Row.

Edwards, M.J. and Grace, R.C. (2006). Analysing the offence locations and residential base of serial arsonists in New Zealand. *Australian Psychologist*, 41(3), 219–226.

Eldridge, J.E. and Jones, J.P. (1991). Warped space: A geography of distance decay. *The Professional Geographer*, 43(4), 500–511.

Engstad, P.A. (1975). Environmental opportunities and the ecology of crime. In R.A. Silverman and J.J. Teevan (eds), *Crime in Canadian Society*. (pp. 193–211). Toronto: Butterworths.

Erlanson, O. (1946). The scene of a sex offence as related to the residence of the offender. *American Journal of Police Science*, 31, 338–342.

Evans, D.J. (1989). Geographical analyses of residential burglary. In D.J. Evans and D.T. Herbert (eds), *The Geography of Crime* (pp. 86–107). London: Routledge.

Everson, S. and Pease, K. (2001). Crime against the same person and place: Detection, opportunity and offender targeting. In G. Farrell and K. Pease (eds), *Crime Prevention Studies Volume 12: Repeat Victimisation*. New York: Criminal Justice Press.

Ewart, B.W., Oatley, G.C. and Burn, K. (2005). Matching crimes using burglars' *modus operandi*: A test of three models. *International Journal of Police Science and Management, 7*, 160–174.

Farrington, D.P (1989). Self-reported and official offending in adolescence and adulthood. In M.W. Kelin (ed.) *Cross-National Research in Self-Reported Crime and Delinquency,* (pp. 399 –423). Dordrecht: Kluwer.

Fritzon, K. (2001). An examination of the relationship between distance travelled and motivational aspects of arson. *Journal of Environmental Psychology*, 21, 45–60.

Gabor, T. and Gottheil, E. (1984). Offender characteristics and spatial mobility: An empirical study and some policy implications. *Journal of Criminology*, 26, 267–281.

Getis, A. (1995). Spatial filtering in a regression framework: Examples using data on urban crime, regional inequality, and government expenditures. In L. Anselin and R. Florax (eds), *New Directions in Spatial Econometrics*. Berlin: Springer- Verlag.

Godwin, M. (1999). *Hunting Serial Predators: A Multivariate Classification Approach to Profiling Violent Behaviour*. New York: CRC Press.

Godwin, M. and Canter, D. (1997). Encounter and death: The spatial behaviour of U.S. serial killers. *Journal of Police Strategy and Management*, 1, 24–38.

Golledge, R.G. (1987). *Analytical Behavioural Geography*. London: Croom Helm.

Goodwill, A.M. and Alison, L.J. (in press). The development of a filter model for prioritising suspects in burglary offences. *Psychology, Crime and Law*.

Gorr, W. and Olligschlaeger, A. (1994). Weighted spatial adaptive filtering: Monte Carlo studies and application to illicit drug market modelling. *Geographic Analysis*, 26, 67–87.

Gould, L. (1969). The changing structure of property crime in an affluent society. *Social Forces*, 48, 50–59.

Green E.J., Booth, C.E. and Biderman, M.D. (1976). Cluster analysis of burglary M/Os. *Journal of Police Science and Administration*, 4, 382–287.

Groth, A.N., Longo, R.E. and McFadin, J.B. (1982). Undetected recidivism among rapists and child molestors. *Crime & Delinquency*, 28, 450–458.

Grubin, D., Kelly, P. and Brunsdon, C. (2001). *Linking serious sexual assaults through behaviour*. Home Office Research Study 215.

Guerry, A.M. (1833). *Essai sur la Statistique Morale de la France*. Paris: Crochard.

Hakim, S., Rengert, G.F. and Shachmurove, Y. (2001). Target Search of Burglars: A Revised Economic Model. *Papers in Regional Science*, 80, 121–137.

Harbort, S. and Mokros, A. (2001). Serial murderers in Germany from 1945 to 1995: A descriptive study. *Homicide Studies*, 5(4), 311–334.

Harries, K.D. (1980). *Crime and the Environment.* Springfield: Charles C. Thomas Press.

Harries, K. (1999). *Mapping Crime: Principle and Practice.* National Institute of Justice. NJC 178919.

Harries, K. and LeBeau, J. (2007). Issues in the geographic profiling of crime: Review and commentary. In press.

Hartley, L. and Morrissey, P. (2005). *The Thames Gateway Crime and Design Project.* Paper presented at the 3rd National Crime Mapping Conference: Jill Dando Institute of Crime Science. Stream 1b: Profiling Neighbourhoods. 12th April 2005: London.

Hayden, C., Williamson, T. and Webber, R. (2007). Schools, pupil behaviour and young offenders: Using postcode classification to target behaviour support and crime prevention programmes. *British Journal of Criminology*, 47, 293–310.

Hesseling, R.B.P. (1992). Using Data on Offender Mobility in Ecological Research. *Journal of Quantitative Criminology*, 34, 95–112.

Holmes, R.M. and Holmes S.T. (1996). *Murder in America.* Beverley Hills: Sage.

Hull, C.L. (1952). *Principles of Behavior.* New York: Appleton Century Croft.

Hunter, J.M. and Shannon, G.W. (1985). Jarvis revisited: Distance decay and service areas of mid-19th century asylums. *Professional Geographer*, 37(3), 296–302.

Johnson, S. and Bowers, K. (2004). The stability of space-time clusters of burglary. *British Journal of Criminology*, 44, 55–65.

Johnson, S.D., Bowers, K. and Hirschfield, A. (1997). New insights in the spatial and temporal distribution of repeat victimisation. *British Journal of Criminology*, 37, 224–241.

Johnson, S.D., Bowers, K.J., Young, C.A. and Hirschfield, A. (2001). Uncovering the true picture: Evaluating crime reduction initiatives using disaggregate crime data. *Crime Prevention and Community Safety: An International Journal,* 3(4), 7–24.

Johnson, S.D., Bowers, K.J. and Pease, K. (2004). Predicting the future or summarising the past? Crime mapping as anticipation. In M. Smith and N. Tilley (eds), *Launching Crime* Science. London: Willan.

Keppel, R.D. and Weiss, J.G. (1992). *Improving the Investigation of Violent Crime: The Homicide Investigation and Tracking System (HITS).* Washington, DC: U.S. Department of Justice, National Institute of Justice.

Keppel, R. and Weis, J. (1994). Time and distance as solvability factors in murder cases. *Journal of Forensic Science, JFSCA*, 39(2), 386–401.

Kind, S. (1987). Navigational ideas and the Yorkshire Ripper investigation. *Journal of Navigation*, 40, 385–393.

Kind, S. (1999). *The Sceptical Witness: Concerning the Scientific Investigation of Crime against a Human Background.* Harrogate: The Forensic Science Society.

Kitchen, R.M. (1994). Cognitive maps: What Are they and why study them? *Journal of Environmental Psychology*, 14, 1–19.

Kocsis, R.N. and Irwin, H.J. (1997). An analysis of spatial patterns in serial rape, arson and burglary: The utility of the Circle Theory of environmental range for psychological profiling. *Psychiatry, Psychology & Law*, 4(2), 195–206.

Kothari, U. (2002). *Migration and Chronic Poverty*. Institute for Development, Policy and Management, University of Manchester. Working Paper No. 16.

Land, K., McCall, P. and Cohen, L. (1990). Structural covariates of homicide rates: Are there invariances across time and social space? *American Journal of Sociology*, 95, 922–963.

Ladd, F.C. (1970). Black youths view their environment: Neighbourhood maps. *Environment and Behaviour*, 2(1), 74–99.

Laukkanen, M. and Santtila, P. (2005). Predicting the residential location of a serial commercial robber. *Forensic Science International*, 157, 71–82.

LeBeau, J.L. (1978). The spatial dynamics of rape: The San Diego example. Unpublished Ph.D dissertation. Department of Geography, Michigan State University.

LeBeau, J.L. (1985). Some problems with measuring and describing rape presented by the serial offender. *Justice Quarterly*, 2, 385–398.

LeBeau, J.L. (1987a). The journey to rape: Geographic distance and the rapist's method of approaching the victim. *Journal of Police Science and Administration*, 15, 129–136.

LeBeau, J.L. (1987b). The methods and measures of centrography and the spatial dynamics of rape. *Journal of Quantitative Criminology*, 3, 125–141.

LeBeau, J.L. (1987c). Patterns of stranger and serial rape offending: Factors distinguishing apprehended and at large offenders. *The Journal of Criminal Law & Criminology*, 78(2), 309–326.

Leitner, M., Kent, J., Oldfield, I. and Swoope, E. (2007). Geoforensic analysis revisited: The application of Newton's geographic profiling method to serial burglaries in London, UK. In Press.

Levine, N. (1999). *Crimestat: A Spatial Statistics Program for the Analysis of Crime Incident Locations*. Washington, D.C.: U.S. Department of Justice, National Institute of Justice.

Levine, N. (2006). Crime mapping and the *Crimestat* program. *Geographical Analysis*, 38, 41–56.

Listi, G.A., Manhein, M.H. and Leitner, M. (2007). Use of the global positioning system in the field recovery of scattered human remains. *Journal of Forensic Science*, 52(1), 11–15.

Liu, H. and Brown, D.E. (2003). Criminal incident prediction using a point-pattern-based density model. *International Journal of Forecasting*, 19, 603–622.

Lowe, J.C. and Moryodas, S. (1976). *The Geography of Movement*. Boston, MA: Houghton Mifflin Company.

Lundrigan, S. and Canter, D. (2001a). A multivariate analysis of serial murderers' disposal site location choice. *Journal of Environmental Psychology*, 21, 423–432.

Lundrigan, S. and Canter, D. (2001b). Research report: Spatial patterns of serial murder: An analysis of disposal site location choice. *Behavioural Sciences and the Law*, 19, 595–610.

Lynch, K. (1960). *The Image of the City.* Cambridge, Mass: MIT Press.

MacKay, R.E. (1999, December). Geographic profiling: A new tool for law enforcement. *The Police Chief*, 66(12), 51–59.

Maguire, M., Morgan, R. and Reiner, R. (2002). *The Oxford Handbook of Criminology.* Oxford: Oxford University Press.

Mayhew, H. (1861). *London Labour and the London Poor: A Cyclopaedia of the Condition and Earnings of Those That Will Work, Those That Cannot Work, and Those That Will Not Work.* London: Griffin, Bohn.

Meaney, R. (2004). Commuters and marauders: An examination of the spatial behaviour of serial criminals. *Journal of Investigative Psychology and Offender Profiling*, 1(2), 121–137.

Messner, S.F., Anselin, L., Baller, R.D., Hawkins, D.F., Deane, G. and Tolnay, S.E. (1999). The spatial patterning of county homicide rates: An application of exploratory spatial data analysis. *Journal of Quantitative Criminology*, 15(4), 423–450.

Miethe, T.D. and McDowall, D. (1993). Contextual effects in models of criminal victimization. *Social Forces*, 71, 741–759.

Mizutani, F. (1993). Home range of leopards and their impact on livestock on kenyan ranches. *Symposium Zoological Society London*, 65, 425–439.

Mizutani, F. and Jewell, P.A. (1998). Home-range and movements of leopards (Panther pardus) on a livestock ranch in Kenya. *Journal of Zoology, London*, 244, 269–286.

Molumby, T. (1976). Patterns of crime in a university housing project. *American Behavioral Scientist*, 20, 247–259.

Morenoff, J. and Sampson, R.J. (1997). Violent crime and the spatial dynamics of neighbourhood transition: Chicago 1970–1990. *Social Forces*, 76, 31–64.

Nee, C. and Taylor, M. (2000). Examining burglars' target selection: Interview, experiment or ethnomethodology? *Psychology, Crime & Law*, 6, 45–59.

Nelson, S. and Amir, M. (1973). The hitchhike victim of rape: A research report. In I. Drapkin and E. Viano, (eds), *Victimology: A New Focus, Vol. 5* (pp. 47–64). Lexington, MA: D.C. Heath.

Nichols, W.W. Jr. (1980). Mental maps, social characteristics and criminal mobility. In D.E. Georges-Abeyie and K.D. Harries, (eds), *Crime: A Spatial Perspective* (pp. 156–166). Columbia University Press.

Paulsen, D.J. (2006). Connecting the dots: Assessing the accuracy of geographic profiling software. *Policing: An International Journal of Police Strategies and Management*, 29(2), 306–334.

Paulsen, D.J. (2006). Human versus machine: A comparison of the accuracy of geographic profiling methods. *Journal of Investigative Psychology and Offender Profiling*, 3, 77–89.

Paulsen, D.J. (2007). Improving geographic profiling through commuter/ marauder prediction. In Press.

Pettiway, L.E. (1982). Mobility of burglars and robbery offenders. *Urban Affairs Quarterly,* 18(2), 255–270.

Phillips, P.D. (1980). Characteristics and typology of the journey to crime. In D.E. Georges-Abeyie and K.D. Harries, (eds), *Crime: A Spatial Perspective.* Columbia University Press.

Polvi, N., Looman, T., Humphries, C. and Pease, K. (1990). Repeat break and enter victimisation: Time course and crime prevention opportunity. *Journal of Police Science and Administration,* 17(1), 8–11.

Pyle, G.F. et al. (1974). *The Spatial Dynamics of Crime.* Department of Geography Research Paper No. 159. Chicago: The University of Chicago.

Ratcliffe, J.H. (2002). Aoristic signatures and the temporal analysis of high volume crime patterns. *Journal of Quantitative Criminology,* 18(1), 23–43.

Ratcliffe, J.H. (2003). Suburb boundaries and residential burglars. *Trends and Issues in Crime and Criminal Justice,* no.246. Canberra: Australian Institute of Criminology.

Ratcliffe, J.H. (2006). A temporal constraint theory to explain opportunity-based spatial offending patterns. *Journal of Research in Crime and Delinquency,* 43(3), 261–291.

Ratcliffe, J. and McCullagh, M. (2001). Crime repeat victimisation and GIS. In A. Hirschfield and K. Bowers. (eds), *Mapping and Analysing Crime Data: Lessons from Research and Practice.* Taylor and Francis: London.

Rengert, G.F. (1975). Some effects of being female on criminal spatial behavior. *The Pennsylvania Geographer,* 13(2), 10–18.

Rengert, G.F. (1981). Burglary in Philadelphia: A critique of an opportunity structure model. In P.J. Brantingham and P.L. Brantingham (eds), *Environmental Criminology* (pp. 189–201). Beverly Hills: Sage Publications.

Rengert, G.F., Piquero, A.R. and Jones, P.R. (1999). Distance decay re-examined. *Criminology,* 37(2), 427–425.

Rengert, G.F. and Wasilchick, J. (1985). *Suburban Burglary: A Time and a Place for Everything.* Springfield, Illinois: Charles C Thomas.

Repetto, T.A. (1974). *Residential Crime.* Cambridge, MA: Ballinger.

Rey, S.J. and Anselin, L. (2006). Recent advances in software for spatial analysis in the social sciences. *Geographical Analysis, 38,* 1–4.

Rhodes, W.M. and Conly, C. (1981). Crime and mobility: An empirical study. In P.J. Brantingham and P.L. Brantingham (eds), *Environmental Criminology* (pp. 167–188). Beverly Hills: Sage Publications.

Rich, T. and Shively, M. (2004). *A Methodology for Evaluating Geographic Profiling Software: Final Report.* Cambridge, MA: Abt Associates Inc.

Richardson, H.W., Gordon, P., Jun, M.J., Heikkila, E., Peiser, R. and Dale-Johnson, D. (1990). Residential property values, the CBD, and multiple nodes: Further analysis. *Environment and Planning,* 22(A), 829–833.

Roncek, D.W. and Bell, R. (1981). Bars, blocks, and crime. *Journal of Environmental Systems*, 11, 35–47.

Roncek, D. W. and Francik, J. M. A. (1981). Housing projects and crime: Testing the proximity hypothesis. *Social Problems*, 29, 151–166.

Roncek, D. W. and Maier, P. A. (1991). Bars, blocks, and crimes revisited: Linking the theory of routine activities to the empiricism of hotspots. *Criminology*, 29, 725–755.

Roncek, D.W. and Pravatiner, M. A. (1989). Additional evidence that taverns enhance nearby crime. *Sociology and Social Research*, 73, 185–188.

Rose, H. M. and Deskins, D. R. (1980). Felony murder: The case of Detroit. *Urban Geography*, 1, 1–21.

Rossmo, D.K. (1995). Place, space, and police investigations: Hunting serial violent criminals. In J.E. Eck and D.L. Weisburd (eds), *Crime and Place: Crime Prevention Studies, Vol. 4* (pp. 217–235). Monsey, NY: Criminal Justice Press.

Rossmo, K. (1997). Geographic profiling. In J.L. Jackson and D.A. Bekerian (eds), *Offender Profiling: Theory, Research and Practice* (pp. 159–176). New York: John Wiley and Sons.

Rossmo, K. (2002). *Exploring the Geo-demographic Relationship between Stranger Rapists and their Offences.* Interim Report for Police Foundation, Washington, DC.

Rossmo, K. (2005). Geographic heuristics or shortcuts to failure?: Response to Snook et al. *Applied Cognitive Psychology*, 19(5), 531–678.

Santtila, P., Korpela, S. and Hakkanen, H. (2004). Expertise and decision making in the linking of car crime series. *Psychology, Crime & Law*, 10(2), 97–112.

Santtila, P., Zappala, A., Laukkanen, M. and Picozzi, M. (2003). Testing the utility of a geographical profiling approach in three rape series of a single offender: A case study. *Forensic Science International*, 131, 42–52.

Sarangi, S. and Youngs, D. (2006). Spatial patterns of Indian serial burglars with relevance to geographical profiling. *Journal of Investigative Psychology and Offender Profiling*, 3, 105–115.

Scott, D., Lambie, I., Henwood, D. and Lamb, R. (2006). Profiling stranger rapists: Linking offence behaviour to previous criminal histories using a regression model. *Journal of Sexual Aggression*, 12(3), 265–275.

Scott, R. (2005). Targeting resources using Geodemographic profiling. *3rd National Crime Mapping Conference: Jill Dando Institute of Crime Science.* Stream 3b: Reassuring the Public. 13th April 2005: London.

Shaw, C. R. (1929). *Delinquency Areas.* Chicago: University of Chicago Press.

Shaw, K.T. and Gifford, R. (1994). Residents' and burglars' assessment of risk from defensible space cues. *Journal of Environmental Psychology*, 14, 177–194.

Sherman, L.W., Gartin, P.R. and Buerger, M.E. (1989). Hotspots of predatory crime: Routine activities and the criminology of space. *Criminology*, 27, 27–55.

Sherman, L.W. and Weisburd, D. (1995). General deterrent effects of police patrol in crime "hot spots": A randomized controlled trial. *Justice Quarterly*, 12(4), 625–648.

Smith, T.S. (1976). Inverse distance variations for the flow of crime in urban areas. *Social Forces*, 54, 802–815.

Snook, B. (2000, December). *Utility or Futility? A Provisional Examination of the Utility of a Geographical Decision Support System*. Paper presented at the meeting of the Crime Mapping Research Center, San Diego, CA.

Snook, B. (2004). Individual differences in distances travelled by serial burglars. *Journal of Investigative Psychology and Offender Profiling*, 1(1), 53–66.

Snook, B., Canter, D. and Bennell, C. (2002). Predicting the home location of serial offenders: A preliminary comparison of the accuracy of human judges with a geographic profiling system. *Behavioral Sciences and the Law*, 20, 109–118.

Snook, B., Cullen, R.M., Mokros, A. and Harbort, S. (2005). Serial murderers' spatial decisions: Factors that influence crime location choice. *Journal of Investigative Psychology and Offender Profiling*, 2(3), 147–164.

Snook, B., Taylor, P.J. and Bennell, C. (2004). Geographic profiling: The fast, frugal, and accurate way. *Applied Cognitive Psychology*, 18, 105–121.

Snook, B., Wright, M. House, J.C. and Alison, L.J. (2006). Searching for a needle in a needle stack: Combining criminal careers and journey-to-crime research for criminal suspect prioritization. *Police Practice and Research*, 7(3), 217–230.

Snook, B., Zito, M., Bennell, C. and Taylor, P.J. (2005). On the complexity and accuracy of geographic profiling strategies. *Journal of Quantitative Criminology*, 21(1), 1–26.

Snow, J. (1855). *On the Mode of Communication of Cholera*. Explanation of the map showing the situation of the deaths in and around Broad Street, Golden Square. Retrieved February 25, 2006, from http://www.ph.ucla.edu/epi/snow/snowbook2.html.

Stephenson, L.K. (1974). Spatial dispersion of intra-urban juvenile delinquency. *Journal of Geography*, 73, 20–26.

Stephenson, L.K. (1980). Centrographic analysis of crime. In D.E. Georges-Abeyie and K.D. Harries. (eds), *Crime: A Spatial Perspective* (pp. 146–155). Columbia University Press.

Tamura, M. and Suzuki, M. (2000). Characteristics of serial arsonists and crime scene geography in Japan. In A. Czerederecka, T. Jaśkiewicz-Obydzińska and J. Wójcikiewicz (eds) *Forensic Psychology and Law: Traditional Questions and New Ideas* (pp. 259–264). Kraków, Poland: Institute of Forensic Research in Cracow, Poland.

Taylor, P.J. (1977). *Quantitative Methods in Geography*. Prospect Heights, IL: Waveland Press.

Tita, G. and Griffiths, E. (2005). Traveling to violence: The case for a mobility-based spatial typology of homicide. *Journal of Research in Crime and Delinquency*, 42(3), 275–308.

Tolman, E.C. (1948). Cognitive maps in rats and men. *Psychological Review*, 55, 189–208.

Tolnay, S.E., Deane, G. and Beck, E.M. (1996). Vicarious violence: Spatial effects on Southern lynchings, 1890–1919. *American Journal of Sociology*, 102, 788–815.

Townsley, M., Homel, R. and Chaseling, J. (2000). Repeat burglary victimisation: spatial and temporal patterns. *Australian and New Zealand Journal of Criminology*, 33, 37–63.

Townsley, M., Homel, R. and Chaseling, J. (2003). Infectious burglaries: A test of the near repeat hypothesis. *British Journal of Criminology*, 43, 615–633.

Trickett, A., Osborn, D.R., Seymour, J. and Pease, K. (1992). What is different about high crime areas? *British Journal of Criminology*, 32, 81–89.

Turner, S. (1969). Delinquency and distance. In T. Sellin and M.E. Wolfgang (eds). *Delinquency: Selected Studies* (pp. 11–26). New York: John Wiley and Sons.

Van Koppen, P.J. and De Keiser, J.W. (1997). Desisting distance decay: On the aggregation of individual crime trips. *Criminology*, 35(2), 505–513.

Van Koppen, P.J. and Jansen, R.W. (1998). The road to robbery: Travel patterns in commercial robberies. *British Journal of Criminology*, 38(2), 230–246.

Walker, J., Golden, J. and Van Houten, A. (2001). The geographic link between sex offenders and potential victims: A routine activities approach. *Justice Research Policy*, 3(2), 15–33.

Warren, J., Reboussin, R., Hazelwood, R.R., Cummings, A., Gibbs, N. and Trumbetta, S. (1998). Crime scene and distance correlates of serial rape. *Journal of Quantitative Criminology*, 14(1), 35–59.

White, R.C. (1932). The relation of felonies to environmental factors in Indianapolis. *Social Forces*, 10(4), 498–509.

Wiles, P. and Costello, A. (2000). *The 'Road to Nowhere': The Evidence for Travelling Criminals*. Home Office research study 207.

Yokota-Sano, K. and Watanabe, S. (1998). An analysis on the repetition of criminal *modus operandi*. *Reports of the National Research Institute of Police Science, Research on Forensic Science*, 3, 49–55.

Young, G. (2003). Mapping mayhem: The geography of crime. In *ComputerEdge*, August 2003.

Youngs, D., Canter, D. and Cooper, J. (2004). The facets of criminality: A cross-modal and cross-gender validation. *Behaviormetrika*, 31(2), 1–13.

Index

Note: Page numbers in **bold** type following the title of a paper indicate where the paper is printed in full in this volume, with numbers in ordinary type indicating where it is referred to by other authors.
Where a title is followed by page numbers in ordinary type only, the full paper can be found in the companion volume *Applications of Geographical Offender Profiling*.
Page numbers in italic type refer to information in figures or tables.

A → C equation 4
accomplices 117, *118*, 119, *120*, 124, 172
action space of criminals 87-8, 153, 233
affective motivation of offenders 82, 128-9
age of offenders 89, 146
   impact on mobility 88, 225, 226
Amir, M. 83, 221, 233
anchor points 7, 153-4, 167, 265, 267
animal studies, spatial behaviour of
   leopards 3, **41-79**
arson, proportions of marauders and
   commuters found in studies *10*
assault, journey to crime distances *118*
asymptotes 45, 47, 50, 53, *54*, 56, 68
awareness space of offenders 87-8, 89, 93-
   4, 96, 97-8, 153, 154

Baldwin, J. 83-4, 89, 102, 235
banks, vulnerability to crime 94
basic search areas of offenders 83-6
behaviour in space 188-9
Bennell, C. *Linking Commercial Burglaries
   by Modus Operandi: Tests Using
   Regression and ROC Analysis* 11
Bennett, T. 233
Bevis, C. 95
Bianchi, K (Hillside Strangler case) 152
bias in data on criminal spatial activity 12,
   236-7
Black, R. 215, 217
Boalt, G 119

bobcats, home range size 72, 73
body disposal sites of serial murderers
   231-46
Bossard, J.H.S. *123*
Bottoms, A.E. 83-4, 89, 102, 235
Bradford, U.K., Yorkshire Ripper case 24,
   26, 28-9, 153
Brantingham, P.L.and P.J. 8, 14, 128-9,
   130, 131, 154
   Notes on the Geometry of Crime **81-
   107**, 149, 150, 221-2, 224, 233
Brent, R.K. 88
Bromley, R.J. 3, 5, 265
buffer zone 115, 124, 131, 154, 155, 182,
   188, 242
Bullock, H.A. 81, 83, *124*
Buono, A. (Hillside Strangler case) 152,
   153, 236
Burgess, E.W. 91-2
burglary 131-2, 186, 211
   age of offenders 89
   choice of target 216
   journey to crime distances 83-4, 87-8,
   100, 129, 138-9, *140*, *144*, 146, 182-3
   linking of crimes 11
   mental maps of offenders 254-6
   offence patterns 189-90
   proportions of marauders and
   commuters found in study *10*
   Sheffield (U.K.) study 165-75
business areas 134, *135*